HEROES

ALSO BY PETER C. NEWMAN:

Selected Titles

Flame of Power: *Intimate Profiles of Canada's Greatest Businessmen*

Renegade in Power: *The Diefenbaker Years*

Defining Moments: *Dispatches from an Unfinished Revolution*

The Distemper of Our Times: *Canadian Politics in Transition, 1963–1968*

Home Country: *People, Places, and Power Politics*

The Establishment Man: *A Portrait of Power*

Company of Adventurers, *Volume I*

Caesars of the Wilderness *(Company of Adventurers, Vol. II)*

Merchant Princes *(Company of Adventurers, Vol. III)*

Empire of the Bay

The Canadian Revolution, 1985–1995: *From Deference to Defiance*

The Canadian Establishment, *Volume I*

The Acquisitors *(The Canadian Establishment, Vol. II)*

Titans: How the New Canadian Establishment Seized Power

(The Canadian Establishment, Vol. III)

Sometimes a Great Nation: *Will Canada Belong to the 21st Century?*

Here Be Dragons: *Telling Tales of People, Passions and Power*

The Secret Mulroney Tapes: *Unguarded Confessions of a Prime Minister*

Izzy: *The Passionate Life and Turbulent Times of Izzy Asper,*
Canada's Media Mogul

HEROES

Canadian Champions, Dark Horses and Icons

P E T E R C. N E W M A N

HarperCollins*PublishersLtd*

FIRST EDITION

HarperCollins books may be purchased for educational, business, or sales
promotional use through our Special Markets Department.

HarperCollins Publishers Ltd
2 Bloor Street East, 20th Floor
Toronto, Ontario, Canada
M4W 1A8

www.harpercollins.ca

Library and Archives Canada Cataloguing in Publication
Newman, Peter C., 1929–
Heroes : Canadian champions, dark horses and icons / Peter C. Newman.

ISBN 978-1-55468-422-9

1. Heroes–Canada–Biography. 2. Canada–Biography. I. Title.
FC25.N49 2010   971.009'9   C2010-903099-0

Printed and bound in the United States

RRD 9 8 7 6 5 4 3 2 1

With adoration and profound gratitude for my parents,
Oscar and Wanda Neumann, the shining lode stars
who guided me on my journey

Contents

INTRODUCTION
We'd Rather Be Clark Kent

HEROES REFLECT THE NATIONS that anoint them—and Canada is no exception. Latin American countries tend to pick dictators who spend most of their time on palace balconies, hectoring befuddled mobs. The British have been reduced to worshipping bedevilled rock stars who eat live bats, and to chasing un-hung derivative traders. To Americans, contemporary heroes tend more toward androgynous constructs like Madonna, drug-chewing baseball batters like Mark McGwire or any number of upwardly nubile beauties with kneel-and-duck love lives, temporarily out on rehab passes. Historically, the Yanks have benefited no end from the hero factory run by Walt Disney, who made demigods out of such frontier reprobates as Davy Crockett and Francis Marion, better known as "the Swamp Fox."

Most Canadian heroes—the few who have historically attained and managed to retain that state of grace—share one tragic qualification: they died in brave circumstances.

There are exceptions, of course, like most of my personal choices, cited in the pages that follow. This breaks the mould of unassuming Canadians, who by habit and temperament do not recognize heroes because that might hint of boasting. Most Canadians regard heroes—or at least the celebration of heroism—as an emotional extravagance, reserved for Americans and other RAH! RAH! species. Those heroic few who can claim that category find themselves in an existential state with a shorter shelf life than boysenberry yogourt. We have little talent for excesses of any kind and little patience for anyone who believes that heroism is worth achieving—except by inadvertence. There exists a vague link between heroes and weather, which remains Canada's most essential reality. Our frigid climate reflects the selectivity of how we pick our heroes: many are cold, but few are frozen.

We're the only country on earth whose citizens dream of being Clark Kent instead of Superman.

One example: Ottawa has struck our own versions of the Victoria Cross, the ultimate badge that recognizes exceptional military valour. But none have been awarded. This despite the fact that our troops have been engaged in a brutal war for most of eight years and our soldiers have been as brave as, or braver than, American GIs, who inevitably return home in uniforms aglow with Technicolor ribbons, signifying a bouquet of medals. "The true heroes," wrote the late political pundit Murray Kempton, "are those who die for causes they cannot take quite seriously." What our brave troops lack in evidence, they make up for in conviction.

———————

CANADA'S MOST COURAGEOUS historical epics—the magnificent journeys of the *voyageurs;* the building of the Canadian Pacific Railway; the *St. Roch's* pioneering traverse of the Northwest Passage; the taking of Vimy Ridge in the First World War; the manning of the fighting corvettes that won the Battle of the Atlantic in the Second World War—these and similar events share a common thread. They exemplified the anonymous bravery and collective endurance of their participants, rather than being remembered for the many individual acts of heroism involved.

Even the few historical heroes we do recognize have not travelled an easy road to glory. They have been mainly lost explorers, slyly hoping they would discover a shortcut to Cathay's treasured spices around each river bend. And then there were the stubborn Arctic pioneers who went against nature's barriers of rock-solid ice, attempting to discover a then-impassable Northwest Passage. Butting pack-ice was not considered to be a truly heroic pastime.

There have been some curious lapses in our choices. The St. Malo navigator Jacques Cartier, for example, is credited with Canada's "discovery" and thus widely hailed, but the Genoa merchant-adventurer John Cabot made his landfall in Newfoundland and Cape Breton thirty-seven years earlier. Until the relatively recent celebration of the anniversary of his voyage, the only memorials to Cabot were the scenic trail looping around northern Cape Breton Island and the plaque on a drafty baronial tower on Signal Hill in St. John's, better known as the location of Guglielmo Marconi's earliest trans-Atlantic signal transmission. If Cabot had only landed in what is now the United States, he would have been more famous than Christopher Columbus. (The Americans celebrate the Spanish navigator as their discoverer, though he didn't get close enough to sight North America's coastline and mistook Cuba for Japan.)

There is additional irony in the Marconi connection. In 1902 the Laurier government awarded $80,000 to the Italian inventor for his wireless radio station, turning its back on Reginald Aubrey Fessenden from the Eastern Townships of Quebec, who had earlier developed a system of voice transmissions as compared to Marconi's primitive Morse code messages. Fessenden was hired away by the U.S. Weather Bureau, where he broadcast daily reports from his laboratory at Cobb Island on the Potomac to a receiving station at Arlington, Virginia. He was never recognized during his lifetime in his home country.

Generals James Wolfe, Louis-Joseph de Montcalm and Isaac Brock were more appropriate Canadian heroes, since they died in battles without knowing their outcomes, but the memory of our most daring privateer, Antoine Laumet dit de Lamothe Cadillac, is perpetuated only by General Motors.

There is little consensus on the nature of Canadian heroes except that they're usually not politicians. Even Pierre Trudeau, the magnetic Liberal leader who inspired a generation, lost his crown in 1979, to—guess who? That's right—Joe Clark, the nerd who never set the world on fire except by accident. It was because the High River politician couldn't master the addition tables that he was defeated in a Commons budget vote nine months later—and the guy with the red rose in his lapel retrieved high office by default. Most of our public figures are equivocating politicians who promise they'll take care of us from erection to resurrection. Then dump us between election campaigns, spending their time in office appointing friends to high places and playing footsie with whatever American bigwig happens to be occupying the White House.

———

WE DO NOT officially mark the anniversary of our founding father's birth, Sir John A. Macdonald, but celebrate Queen Victoria's birthday instead—long after that routine occasion has been forgotten in her mother country. A rare exception to our antihero worship is the Group of Seven, who glorified Ontario cottage country by turning it into stunning landscapes; they certainly took on heroic dimensions. Though most Canadians assumed that Tom Thomson fronted the big Seven, it was formed two years after he died. (That didn't stop him from gaining heroic status, since he drowned under mysterious circumstances at the height of his fame.)

Our antihero attitude extends even to entertainers. If they're successful, they can't be real. Anne Murray, one of our first world-class pop singing stars, saluted by *People* magazine as the Madonna of Sunnybrook Farm, received this back-handed tribute from the music critic Larry LeBlanc: "If you close your eyes and think of a naked Anne Murray, parts of her always come up airbrushed."

The most conspicuously heroic Canadian of recent times was, of course, Terry Fox, the young British Columbia athlete, ravaged by cancer, who in 1980 hobbled halfway between our coasts. His heroic stature was confirmed when he was pinned with the Order of Canada just before he died the following year. (What's-his-name, who followed Fox's path while suffering from precisely the same affliction, actually completed his trek and raised $13 million for cancer research. But Steve Fonyo, who didn't look or behave heroically, has since been relegated to obscurity so chilling that he has remained visible only as a result of a series of petty crimes and misdemeanours.)

Similarly, no one made much fuss about Dr. Norman Bethune until he was sanctified in his heroic status by dying while on military duty; in 1939, as a member of Mao Tse Tung's Communist forces, he neglected a cut finger after operating on an infected soldier. Becoming a Canadian hero is a tough gig. Heroes can't be manufactured. They materialize unbidden, like cats appearing on laps.

Recognizing heroics is twice as problematic in the Age of Internet, a medium that has more bytes than bite, and has so far cast up only one *fin-de-siècle* antihero: the pathetic Matt Drudge. Within the new Internet culture, anarchy is always the flavour-of-the-month, with no one in charge of anything and every hacker capable of bringing the www.com world crashing into chaos. Heroism is not a function of Internet, unless you count fighting your way past all those RAMs of Viagra ads that pollute the digital universe.

Even when Canadians are placed in such potentially instant heroic circumstances as sports competitions, they tend to excuse themselves for winning and hope that with any luck, it would never happen again. In few other countries would a rising tennis star like Marjorie Blackwood set her long-term sights on being "among the top forty tennis players"—instead of going for gold. Quebec's Olympic champion speed skater Gaétan Boucher once explained why he competed in the American, instead of our, way: "Canadians come to me and say, 'So, you came in tenth, eh? Well, that's not too bad.' But it is. Compare that with the Americans. They do everything to win, not to finish tenth."

Heroes require contexts. The bounce and bravado that characterize most countries' national will prompts their citizens to focus on inordinately courageous, charismatic and resolute figures who fit the heroic mould. These larger-than-life totems become touchstones to live by and maintain a society's vibrancy. By its example, heroism is a tonic that heals and recharges. The urgency of time on the march has been my taskmaster; the hunt for personal heroes, my self-defeating quest. I picked my personal candidates for this book based on admiring their courage, dedication to country and loyalty to their craft or personal crusades. They remained true to themselves and loved Canada, as I do. They were patriots with balls—a rare combination.

I consider myself politically neutral; I attack everybody, though I maintain some strong preferences among individuals.

I have found that the measure of commitment and integrity a man or woman brings to the political wars is far more significant than the banner under which they travel. Above all, heroes must be doers, go-getters who can turn destiny into history. Garibaldi, de Gaulle, Lincoln, Churchill and Mother Teresa come to mind. (Sir John A. Macdonald's inclusion is suspect, since he founded this country while he was often falling-down drunk and it's not clear whether he was following some grand vision or AA's Twelve Steps.)

Faced by a massive loss of faith (in politics but not in democracy), Canadians have begun to fashion their own belief systems. In a sub-Arctic update of Pirandello, we've become thirty-four million characters in search of an author. Who can maintain heroic status in an age when we are assaulted by such phenomena as round-the-clock rap music, psychic hotlines, "Viagra-Light" for codgers who just want to cuddle, and Lady Gaga?

Our national trait of modesty has long been explained as the levelling influence on a country whose inhabitants have often been forced to cooperate for survival. But with mainly the uninspiring imperative of outlasting a cold climate to spur us on, and a prime minister whose idea of manifest destiny is to perpetuate his hold on power by not allowing cabinet ministers to sneeze without his permission, we have a long way to go before we can claim heroism as our national characteristic.

Given the debased nature of our public discourse, Canadians continue to huddle under the polar moon, satisfied with their freedoms-from instead of exploiting their freedoms-to. Becoming

Canadian requires no conversion to a new faith or allegiance to anything more profound than knowing on your citizenship test that Mackenzie King was not a royal.

Founded on social compact instead of the U.S. ethic of individual allegiance, Canadian nationhood seems threatened less by the Americans taking over every profitable activity except selling hand-carved Inuit chess sets than by our lack of self-confidence. This country remains fallow ground for heroism. Risk takers—and every hero must be one—cannot play to a public that ranks our pledge to preserve peace, order and good government above the Yanks' pursuit of hedonism and happiness.

Chances are that we will fumble past the next millennium by pretending that survival is a glorious option—and talk ourselves into the twenty-second century. That's hardly a heroic formula. But it helps to make it through the night.

PART 1
The Arts

Margaret Atwood: The Corrugated Madonna

BECOMING A METAPHOR is never easy, and Margaret Atwood, with her wintry eyes and corrugated hair, tries hard to conceal herself in her books, leaking information in careful bits and smaller morsels, salting literary instinct with mundane detail and publishing the results.

Her novel *Life Before Man* is populated with heroines and antiheroes driven by the conviction that they ought to become pivotal characters in their own lives. There are women like Lesje Green (half Lithuanian and three-quarters Jewish), who discovers that risking your life is less important than risking your soul. And men such as Nate Schoenhof, who has given up his law practice to carve toy rocking horses but never quite realizes that the forces that drove his ambitions didn't come out of the same faucet as those that control his emotions. In typical Atwood fashion, her cast of characters meets its come-uppance, torturing one another with ancestry and recriminations, ultimately drowning in the existential quicksand that is an Atwood specialty.

It is in the architecture of her prose that Atwood's novels achieve their power. She can build an entire page around the difference between a pause and silence, call down revelations as disturbing as thunderclaps, yet seldom pauses to deliver a tangential thought or phrase. Her art is rooted in an ability to step back from herself, calibrate her characters' emotions, acknowledge the absurdity of life—then create comedy out of hurt or vice versa. She understands that love, however tempting, inevitably casts its partners back into the loneliness that first disposed them to one another—until their isolation becomes intolerable and they are driven back together, more needy than before. "Dreams are not bargains," she reminds us. "They settle nothing."

Even when Atwood occasionally slips into girlish chatter or tries too hard to turn her scenes into symbolic crossword puzzles, her literary lapses become her signature, like uneven threads in a handmade wall hanging. Her writing has always been an exploration of the reality in which we live. In the process, she provides us with a sense of place. "I don't think Canada is 'better' than any other place," she once told me, "any more than I think Canadian literature is 'better'; I live in one and read the other for a simple reason—they are mine, with all the sense of territory that implies. Refusing to acknowledge where you come from is an act of amputation. By discovering your place you discover yourself."

Life Before Man may not be *the* great Canadian novel, but it is a significant book which proves, yet again, that Peggy Atwood is one of those rare writers with the natural pitch of a street-corner minstrel and the agitating talent of a born truth teller. All Hail, Atwood.

—1979

The Tempestuous Vision of Irving Layton

ACCORDING TO KEITH SPICER, the essayist and *bon savant* chosen in the mid-1980s to head the Citizens' Forum on Canada's Future, our destiny ought to be articulated by poets, not the professors, politicians or hectoring new-wave singers who brought this country to the brink of disintegration. So I found it entirely appropriate to seek out the wit and wisdom of the man Northrop Frye described as "the best English-language poet in Canada"—the self-styled literary colossus, Montreal's Rabelaisian superman of letters, Irving Layton.

The author of fifty-four books translated into seven languages, twice nominated for the Nobel Prize for Literature, Layton lists his favourite recreation as "polemicizing," a search for ways to perpetuate his inelastic faith in himself as a *bon vivant*, freethinker and Olympic-grade lover. His seventy-eight years have not slowed him down exactly, but instead of being

a freelance firecracker attempting to explode every social shib-
boleth within range, he has become a verbal cannon, aiming big
salvos at big targets.

We meet at the Hostaria Romana, a downtown Montreal
pasta joint he describes as having "exquisite food, served as if
the guests were royalty." The spaghetti Bolognese turns out to
be mediocre, but the conversation is wonderful. "Civilization
has never been in greater danger," Layton begins, characteristically ignoring the dubious comforts of understatement. "But I
don't regard that danger as a menace or a bad thing. On the contrary, with danger, you have the possibility of change and hope,
an opportunity to do something different. Everything becomes
negotiable, because there's the possibility of doing things in a
fundamentally new way. Too often in the past we've drawn back
and resisted the opportunity for genuine improvement."

Unlike most Canadians, who tend to blame everything from
the Maple Leafs hockey team's perpetual losing streak to the
clouds of locusts chomping on Alberta's barley fields on the lousy
politicians in charge of our destinies, Layton shrugs them off as
being irrelevant. He puts down Jean Chrétien as never having had
the character, stamina or personality required by Canada's precarious situation. "You've got to have not only the right man but
the right moment," he explains. "This is the right moment, but
we don't have the right man." Quebec premier Robert Bourassa
he praises as a "cool-headed economist who understands that the
most important thing is to feed and clothe people, so you can't go
wild with your nationalism."

Only Pierre Trudeau earns the poet's broiling wrath. "He thinks he's a visionary," Layton begins winding himself up. "But a certified visionary must understand the elements he's working with, and Trudeau ignores the French-Canadian fact. He always struck me as being very opinionated, highly dogmatic and, above all, arrogant. His pit-bull attitudes are based on his inability to listen; he feels so superior to everybody because of his training as a Jesuit and his observance of the catechism of Angry Anglohood. In short, his temper and his rooster masculinity militate against his ability to govern."

Partly because he has travelled and read so widely, Layton views Canada's perpetual constitutional crisis from a worldwide perspective. "I see the quest for independence, whether it's in Quebec or Eastern Europe, springing out of the alienation of the individual from a world he never made. I see modern man as being alienated from God, from nature and, finally, in this last stage, from himself. We feel afraid, forlorn and comfortless, seeking a touch of warmth, like lost sheep plunging back into a flock that follows no direction." Amen.

That's a mild rant for a rainy Tuesday noon hour, but Layton is just getting started and turns less forgiving with every slurp of pasta. "I can't help feeling," he glooms, "that we're now in a situation analogous to the fourth or fifth centuries, during the fall of the Roman Empire, when the barbarian hordes were knocking on the gates. Those barbarians were external. Ours are internal, in the sense that they're our own citizens who have shaken off the restraints of civilization. It's even true of the arts. Will we ever see another Milton, Shakespeare, Racine or T.S. Eliot? Forget it. That kind of greatness is gone forever, destroyed by technology and the forces of so-called education. If you want great poetry today, don't go to the poets who are all busy writing their sweet little lyrics, God bless them. If you want great poetry today, go to films and music."

Curiously, Layton's pessimism excludes the future of Quebec, because he feels its society is firmly rooted in a distinct history, religion, language, literature and memory. That's where the grievances and the difficulties come in, he believes, because English Canada lacks such unifying anchors. This doesn't only mean English Canada would have a tough time facing the determined collective will of French Canada, but that those of us outside Quebec are much more open to the destructive forces of the modern world. "Menaced by the Anglos, the French Canadians pull in," he explains, "because they feel they're protecting something valuable against the onset of mediocratization and homogenization. English Canadians don't have much intellectual baggage whatsoever. None at all, really. So they have very little to protect and not much will to fight back."

The third glass of Pinot Grigio has turned lukewarm between us, and Layton grows silent for a few precious nanoseconds as his audience—the bevy of gathered waiters, who stand around like cashiered hedge fund managers—agree with him.

But the poet ends on an up note. "I have two deities," he confides. "My main deity is chance; the other is love. I'm a great believer in chance. I was born circumcised, which gave me the vanity and egotism of a saviour, and made my mother favour me. I was the only one in her brood of seven who attended high school, because our family couldn't afford the fees. She felt that if I turned out to be the Messiah, I should know the English language, history and so on. I've been a great believer in chance ever since." Layton hints that Canada may be salvaged by just such a confluence of good fortune.

I can't resist. "Surely," I plead with him, "as a putative Messiah, you can save this country." His eyebrows shoot up, not sure whether I'm joshing. "I don't think I can save it," he replies, sadly shaking his great mane of grey curls.

Then he quickly recovers his customary triple-A chutzpah. "I shouldn't be overcome by such modesty all of a sudden," he snorts. "Maybe after I've had another drink . . ."

—1997

A Fond Farewell to Robertson Davies

"ALL MORTALS ARE REPLACEABLE" runs the modern mantra, betraying the ethic of programmed obsolescence that has come to dominate North American culture. There are exceptions, and one of them, Robertson Davies, died recently, leaving a gap in the Canadian ethos that cannot be filled.

A society can afford to lose only so many voices of wisdom and civility before it feels cut loose from its spiritual moorings. In the past decade, that list of departed Canadian beacons of enlightenment has included Morley Callaghan, Marian Engel, Barbara Frum, Northrop Frye, Margaret Laurence, Bruce Hutchison, Roger Lemelin, Arthur Lower, Hugh MacLennan and Sandy Ross. The greatest of them was Robertson Davies. A writer of serious mien with a bespoke twinkle in his eyes, he left open the natural speculation by anyone he met: whether he resembled God or did the Supreme Deity sport a bearded countenance like his?

No matter. "Rob," as he was known to his friends, championed mid-nineteenth-century thought and sentiment, describing himself as the most reluctant of patriots, finding Canada hard to endure yet impossible to flee. "God, how I tried to love this country," exclaims a character in his play *Fortune My Foe.* "I have given all I have to Canada—my love, then my hate, and now my bitter indifference. But this raw, frost-bitten country has worn me out, and its raw, frost-bitten people have numbed my heart."

In less lofty language, he once explained to me in private that while he had many chances to live elsewhere, he just couldn't bring himself to leave. "I belong here," he told me, with a pained expression. "To divorce yourself from your roots is spiritual suicide. I just am a Canadian. It's not a thing you can escape from. It's like having blue eyes."

Well, not quite. The life Davies chose for himself hardly qualified him as one of your McKenzie-Brother, run-of-the-brew, prototypical Canadian hosers. After graduating from Upper Canada College and Oxford's Balliol College, he created an intellectual haven for himself as founding Master of the University of Toronto's Massey College. Inside its elegant, very un-Canadian walls, he moved among his Fellows in their gowned splendour, looking extraordinarily magnificent in his necromancer's beard, living in the Master's Lodge, the BMW in his private driveway, presiding at High Table, sniffing snuff out of an ivory horn, sipping claret and responding with supreme indifference to charges that the institution he headed was snobbish, sexist, anachronistic and perhaps even a little absurd. The place reflected perfectly his view of life and his genius for civilized eccentricity that he so brilliantly captured in his novels. They felt so authentic because they were, in spirit if not in detail, autobiographical with never a touch of plea bargaining.

All the while that he presided over Massey, stressing tradition over practicality, the Master was playing a splendid joke on his detractors. In 1970, after writing a stack of novels, plays and works of theatrical criticism that brought him mild approval at home and virtually no notice abroad, Davies published *Fifth Business* to universal international acclaim. Saul Bellow and John Fowles, then the English-speaking world's leading fiction writers, were loud in their praises, as was the *New York Times* and just about every other reviewer except *Mother Jones.* Davies had finally found his place at the pinnacle of literary acclaim, which was only proper, since that was where he had always meant to be. That success was repeated with *The Manticore* and his six subsequent novels.

I spent much of an afternoon chatting with the illustrious author at his cozy Massey College digs, later attending one of his High Table dinners. He sat there at the head of the tableaux, theatrical in appearance, almost ostentatiously dated in his manner. You expected him to wear a Cromwellian collar while debating whether Thomas More, Lord Chancellor to Henry VIII, was a fanatical heretic or a saint. "I am very interested in the condition of sainthood," he confided, presumably including his own. "It is just as interesting as evil."

Unexpectedly, we moved to the subject of pornography. "It is a cheat," he declared. "It is an attempt to provide a sexual experience by second-hand means—rather like trying to find out about a Beethoven symphony by having somebody hum a few bars. It's not the same thing. Sex is primarily a question of relationships; pornography—a twenty-second best." Davies hated nothing worse than what he called "young fogies"—those pretenders who everlastingly harped on the fact that they *were* young but thought and acted with a degree of caution that would be excessive in their grandfathers. "They are the curse of the world," he thundered. "They don't even know what they are conserving."

While he had great respect for his craft, Davies categorized himself as a simple storyteller. "I think of an author as somebody who goes into the marketplace and puts down his rug and says, 'I will tell you a story,' and then passes the hat. When he's taken up the collection, he tells his story, and just before the denouement, passes the hat again. If it's worth anything, fine. If not, he ceases to be an author."

Our conversation kept coming back to why he felt so alienated from and yet obsessed with being—and remaining—Canadian. "Canada demands a great deal from people," he said, emphasizing each syllable like a preacher mouthing a benediction. "It is not, as some countries are, quick to offer in return a pleasant atmosphere or easy kind of life. I mean, France demands an awful lot from her people too, but France also offers gifts in the way of a genial, pleasant sort of life and many amenities." "Canada is not really a place where you are encouraged to have large spiritual adventures," he lamented.

"A lot of people complain that my novels aren't about Canada. I think they are, because I see Canada as a country torn between a very northern, rather extraordinary, mystical spirit, which it fears, and its desire to present itself to the world as a Scotch banker. This makes for tension, and tension is the very stuff of art, plays, novels—the whole lot."

Like his books, Davies' conversation was peppered with the supernatural, and he ended the evening by returning to sainthood, almost as if he felt he should claim its halo. "Most saints have been unbearable nuisances in life. Some were reformers, some were sages, some were visionaries, but all were intensely alive, and thus a rebuke to people who were not. So many got martyred because nobody could stand them. Society hates exceptional people, because such people make them feel inferior."

Robertson Davies was, if not a saint, certainly a genius. It was to his credit and to our gain that he was such a magnificent storyteller—and that he was ours.

—1997

The "Fillum" Moguls Who Made Me

JOAN DIDION, who chronicled the psychic extravagances of the California lifestyle, once observed that the oral history of Los Angeles was written in piano bars: "People tell each other about their first wives and last husbands. 'Stay funny,' they say, while listening to 'Moon River,' 'Love for Sale' and 'Send in the Clowns.'"

In the Toronto of the 1970s, the bar was Club 22 and the clowns were the hucksters who breach-birthed the Canadian movie industry on the premises, tucked into a corner of the Courtyard Café, at St. Thomas and Bloor. The bar was part of the Windsor Arms Hotel, purchased in 1963 by George Minden, a U of T philosophy and English graduate who picked his friends by whether or not they knew when to laugh at the bassoon joke in Brahms' *Academic Festival Overture*. His watering hole became the epicentre of the city's—and the country's—cultural renaissance. If Toronto was downtown Canada, the Courtyard was uptown Toronto.

A combination of Beverly Hills' Polo Lounge, Elaine's and Sardi's in New York (where the stars went to be private in public), Blakes in London and the Gaslight in Paris, it was my hangout. During his fourteen-year gig, Paul Drake, the resident pianist who later married into Belgian royalty, became Club 22's chief animator and musical host. Among the many visitors was an aging Debbie Reynolds, who arrived with eighty suitcases. (Asked about her love life, she confided: "I haven't forgotten how, I just don't remember *why.*") One of the highlights Drake recalled was the night Christopher Plummer, celebrating the premiere of his film *Murder by Decree,* rose unsteadily in his seat to proclaim with Shakespearean cadence and customary dignity: "We live in a world where celebrities hold the proxies for our identities . . ." Only to be drowned out by the drunken cheers of the pseudo-celebs.

It was the kind of place where macho males were judged by the angles of their cigars. Except for the odd Hollywood agent temporarily slumming in the Great White North, Club 22's clientele was Canadian. Well, un-Canadian, really—much too ballsy to qualify for citizenship, except retroactively. (One exception was a Hamilton-born visiting Hollywood director of horror movies who never removed his sunglasses—with mirrors on the inside— and kept muttering: "Gonna lie doggo in ma' Tuscanny shack" while snorting cocaine off his Porsche key.)

They were self-proclaimed geniuses who lived off each other by pitching movies. Walking into Club 22 was like visiting a zoo at feeding time. The restless titter of macho *machers* making deals to make deals kept the place buzzing, and the buzz was always about future films, or "fillums," as the patrons described their art form.

The Toronto movie boom of the 1970s was uncannily like the Leduc oil strike of the 1940s: everybody pretended to be what they claimed they were, holding on to their precious piece of the action. The movies they made have long been forgotten, but they portrayed—occasionally brilliantly but mostly middling—truths that were large and small, yet essentially Canadian.

What the big screen demanded was alchemy, and that was in short supply. "We're going straight to cult," a frustrated Cabbagetown movie mogul announced, then jauntily began lining up his next blockbuster. The movie people felt most alive as they tested their nerves, digging their tax shelters, waiting out the offers, swinging on a bankable star who had told them she "would kill" to be in their movie but hadn't shown up yet. The trick was to stay in the game.

The extras were mostly CBC types, showbiz hangers-on, camp followers of more than two sexes, not to mention the whiskey priests flaunting their self-appointed authority as they toyed with the pine nuts floating in their chilled cucumber soup.

Scattered among the plush-brown banquettes were the real *machers:* Bill Marshall (the only one with a private phone at his table), Bob Cooper, Robert Cohen, Jon Slan, Garth Drabinsky, David Perlmutter, George Mendeluk, and Fil Fraser from Calgary, whose *Why Shoot the Teacher* was a Canadian breakthrough film. The entertainment lawyer Michael Levine was everywhere, acting as executive producer to more movies than he later claimed.

The star of the circus was Mike McCabe, my political pal from Ottawa days, then head of the Canadian Film Development Corporation, which provided the industry's momentum and seed money. Brash, confident, done up in bushy beard and safari jacket, he turned Canada into the world's third-largest film production centre, with $150 million invested in new movies during its top year.

The self-described starlets who nightly sat around Club 22 waiting to be discovered were convinced that to be an actress you only had to look like one. The sexual thermostat was always set on high. Late one night, I noticed a Club 22 regular posing as a producer (mussed haircut, peasant body shirt, Riviera jeans) leaning over a stunning brunette and conversationally asking her what she liked doing best. "Balling," she replied, assuming this was an appointment for her screen test. The confused would-be seducer backed away, and the jilted bride started to cry, her perfectly formed tears refracted by the ceiling spotlights, glittering like a spill of diamonds.

At the bottom of the movie industry's pecking order were the writers, of course, charged with the unglamorous job of turning the wild, late-night Club 22 fantasies, jotted down on table napkins, into filmable shooting scripts. "Our position," declared Frank Pierson, the visiting head of the Screen Writers Guild, "is that hopefully, someday, the industry can forget the old joke about the Polish starlet who thought she could get ahead by fucking the writer."

Not being Polish, I can't pretend that I was part of the scene, but I was there, and what I caught, like a galloping fever, was the kinetic energy and unbridled optimism afloat in the Courtyard and its piano bar. If these guys could make movies out of cigar smoke and chutzpah, I could transform the comatose monthly *Maclean's,* whose editorship I had recently inherited, into a profitable weekly newsmagazine.

It was here in Club 22 that Canada's weekly news magazine was conceived, and those optimistic improvisers of Canada's cult fillums were its godfathers.

—2005

Terry Fox on the Run

FEW CANADIAN BUSINESSES have more richly earned a shoddy reputation than our indigenous film industry. Touted as the mirror of our identity and the high road to fortune for tax-shelter-happy dentists, it wiped out its investors, did little to define the nation and spawned a motley crew of deal makers who, if there were any justice, should have been circus barkers for freak shows.

In the mid-1980s, into this artistic abattoir arrived *The Terry Fox Story,* about the cancer-stricken amputee determined to cross Canada. The movie, much like Fox himself, overcame many seemingly insurmountable obstacles. Yet it may well have been the most artistically coherent, and certainly the most authentically Canadian, of the many weak attempts to make a film worthy of its subject.

Eric Fryer, who brilliantly portrayed Fox, was so believable, it hurt. At first, Fryer as Fox (in the movie, as in real life) ran alone, with no fanfare or support systems. The journey started with the simple ceremony of sticking his artificial foot into the Atlantic Ocean at Cape Spear in eastern Newfoundland. Doggedly, he began to hobble the eight thousand clicks home. In the harsh morning light, huddles of well wishers in tiny Newfie outports, as luminous as figures in Renoir canvasses, coalesced to wish him luck. There was a lame Patrick Watson, in a brilliant cameo, hobbling out to deliver an obscene but heartfelt benediction.

Inexorably and almost imperceptibly, Fox's pilgrimage developed its own field of force. The kid started to draw crowds and media groupies. The movie's pace took off when Fox was joined by Bill Vigars, a Canadian Cancer Society official (played by Robert Duvall). A noble-looking but uncompromising mentor with a devilish countenance, Vigars turned the lonely trek into a "Marathon of Hope."

The film had serious flaws. The music, by Bill Conti, was bubbly elevator-style fluff, more suitable for afternoon TV soaps. What the film needed was some hard-edged, early Lightfoot or the evocative chants of Stan Rogers. The indoor lighting was poor throughout, and the first thirty minutes threatened to turn the film (literally) into a sleeper.

The Terry Fox of this movie was just an athletic kid given only six short months to live, wanting to make the best of it. The

undeniable courage was there, but at first he couldn't work up
the nerve to break the news to his father that he intended to run
across Canada. When his mother told her husband for him, the
response was a flat and very Canadian "When?"

What raised the film beyond its pedestrian potential was
the camera work of Richard Ciupka and the direction of Ralph
Thomas. Ciupka captured subtle shifts in landscape and the differences of shadings of light as plot and character moved across
the lanscape, from Newfoundland in spring to Ontario in deep
summer. The wispy mists of dawn over a Quebec cornfield,
the mauve shadings of twilight in the lush farmlands of the St.
Lawrence Valley were less a backdrop than the movie's dominant
theme.

The country was playing itself, and it was a star. Every town
was a landmark; the road became the movie's narrative arc. There
was an austere chill in the land across which Fox struggled—a
parallel but very different texture from Ingmar Bergman's tidy
Sweden or Richard Attenborough's teeming India. This was
Canada, with its isolation and haunting potential, its dominant
reality: an empty land filled with wonders.

By the time Fox approached Thunder Bay in what turned
out to be the tragic end of his run, he was alone again, lost to
the destinies that dominated his brief life. But alone or not, he
became what he wanted to be, and in the last week of his trek, he
pronounced his own epitaph: " . . . Life is about reaching out to
people—and having them touch you back."

Terry Fox was determined to cross Canada "from telephone pole to telephone pole." His interrupted ordeal is
commemorated by this jewel of a film, which managed to sus-
pend disbelief without romanticizing his odyssey.

— 1980

Jack McClelland: The Authors' Publisher

AT THE HEIGHT of the 1981 publishing season, when bookstores in western Canada started running out of *The Acquisitors*, the second volume of my series on *The Canadian Establishment*, my publisher, Jack McClelland, reacted in typical style. Instead of loading boxes of books aboard trains or planes, he hired half a dozen trailer trucks and dressed their drivers in rented tuxedos. I was never quite certain what the ultimate purpose of this exercise was meant to be, since no one except McClelland and me—who waved off the brave convoy with appropriate formality and exaggerated bravura gestures—paid the slightest attention to the strange caravan snaking its way across country.

But it was vintage McClelland, and I was reminded of this small incident when it was announced that, after twenty-nine years at the operating helm of his publishing house, McClelland was assuming less onerous duties as chairman of the board. He was my mentor and advocate, who launched and nurtured my writing career. He almost single-handedly endowed the country with its indigenous popular literature, publishing authors, instead of printing books. Until then, domestic volumes had been sold in obscure corners of our few bookstores, in modest sections self-consciously labelled CANADIANA. Jack willed us into the mainstream.

His publicity ploys and promotional gimmicks gilded the McClelland legend, such as his annual skating appearance on the rink in front of Toronto City Hall, where he handed out free Canadian paperbacks to anyone who confessed that reading was their pleasure. Or his hiring a tough-looking professional wrestler to page me throughout a Conservative convention, following publication of my controversial biography of John Diefenbaker. (It was during that convention that several western Tories threatened to "tear off my writing arm"—which was a slightly dated sanction, since by then, I had moved from my poison pen to a typewriter; but their intent was unmistakable.)

To those of us who were fortunate enough to be his authors, Jack McClelland was very much more than a good promoter and a great publisher. He was, above all, a sensitive and shrewd editor, spotting the weaknesses in a sentence, paragraph, page or book, writing casual fix notes that magically resolved literary blocks. More than that, he was what all authors need when facing the terror of blank pages and blanker minds: an understanding friend who appreciated the essential loneliness of our craft. He would do anything for his authors, not excluding the arrangement of bail or abortions.

A surprisingly modest individual (and closet war hero as commanding officer of a motor torpedo boat in the Mediterranean during the worst days of the Second World War), McClelland was an irreplaceable and irrepressible force of nature. But at times his sense of the ridiculous ran away with him. A certain Rosedale society lady, whose chauffeur's uniform I had described in my first Establishment book as having specifically been ordered to match the bottom of her swimming pool, took my words to the Supreme Court of Ontario, accusing me of having made fun of her. McClelland did not take kindly to the lawsuit. It was only with great difficulty that Julian Porter, our ubiquitous lawyer, convinced him not to appear in the judge's august chambers dressed in a white toga, prepared to bear witness that its colour matched the bottom of his bathtub. Now, *that's* a loyal publisher.

—1982

Hugh MacLennan: Charting Canada's Psyche

IF CANADA EVER had a spiritual town crier—the James Boswell of our aspirations and afflictions—it was Hugh MacLennan, the Montreal novelist and humanitarian who has died at eighty-three. The author of seven major works of fiction, the best of which, *The Watch That Ends the Night*, ranked as one of the great Canadian novels, and six magnificent essay collections, he was an ardent Canadian, as much in his life as in his writing. To toughen himself to the local climate, he spent ten years of his youth living in a tent at the back of his parents' Halifax house. And despite international honours that included a Rhodes Scholarship, a Guggenheim Fellowship and a PhD from Princeton, he never considered living or teaching anywhere but in Canada. His five Governor General's Literary Awards notwithstanding, the favour was not returned. His best-known work, *Two Solitudes,* which became the fountainhead for defining the shared loneliness that is at the heart of the Canadian experience, brought him initial royalty cheques of only $4,500. Worse, although he had taught English literature with distinction at McGill University for more than three decades and inspired generations of young writers, in 1985 he was unceremoniously evicted from his modest office and left to drift.

None of this soured his writing or his outlook. His prose was saturated with wisdom, humour and tenderness, the passionate cry of a writer determined to assert the unfashionable view that existence is more than a meaningless accident. He was at his best chronicling slow lives, examining men's and women's feelings, portraying their self-imposed distances and their subconscious protection of one another. The truth that he revealed was not in the least sensational. Just truth.

A friend and mentor, MacLennan wrote the introduction to one of my books and became a prolific contributor to *Maclean's* when I was its editor, publishing thirty-three major articles in the magazine. When I asked him how he picked his themes, he replied, in that melancholy Calvinistic burr of his, that they picked him. "You get things through the pores," he explained and left it at that. Released from the novelist's bonds of plot and characterization, his essays succeeded in portraying what U.S. literary critic Edmund Wilson called "a point of view surprisingly and agreeably different from anything else I knew in English: a Canadian way of looking at things." In one of his essays, he warned against our absorption by the Americans and advised Canadians to act "in the spirit of a girl in the backseat of a taxi, with one eye on the meter and the other on the profile of the determined man who took her out that night."

Equally scornful of anything British or American, MacLennan jealously guarded his Celtic heritage. Born in Glace Bay, Nova Scotia, in 1907 to surgeon Samuel J. MacLennan and his wife, Katherine, he credited his Highland roots for the sensitivity of his perceptions. "A Celt," he once confided, "hears a dog-whistle sound that an Anglo-Saxon simply doesn't get." Contemptuous of academic aesthetes, whose books he dismissed as "poetry of the menopause," he believed that a writer must be engaged with the issues of his time, echoing D.H. Lawrence's dictum that "the novel treats the point at which the soul meets history."

He was obsessed with Pierre Trudeau. "The light in his eyes has a subtle and curious Gioconda-like intensity. I doubt if even the painter of Mona Lisa herself could capture it," he wrote me, and then blasted Trudeau for being a cheapskate. "He once invited Peggy Atwood and me to 24 Sussex for lunch, at the end of which he departed in his limousine, and it took us an hour to get a taxi to the airport."

MacLennan's last years were filled with suffering. After he was expelled from his McGill office (he never complained; I only found out about it through a change-of-address card), his second wife, Frances Aline (first wife, Dorothy Duncan, had died in 1957), was struck by lightning and suffered brain damage, while he was afflicted with a rare form of MSG food poisoning. "The symptoms are preposterous," he wrote. "One wakes up and believes one is dead."

None of that diluted his passion for life or for his country. "I have really enjoyed my existence," he noted in the last letter I received from him. He complained that Canadian politics were running at least forty years behind the times and that Quebec had gone crazy as never before. He felt not at all certain that Canada would, at last, amount to anything: "Some fibre went out of us."

No fibre ever went out of Hugh MacLennan. He was a fine man and a great writer, and we were lucky to have lived in a time and place that had him for its town crier.

—1978

Remembering Pierre Berton, the Big Foot of CanLit

WHEN I HEARD the news of Pierre Berton's passing, I reacted with grief, disbelief and dismay. Grief because he had been such a loyal friend; disbelief because he had been the essential curator of the Canadian Dream; and dismay because he was quite simply irreplaceable.

He was the first to take a shot at defining the poignant mystique of our national identity: "The country is still an unknown quantity," he wrote, "as elusive as the wolf, howling just beyond the rim of the hills. Perhaps that is why it holds its fascination." (I never accepted Berton's more popular definition that "a Canadian is somebody who knows how to make love in a canoe." All you had to do was to scan his six-foot-plus frame to know that was a non-starter. Besides, I tried it. No way, José.)

Berton's books, TV series, sermons and other public utterances celebrated his country so convincingly that he almost single-handedly made patriotism an acceptable form of behaviour in polite circles of Canadian society, instead of the semi-subversive emotion it had once been. He did this by recreating Canadian history as a heroic pageant worthy of a significant nation instead of a self-governing colony, as we were so dismissively labelled.

Berton's approach to history had a knack for the unexpected. In one of his later volumes, *Marching as to War*, he argued that counter to their image of themselves, Canadians have never been citizens of a peaceable kingdom. He made a convincing case that in the four wars we fought between 1899 and 1953—in South Africa, twice in Europe and in Korea—Canadians became involved because they wanted to be. The politicians declared war in order to follow the will of the people, not the other way around.

He gained equal fame as a TV panelist and interviewer, managing editor of *Maclean's,* raconteur, army-of-one and frequent accessory-before-the-fact of countless worthy causes. In his political heyday, there were few public petitions championing liberal or left-wing causes that didn't lead off with his name and financial support. He brought to his writing the bias of a social democratic activist. He hesitated not a moment before pledging his loyalty and dollars to the most obscure of humanitarian crusades—bellowing over his portable telephone while lounging poolside at his country estate in Kleinburg, Ontario.

That was where he found his greatest solace, among his extended family and especially with his wife, Janet, who was his anchor. The bluster that marked his daily passage through a crowded lifetime was just that: bluster. His body language could be deafening. He was a tough hombre when it came to writing or editing but treated nearly everyone who came in contact with him kindly and generously—unless they were public relations flacks. He banned these self-inflated messengers from the *Maclean's* editorial floor.

Before his energy was gutted by the heart failure from which he suffered in his final years, his strident physique lent force to his habit of emphasizing his convictions in a voice that must have frightened every stray moose for miles around and left little room for argument. He was a large man with large appetites, the Big Foot of CanLit. Passionate and opinionated, he was unmarked by the gloomy introspection of his calling. His Yukon heritage not only produced some of his best books (*Klondike, The Mysterious North, Drifting Home* and *Prisoners of the North*), but also kept him from becoming a full-fledged member of the Toronto literati with their self-indulgent chatter and habits. That was what kept his focus so clear and his prose so accessible.

Deference to established academic authorities was never his long suit. Berton not only survived his academic critics, but bested them. He understood better than they that history is made up of individual and collective memories refined, the sequence of encounters between character and circumstance. And that Canada's history needed to be told not just through facts, but also with feelings. That Canada will always have more geography than history but that we cannot learn to appreciate the former unless we better understand the latter.

The last time we appeared together was at the Vancouver International Writers Festival in the fall of 1998, at a shindig to celebrate the merits of popular history. He walked in with the aid of a cane, appearing drawn and debilitated. But once we started declaiming the glories of our trade, he came alive, the energy visibly flowing back into his body and his hog-caller's voice back at full volume. "The whole secret," he told the audience, "is to make history read like a novel." That, of course, was exactly what I—and most of the non-fiction writers in the hall—had been trying to do, but we lacked his panache and self-confidence. If he had written music instead of prose, his scores would have carried instructions for the orchestra to play "bravura with abandon." Subtlety was not his strength.

After our presentations, Pierre and I walked over for sandwiches at the Hotel Vancouver. "It's now called the fucking Fairmont," he snorted in the disparaging tone appropriate to any historian of the CPR who had condemned the acquisition of the railway's hotel chain by American owners who changed its name. "We have to preserve the fabric of our nationhood through things like medicare and the gun laws, and all that stuff that is different from the Yankees. We are different," he insisted that day. "Our background is different. Our history is different. The geography is different. We have to sing our own songs and create our own heroes, dream our own dreams—or we won't have a country at all."

What made Berton's five dozen books so valuable was his eye for anecdotes, those tidbits of observable trivia that illuminate

human character. His description of the shameful banishment of
twenty-one thousand Japanese Canadians from their homes and
businesses on Canada's West Coast during the Second World War
began not with a statistical summary of their financial losses but
with the story of Toshiko Kurita, a Japanese Canadian woman
who was quietly walking to her suburban home when a white
man came up to her and spat full in her face.

Following that long-ago encounter in Vancouver, I knew that
the wellspring of my friend's talent would never run dry: that
it might die with him but not before him. Now he is gone, but
his books will outlast him. We must celebrate the unparalleled
relevance of Pierre Berton's accomplishments. We shall not read
his like again.

—2001

June Callwood: A Passion for Compassion

ITALIANS HAVE SAINTS.

The Japanese have National Treasures.

We had June Callwood.

Every country is a mystery composed of the lives of men and women, bound loosely together in common citizenship and a "Republic of Dreams." But each generation is fortunate enough to be blessed with the presence of a few unusual individuals who have the ability to move outside their own concerns and take up the plight of others, often strangers, and help one another in the agonizing proximity of poverty, disease and damnation.

June Callwood was one of those rare compassion dispensers, a woman for all seasons, who once advised a group of McMaster University social science students: "I wish that you suffer enough guilt to grow a conscience—but not so much as to sour your life."

The last time I saw her, at a December 2006 reception for Stéphane Dion, the freshly minted Liberal leader, she seemed to be having a good day, and when she got up to leave, she danced a little jig and winked at me, not for a moment acknowledging that we both knew how fatally ill she was. We never met again. Looking back on that magic moment, I was reminded of Pablo Picasso, who once wisely observed that it takes a long time to feel young.

Her own youth was a drab endurance test, with an absent father, an aloof mother and no steady family income. Growing up, she existed on potatoes and water for days at a time. She began her journalism career at the *Brantford Expositor* in 1941, then joined the *Globe and Mail,* where she met the love of her life, sportswriter Trent Frayne, though she continued to use her own surname because the paper did not employ married women at the time.

Writing became her profession, but compassion remained her calling. She helped establish no fewer than fifty epicentres of social activism, including hostels for abused women and the first AIDS hospice in the country. She never let up in her struggle for justice and freedom, but she did it with such good humour that few could refute her causes. "She sees the good things people do, however small, instead of being consumed by the bad stuff that can be ragingly conspicuous," wrote her biographer Anne Dublin. "By embracing the good, she found the passion she needs to fight for it."

Callwood wrote more than two dozen books under her own

name and was the ghost writer of many more. My favourite was her *Portrait of Canada,* a lively and evocative portrayal of her country at a time when its history was supposed to be so dull that only academics were fit write it. In her take, she mischievously pointed out that "Canadians are the third-largest ethnic group in America."

Much of her best writing was published in magazines. During the 1950s I served with her at *Maclean's* under the fabulous editorial duo of Ralph Allen and Pierre Berton. They never wasted a word. She had a favourite story about how abruptly stories were assigned in those days:

Berton: "We'd like a piece on the universe."

Callwood: "The universe?"

Berton: "Yeah. The universe. Deadline in two weeks."

Callwood: "Fine."

Her home life was solid, but she was not immune to personal tragedies such as the accidental death of her youngest child, Casey, and her own cancer, which was diagnosed in November 2003. She spent sixty-six years in journalism and won every award going plus some created specifically for her. But her greatest concern was for the protection of civil rights. "Very often, our view of civil liberties . . . [is] shaped primarily by something in our Canadian bones," she maintained. "That gut reaction, a conservative reaction, is what makes us a distinctive people. We are not Americans who happen to have drawn the worst climate and best geography; we are a different people, and this is nowhere more apparent than it is in the area of civil rights."

That was the bedrock of her belief system, and she personalized it. "Each person is like a stone in a pond," she observed near the end of her life. "Individual actions, good or bad, send out tiny ripples that change the surface of the public pond. People, by choice, can spread warm understanding or cold indifference."

Her own choice was crystal clear.

—2007

Jack Poole: The Shy Birth Father
of the Vancouver Olympics

LIKE THE PULL of an invisible whirlwind, the proud forest of Vancouver skyscrapers attracted a posse of unorthodox business tycoons whose fiscal fantasies had a habit of coming true. The greatest and yet most modest of them was John W. Poole, the co-founder and moving spirit of next year's Olympic Games, who died just before the Olympic furor started, after an epic battle with pancreatic cancer.

Unlike most of his Vancouver contemporaries, who tended to regard themselves as Sungods cavorting on the playing fields of the Lord, Poole was never satisfied with his skyline-altering achievements. He rightly described himself as "an un-public person," and in his pre-Olympic days, his name seldom appeared in the press. He was ill at ease with journalists, especially when being interviewed in his eighteenth-floor chairman's office at Daon Development Corporation, which was large enough to hold a platoon of foot soldiers, complete with camp followers. On one such occasion, his nervous answers to my nervous questions about his next megaproject left me with the impression that he was as apprehensive as a wrestler sweating in the ring, convinced his championship rounds would never come. As it turned out, this was a fairly accurate reading of his withdrawn personality, since Poole had indeed spent part of his youth as a semi-successful professional wrestler.

A photogenic six footer, the youthful Poole, who grew up in Mortlach, Saskatchewan, graduated in civil engineering from the University of Saskatchewan when he was seventeen. He married his high school sweetheart, Darlene. Though he jobbed around Alberta for a while, his lucky gusher was not an oil well but his meeting with a financially brilliant misanthrope named Graham Dawson. A perpetually angry visitor to our discontented earth, Dawson never learned to spend his money happily and tried to impose Upper Canadian puritanism on Vancouver's Lower Granville hedonism.

When Poole and Dawson became co-founders of Daon, their two-bit construction company was struggling on the down side of breaking even. To give the upstart firm what then passed for *gravitas,* the partners hired former Lions quarterback Joe Kapp as their in-house celebrity.

In 1976, during a brief holiday to California, Poole counted up the houses-for-sale want ads in the *Los Angeles Times* and was stunned to discover there were only 1,400 vacancies in a city of 3.6 million. "We thought, Gee, can this really be as good as it looks—well, it wasn't, it was a hell of a lot better," he told me.

Within the next twenty months, Poole had amassed California's largest land bank and expanded into half a dozen

American metropolitan areas. By 1980, with net income running an incredible $1 million a week, Daon had become the second-largest publicly owned real estate firm in North America. His personal holdings of Daon shares were worth $100 million, which bloomed forth an annual dividend of more than $1 million.

Unlike his Howe Street peers, who expended their extra energy on exotic hobbies, such as squiring young chicks in aubergine bikinis, who, they seriously claimed, were a useful hedge against inflation, Poole stuck to raising Hereford and Simmental cattle on his 160-acre ranch near Surrey. After years of hesitating, he did purchase an expensive motor yacht, but his log book seldom showed more than a dozen outings a year.

Those who knew him best realized that he lived on the tongue of the wind, a man driven more by his dreams for others than for himself. One of the twenty-first century's hallmarks is that no one is indispensable—that, like it or not, most of us have become interchangeable.

Not Jack Poole.

Every country is a mystery composed of the lives of strangers who meet at great occasions such as the Olympics and feel good about their country and better about themselves. Such spectacles inevitably have more than one founding father. But suffice it to say that those who are in the know quite simply insist, "There would have been no Olympics without Jack."

—2009

Marshall McLuhan: Calling Planet Earth

MARSHALL MCLUHAN SLUMPS through the doors of the midtown Toronto restaurant with an oddly rolling motion, like that of a shore-bound sailor, squinting into the half-light, testing his senses against the glum, plastic dining room. At fifty-nine, white-haired and full of honours, McLuhan has grown a little weary of watching the world through his famous rear-view mirror. His Delphic ideas, which once made him sound like a distant interplanetary intelligence, became the dominant cultural insights of twentieth-century life, so that even the girls who enhanced the mystery of their sexuality with tinted stockings and dark glasses were subconsciously responding to his message.

"I heard a story the other day," McLuhan says as we begin a long, relaxed lunch, "about a Scot who comes on the scene of a motor crash. The injured are lying around, and poking one of the survivors in the stomach with his walking stick, he asks: 'Has the insurance adjuster been here yet?' Not yet, is the reply, prompting the Scotsman to ask, 'Do you mind if I lie down beside you?'" The hour or two we spent together every month or so bristled with one-liners such as his imaginary quote from the Greek god Zeus, warning his fellow deity, "Narcissus, watch yourself!"

When I was a University of Toronto student in the fifties, McLuhan used to be pointed out on the campus as that kooky author of *The Mechanical Bride,* and in those days he always seemed painfully intense. Now there was a playful aura about him; he had turned himself into an intellectual minstrel, almost a court jester, coining apocryphal slogans for an apocalyptic age. As a fellow diner got up and paid for his meal, McLuhan winked at me. "Money is the poor man's credit card," he said, and seconds later told a story about a man who went on a date with Siamese twins: "The next day a friend wanted to know if he'd had a good time, and his answer was 'Well, yes and no.'"

His humour was infectious, but Canadian critics had been inordinately harsh on McLuhan's two most recent books, and I asked him why he stayed in Canada instead of moving permanently to the U.S., where several Ivy League universities offered amenable surroundings, amiable colleagues, large salaries and the respect of his peers. Even though he had had dozens of attractive offers—and did leave temporarily to occupy such prestige-encrusted posts as the Schweitzer Chair at New York's Fordham University—he always came back. "It's a nuisance having my books criticized. It's like being caught with your fly open," he admitted. "It confuses my students. But I don't think I've ever had more than half a dozen students who read anything I've written anyway. They're not interested in my stuff, and they know very well that if they use it anywhere in their essays, it's going to be held against them. I warn them never to quote me. Some of my fellow academics are very hostile, but I sympathize with them. They've been asleep for five hundred years, and they don't like anybody who comes along and stirs them up. Still, I experience a great deal of liberty here in Toronto that I wouldn't get in the States, because I'm taken quite seriously there. The fact that Canadians don't take me seriously at all is a huge advantage. It makes me a free man."

The pop culture we've adopted from the U.S. discards its gurus with alarming haste, and McLuhan by this time was not being listened to quite as attentively as he once was. Yet his intuitive leaps, the quality of his probes into a dim future where not only facts, but also the very dimensions that contain them would be changing, remained as relevant as ever. "The new human occupation of the electronic age has become surveillance, CIA-style," he decreed. "Espionage is now the total human activity—whether you call it audience rating, consumer surveys and so on. All men are now engaged as hunters of espionage. So women are completely free to take over the dominant role in our society. Women's liberation represents demand for absolute mobility, not just physical and political freedom to change roles, jobs and attitudes, but total mobility. At the same time, Canadian politicians are faced with a serious dropout problem. They're still talking, but fewer people are bothering to listen. The successor to politics will be propaganda, not in the sense of a message or ideology, but as the impact of the whole technology of the times. So politics will eventually be replaced by 'imagery.' Politicians will be only too happy to abdicate in favour of their images, because the image will be so much more powerful than they could ever be."

That's not your usual chatter over a plate of fettucine alfredo, grown cold and sticky. But McLuhan's soliloquy turned more relevant when he zeroed in on his favourite politician, then in power. "Pierre Trudeau must be at least 40 percent Indian because nobody could penetrate his tribal mask," he told me. "Pierre has no personal judgment, but he is always interpreting the whole process that he's involved in. So that when he slides down a banister or hops off a camel, it's not really a way of expressing what it feels like to be Trudeau—it's trying to express what sort of a hell of a hang-up he's in. He'll do anything to snap the tension."

"Marshall McLuhan and John Kenneth Galbraith are the two greatest modern Canadians the United States has produced," British novelist Anthony Burgess once wryly observed. The influence of McLuhan's intellectual pyrotechnics was best caught in a *Financial Post* article by Alexander Ross: "There was a time when every university in Germany had a free period at 11 in the morning, because that was when Hegel was lecturing in Berlin. McLuhan is that kind of man, in our very own midst. So be proud."

Proud we should be, and it was Tom Wolfe, the tart-tongued

New York journalist, who coquettishly inquired: "Suppose McLuhan is what he sounds like, the most important thinker since Newton, Darwin, Freud, Einstein and Pavlov—*what if he is right?*"

To which Marshall McLuhan, with that tight John Wayne smile, which signalled his most telling sallies, replied: "I'd rather be wrong."

—1971

Ralph Allen: The Man from Oxbow

I WAS IN QUEBEC CITY yesterday morning when I heard the CBC announce that Ralph Allen, who was the most influential of the postwar editors at *Maclean's* and my most memorable mentor, had died in the night.

When that cool voice delivered this stunning news, I thought, How can they presume to sum him up in a hundred words? Now I am trying to sum him up in a thousand and that, too, is an impertinent presumption.

I cannot write about Ralph the war correspondent or Ralph the fisherman or Ralph the raconteur. In the decade I knew him, we had what he once called "the tough relationship between editor and writer"; and we were very different men, of different generations, different backgrounds, different personalities. But I don't expect ever again to know a man I can so implicitly trust and so unabashedly revere. It was he who formed the sensibilities and attitudes that allowed me to view Canadian politics "with a mind cleared of cant."

When I first went to *Maclean's* in 1956, Ralph Allen was its editor, and he made all of us who worked for him seem special, bigger than we were, better writers than we knew how to be. He made us feel part of an admirable adventure. He sat, fat, freckled, red-headed, quick-tempered—and irreplaceable—in a corner office, and the world outside looked manageable. When I look back on those heady times, I realize we were only basking in his reflection and the world was not manageable; we were not golden and never again thought that we were.

As an editor he was no hot-eyed radical but a man of reason, a man of civility and no pretence. His natural enemies were *poseurs* of every description—war correspondents who hadn't gone to the front lines and journalists who talked better than they wrote—mediocrity in all its aspects.

He sought excellence relentlessly. He was a hard and exacting editor. In some ways he did not fit the temper of his times; he was something of a puritan (although no prude) and, for a journalist, uncharacteristically dedicated to defending the individual's right to personal privacy.

His sense of integrity and instinct for fairness were such a large part of his character that it was easy to overlook his personal courage, his sensibilities, his wit and his vitality. He could transform the banter of a ten o'clock coffee break into a memory you would savour for a decade.

Even his interoffice memos were graceful, and as he got older, he overcame more and more of his natural shyness and began to talk as he wrote, in flawless cadence and metaphors that ought to have been bronzed. His most serious writing went into his novels. They were autobiographical only in the sense that in each of them there was one character vainly standing up for reason in a mad world. (His evocative *Peace River Country* curiously portrayed a patch of little-known Canadian geography that later turned out to be the home turf of Alvy, my last, most endearing and most enduring wife.)

Ralph's secret was that what he really wanted to be and what he had been best at—like Roy MacGregor, who I think of as his natural heir, both stylistically and ethically—was sports writing and, specifically, hockey: "For 27 glorious minutes last Saturday night Canada came close to rediscovering the only unique part of its inheritance. In spite of what they'll say in the commission on culture and the proliferating expositions and festivals and aids-in-grant to anybody who knows anybody else, the only true Canadian invention is a game called hockey."

Ralph found uncharacteristic joy in his books, and I remember that on the heady day after he finished his last novel, he phoned me and said that it was "damned good." When a volume of mine was published, he sent a note in which he said that "writing a book has always struck me as a very close parallel to going to a war; a great place to have been and a great place to be back from."

"God bless" was how he wished goodbye to friends, and somehow it was a benediction worthy of a pope—although Ralph himself had a Presbyterian conscience and took great pride in claiming he was a lapsed Unitarian.

Ralph Allen was a good man. When I met him first, I was very young and I thought there were lots of good men, that my world would be full of them. But now that I am not young, I know two things: that there are not many good men and that I am forever lucky and forever different because I knew one. God bless.

—1966

Homage to Christina McCall

WHEN I LEFT the austere High Anglican environs of Toronto's Saint Thomas's Church in the chilly spring of 2005, following the equally austere funeral service for Christina McCall, I felt she had been let down. The prescribed psalms, anthems, creeds, litanies and prayers had been performed faultlessly. But they offered little connection to the spirited life they were meant to celebrate. Having been Christina's devoted husband for seventeen years and an admirer for much longer, I felt I had licence to comment on the liturgy she deserved instead of the one she received.

To her many fans, Christina will be remembered mainly for revolutionizing the non-fiction writing style of her generation, using deceptively simple phrases (such as her salute to Pierre Trudeau—"he haunts us still") to describe the conflicting emotions she observed detonating around her. Her powers of observation transported the impact of cinema-vérité to the written word. Cameras never lie, and neither did Christina.

She taught me the essence of womanhood. She was the quintessential WASP *shiksa* who never misplaced her captivating aura. She had an innate sense of fashion, looking as though she had been born with pearls and a cashmere twin set. She was a singular woman—smart, beautiful, with the eyes of a nightingale and a *zaftig* figure, burdened by a hyperactive Presbyterian conscience—decent to the core.

Then there was the other Christina. Somewhere deep inside her, an unsmiling universe represented the dark side of her Irish ancestry that occasionally exploded into black tempers, when her company was best avoided. She resorted to brutal Hemingway cadences to challenge any male who ventured within firing range. But such occasions were more than compensated for by the pleasures of her company when she shared her heightened sensitivities to enlarge the promises of life.

During the 1960s we became an Ottawa power couple, the first English-speaking journalists to entertain Pierre Trudeau at home, along with his spirited Gallic companion, Madeleine Gobeil, then a professor at Carleton and the woman he should have married. Later, after Pierre had become prime minister, I published my second political book, *The Distemper of Our Times,* which included an appendix bursting with top-secret documents. When his cabinet debated whether or not to charge me with breaking the Official Secrets Act, Trudeau cut off the dispute by deciding instead to prosecute the individual who had given me the offending papers. I never knew whether he was defending freedom of the press or if he recalled having rolled around our living room with his sexy soulmate.

In 1971 Christina and I were hired as a team to save *Maclean's,* then a general-interest monthly, by turning it into a weekly news-magazine. As well as being our best writer, Chris tutored new contributors. "She was the most gifted editor I ever saw; her fix notes were often better than the pieces she was working on," recalled *Toronto Life* editor John Macfarlane, who was a senior editor on *Maclean's* staff at the time. "One felt that you kind of had to live up to Christina."

She eventually left the magazine so that we could co-author the ground-breaking first volume of *The Canadian Establishment.* That was when our differences first surfaced: She wanted to attack the very notion of an elite; I hoped to probe, describe and reveal the uses and abuses of its power structure. Our dis-agreements made us realize that we no longer saw the world in the same way. The deterioration in our relationship took most of a decade to marinate, made worse by my self-inflicted workload. When I returned to my desk one sunny Saturday afternoon, I found Christina lying across it, staging a tearful, personal lie-in to protest my atrocious work addiction. It was the saddest moment of our marriage, but I did little to reduce my workaholic habits.

For most of our time together, not a single piece of copy left our various homes that didn't bear the imprint of shared knowledge and joint editing. But as my output increased, I grew to depend more on her than she on me, and I received most of the public credit. I exploited her talents too blatantly for us to remain equal partners, so that while there still was love between us, there was no longer truth, and so, sadly, we had to part.

Years later, just before we both remarried, we exchanged letters. "For 20 years of my life I valued and loved you deeply, and I know that despite the pain that has swamped my spirit since we came apart, you loved and valued me," she wrote. "I think of you at the wheel of your boat with that crazy cap on and have tenderness for what you were and regret for what we might have become. We were lovers for a very long time and I am glad."

So am I, Christina. So am I.

It was her gift of joy, her unique combination of a cold eye and a warm heart that I expected would find echo in the epitaphs proclaimed by the Anglican officiates at her funeral. It was not to be.

Across the years, through the arid days and brooding nights, even after I found joy and happiness with my present wife, Alvy, I've often thought about Christina: the miracle of the love we shared and the tragedy of its loss. Now there is nothing left to say except the Latin blessing with which we parted: *Pax Vobiscum*— peace be with you.

We divorced over religious differences. I thought I was God and she didn't.

—2005

PART 2
Politics

Michael Ignatieff: The Count Comes Home

GREAT POLITICS, REALLY great politics, must be guided by an invisible hand: the spontaneous intersection of instinct and character—caught in a moment's creative impulse.

That's the trick Michael Ignatieff has been trying to master, with mixed results, ever since he returned to the country where he simmered up, which he now wants to lead. Following his Odyssey—which was far longer than Homer's original tale—he arrived home in style, like a rock pitched through a stained-glass window.

Exactly forty months after he had incarnated as a stranger in a familiar landscape that he had abandoned three decades earlier, the count staged a political masterstroke that, in almost any other jurisdiction, would have been categorized as a *coup d'état*. It was, in fact, the most stunning act of immaculate conception in the country's political history. From what had been a standing political start, the genius savant emerged as the interim leader of the Liberal party and thus Canada's alternate prime minister. Paradoxically, his bold manoeuvre ranked as the second prize. Bizarre circumstances had simultaneously placed him in the lead position of a parliamentary coalition preparing to grasp power and ensconce the itinerant intellectual as Canada's twenty-third prime minister.

That didn't happen, but the alchemy with which Ignatieff intended to lead the lost tribe of Grits back into contention did work its initial magic. Universally recognized as one of the most effective public intellectuals of his generation, but new and untried in the black arts of Canadian politics, Ignatieff managed to keep Stephen Harper, his shrewd and formidable opponent, at bay—stranded in the uncomfortable purgatory of minority status.

Having been a suave professor, a daring human rights activist, the author of seventeen controversial books and the most desirable sex crumpet on the BBC's late-night television panels, Ignatieff volunteered for the Mission Impossible task of rescuing Canada's Liberals from themselves. In power longer than any other political movement, including the Russian Communist party, the once mighty Grits had morphed from their comfortable pew as Canada's Natural Governors into a warring rump of something under fifty thousand bitchy party members, aching to be restored to their accustomed glory.

———

THE MOST PERVASIVE influence on Michael Ignatieff's storybook life and turbulent times was his father, George, who became one of Canada's most distinguished diplomats and very nearly our governor general. He was as much of a hero figure as any to be found in Greek mythology: all-powerful, all-wise—and distant beyond belief. Having lost all in the cauldron of the Russian Revolution, his family came to Canada, virtually penniless and tongue-tied. After a private school education, mostly on scholarships, Michael sailed through Harvard, Cambridge, Oxford and the École des Hautes Études in Paris. On his own as an academic and literary entrepreneur, he reached the pinnacle of his professions (all of them) and was rewarded with the esteem of his adopted countries (most of them).

Now he was back home, and it was payoff time.

———

HOW DID HIS story go again? Let's see—in all the great odysseys, from Homer to Joyce, the hero ends up . . . at the beginning. The Hero Comes Home Again. Five words that sum up most of Western literature of the past 2,500 years. It was archetypal, because one of the great life lessons is that we venture outward to journey inward; we seek new continents to discover ourselves.

Michael arrived, eager to prove himself, even if he had to shoot tin cans off fence posts. A brainy hunk whose heart was pure, his early political gambits were as amateurish as those of a one-album country singer stuck with "If Your Phone Don't

Ring, You'll Know It's Me" as his biggest hit. Despite his determination not to treat Canadian politics as the blood sport it
had become, he ought to have been prepared to deal with the
worst of human nature. After all, when he found his true calling, it turned out to be bearing witness to ethnic slaughter on
three continents and writing up the haunting realities of the
carnage. He discovered first hand that the world can be a hor-
rific place. That there are some assumptions, certain "necessary
illusions," that require unquestioning allegiance—like personal
survival, for instance, or keeping your lines open to that Master
of the American Universe, the mental midget who inhabited
the White House at the time.

Michael's dance card was always full. The mythologies that
piled up about his career helped expand his audience and
minimized his risk, though being frightened was not part of his
repertoire. He revelled in the internal screenplays we all believe
ourselves to be living through and turned them into full-fledged
film festivals—the respectful dividends of a well-spent life. He
was always running, between jobs, lectures, book deadlines, continents, distinguished sinecures, reputations—and wives who
taught him that love is given, not earned.

Having arrived back in his original playpen, he was still running, but now he was running to, not away. He was running
home.

WELL, NOT REALLY. Ever since he'd reclaimed his native land, Ignatieff had been running for the country's highest political office. His qualifications were superb on paper, but his quest was hampered by a basic fallacy. The Emperor-has-no-clothes storyline unravelled because it wasn't logical. Academics, journalists and philosophers hunt for truth, or at least the ring of truth; politicians seek power.

The twain don't meet.

Having the mentality of a writer and the aspirations of a politician meant that Ignatieff had to turn himself into an actor. Having written several plays and movie scripts in which he'd acted, Michael Ignatieff knew the different between acting and politics, even if he couldn't always bridge the gap. It all comes down to theme and variations. Theme from the Greek *themis,* meaning "laid down," like a railroad track or a harmony. When a theme is harmonious, musicians and writers can play infinite variations off it; in books, the grace of cadence illuminates every page. When it doesn't compute, there is discord, no matter how skilful the presenter.

Michael Ignatieff is neither arrogant nor particularly demanding. But after ingesting his millionth rubber chicken dinner, he surely must have felt that he'd earned the respect of a grateful nation. After all, he could have remained on the family farm in rural Quebec and cultivated apples or sold tractors, had a few forgotten affairs and grown a valiant moustache. But no. He had a fierce, burning need to control his destiny, borne of not having known Unconditional Love but having experienced Conditional Surrender. He had an agenda. We all do, even if we're not brave enough to admit it. His agenda had much to do with service to the neglected country of his dreams.

Canada is a dangerous place for patriots. I remember being on Rafe Mair's call-in radio show in Vancouver and saying something as innocuous as "I love Canada. I physically love this country." This innocent exchange prompted two reactions. The most immediate was an angry woman from Burnaby who yodelled into the radio station's open line, "Why are you being so darn anti-American, Mr. Smarty Pants?" (The second was in *Frank,* the satirical magazine, which reprinted my quip about physically loving Canada and wryly commented: "We'd give a nickel to see that.")

———

IGNATIEFF'S NEED to serve the nation he so long neglected was almost physical in its intensity and may be his most fascinating trait. Perhaps it flows from guilt for having been away and missed all those Canadian winters. Still, he genuinely believes that it is his destiny to fashion the country in his own image—its good aspect, not the metaphorical country singer part. Having decided to grab the bull by the tail, he has no wish to be a passive player asking for his readopted land to grant him political asylum. He set out to make his Canada the sort of place you could trust—a liberal Canada, a tolerant Canada, an independent Canada—in other words, a Canada where Michael could feel valued and be valuable.

His internal compass has never been set to ideology. He isn't drawn to liberalism or conservatism *per se*. The regional battles of a quixotic Canada mean as little to him as the squabbles of the Flemish and the Walloons. They were merely there to be studied and mastered but did not claim his loyalty. What he was after was power. Period. He had as much influence as it is possible to garner and still not levitate. But he never had power. He had written and thought so much about the tragic, powerless inhabitants of the Third World that he realized the value of being, as Lord Russell once noted, "in charge of the production of intended effects." That's a valid definition of wielding power, and Ignatieff wanted to grab some of it for himself.

———————

THE LIBERAL PARTY he inherited had yet to pass through the invisible membrane that would allow it to be in touch with contemporary realities, moving beyond its historically successful stance, which allowed its elitist apparatchiks to exercise power more or less benignly on the people's behalf.

In private, Ignatieff conceded that he was the Liberals' riskiest choice for leader but insisted there was an upside because he was plugged into the future. His gospel ran on a simple track: that if it's absurd to believe you can change things—reform the party and plug into the urgent priorities of the country's current needs—it was much more absurd not to try.

Entranced journalists remained eager to record his latest acrobatic reversal of the previous day's pronouncements. These *faux pas* were always newsworthy, and for a while they were daily events—except on slow-news days, when there might be more than a single blooper. Those few, ink-stained wretches who actually read most of his fourteen non-fiction books realized that Ignatieff is a great reporter and a master of evocative prose. The even rarer claque who went on to peruse one or more of his novels recognized him as having a talent that exceeded their own, which in the upside-down ethics of Canadian journalism amounted to a cardinal sin.

―――――

HE MAY WELL BE OUR FIRST POSTMODERN LEADER and, as such, ought to be forgiven the worst of his inner contradictions. They are genuine, the life source of any accredited postmodern savant. If indeed he cares more about ideas than people, that's his loss but also his privilege. He recognizes that the essential issues will always remain insoluble, but for all that, remain susceptible to creative improvisation and that greatest of Canada's gifts to the perpetuation of the democratic paradigm: the ability to muddle through.

Ignatieff's prime gift as a leader is his attentive gravity. He is a great listener. His diagnostic eyes give nothing away. It is his eyebrows that signal his passions, hooding his eyes in moments of concentration, huddling together in V-formation on his forehead to emphasize a point. As an intuitive television commentator, he knows that cameras register the most subtle flickers of emotion through their subjects' eyes. That's why they remain hidden.

Like most public speakers, he plays with the ingredients of his increasingly effective stage presence. Great performances are cumulative. You build a speech from moment to moment, metaphor to metaphor, until it finds its own cadence and then becomes a kind of karaoke that serenades a thousand expectant, upturned faces.

Humour remains a foreign country, but his convictions sound genuine, even if the chill of intellectual arrogance has only barely subsided. There are still too many gaps between what he says and what he thinks, so that he has constantly had to keep contradicting himself. His worst gaffe, shortly after his arrival, was to pledge a renewal of the constitutional wars that had drained the country's vitality during the Mulroney years. That was the first time the political cost of his lengthy absence really counted. Had he been here, he would have known that however benign or creative constitutional initiatives might be, their implementation inevitably leads to a quagmire that turns into quicksand.

So many problems. But when you are no stranger to the daily agonies faced by other countries, it is clear that Canada retains a mandate from heaven. Still, to shrug your shoulders and smile is sometimes the only sane response to the preposterous incongruities of human existence.

There is nothing Michael Ignatieff has set out to accomplish that he has not achieved. Till now. The jury is still out on how his ultimate *beau geste* will play itself out.

—2010

Pierre Trudeau: Phantom of the Canadian Opera

"To be a revolutionary is first of all to make sure of permanence and of a good reception. After which intellectual masturbation is permitted."
—Graffiti, Sorbonne University courtyard, May 1968

HE MAGICKED US. Like the star of *The Phantom of the Opera*, Pierre Elliott Trudeau appeared elusive and unfathomable, yet master of the music of the night. He remained the eternal paradox: an egotist with radical ideals. Masked and huddled in his cloak, he controlled the melodrama of Canadian politics for a generation. He was eventually brought to heel by age, circumstance and the imposition on his good humour of having to deal with a wife who had exhausted his patience. Even then, he lingered in the wings long enough to confound his rivals with a booby-trapped legacy, and his ghostly, chain-rattling appearances allowed him to remain a decisive influence, way past his ordained shelf life.

Canadians have always been of two minds about Pierre Trudeau. They admired him and felt good about being envied for having elected the first Canadian PM to become a world-class celebrity. At the same time, they felt betrayed at having been seduced by a supremely detached Jesuit who acted as if his grandeur grew in direct proportion to his aloofness. Compassion cast little light on his interior landscape. Despite his penchant for making outrageous statements and dressing in what then passed for outlandish costumes—leather coats, desert boots, loose-flowing capes and thonged sandals—Trudeau appeared a lot more daring than he really was.

Though they would endure a week of blackflies before admitting it, most Canadians harboured a delicious inner feeling that they had dared to elect—and re-elect—such a fabulous smartass. (After all, he was *our* smartass—and London's *Daily Mail* had picked him as "the world's seventh sexiest man"—which was about right for a Canadian hero.)

As hypnotic as Trudeau's presence proved to be (someone described his style of government as "despotism tempered by epigrams"), his words were less compelling than his body language, which was worth a PhD thesis—or a rock opera. He was the dancing man, sliding down palace banisters, pole-vaulting onto speech platforms or standing his ground during riots directed at him, dodging Molotov cocktails, leaning back—thumbs hooked into his belt loops. The nerve of the man was breathtaking. No other country boasted a head of government who could dance the Arab *moozmaad* in Sheik Yamani's desert tent; practise his pirouettes behind the queen's back at Buckingham Palace; yell *"Mangez la merde!"* at striking mail-truck drivers; skin-dive, high-dive, ride a unicycle; earn a brown belt in judo; date some of the world's most desirable women; and have two sons born on the same day as Jesus Christ. Even his marriage breakup commanded world attention as Margaret "liberated" herself by bar hopping with the Rolling Stones.

Trudeau in office was a Zen adept who could detach himself from whatever political mayhem was happening around him. Yet he saved Confederation by facing down the Front de Libération du Québec in 1970 and winning the referendum on French Canada's future a decade later. He made us aware that politics at its best consisted not of backroom deals but of sharing the passions of our age. He won four general elections and accomplished precisely what he set out to do: bring home Canada's constitution and sponsor a charter of rights and freedoms, which, in effect, was a contract between individual citizens and the state. In theory, at least, every Canadian now constituted a nation of one.

Pierre Elliott Trudeau put us on the map. His candour, his intellectual curiosity, his nose thumbing at the staid traditions of the country's highest political office qualified him as our first existential political hero: the man with the red rose in his buttonhole, who rescued us—finally—from the dusty age of Mackenzie King. He levitated the staid government party into an activist political and social instrument without ever leaving the ground.

———

IT WAS A GLORIOUS SPRING MORNING in that once-upon-a-time spring of 1968 when Pierre Elliott Trudeau, who had just been sworn in as Canada's fifteenth prime minister, welcomed me as I stepped into his as-yet-unfurnished parliamentary office. He had promised to grant me his first interview as PM, and here he was, ready to shrug into my tape recorder.

During his term as justice minister, he had secretly leaked future plans of his department to me, so that my scoops would test public reaction. That first historic day, as I set up my tape machine in his new quarters, I couldn't control my enthusiasm. "Hey, man, I'm so glad you won. Now, I'll get leaks from *all* the ministries . . ."

"Listen," Trudeau shot back, his face hardened into a Rodin sculpture. "The first cabinet leak you get, I'll have the RCMP tap your phone."

Trudeau was legally correct to squash my feeble attempt to poke fun at the Privy Council oath of secrecy. But his reaction to what was obviously a tension-relieving joke was so extreme that our exchange has stayed with me. It was an early warning signal of how fast and how completely power would change the loose-limbed disco dipper, who only hours before had been on the convention floor, doing the boogaloo with a wild-haired blonde under the shimmering Klieg lights.

———

THE ADVENT OF Pierre Trudeau was a going-away gift from Mike Pearson, the previous Liberal prime minister who left office after exhausting years of remarkable legislative achievements. As well as the frustrations of having to operate with minority governments, he daily faced the wrath and histrionic rhetoric of John Diefenbaker, the Tory Renegade, who saw himself as Samson, determined to bring down the whole damn temple. Pearson recognized in Trudeau a man very different from the florid French Canadians who had preceded him. Despite Trudeau's eccentricities of dress, he possessed the qualities Pearson admired. He was the product of a rich and cultivated home, had been educated abroad, had travelled widely, was an avowed intellectual, a political activist and a convinced internationalist.

On April 4, 1967, Pearson moved Trudeau into the prestigious Ministry of Justice and assigned him to reform a badly outdated legal system. During an interview I had with him at the time, Trudeau went directly to the core of his persuasion: "This should be regarded more and more as a department planning for the society of tomorrow, not merely acting as the government's legal advisor. It should combine the function of drafting new legislation with the disciplines of sociology and economics, so that it can provide a framework for our evolving way of life. We have to move the framework of society slightly ahead of our times . . ."

Eight months later, he presented a reform package to the Commons, and while defending his ideas on television, pronounced the magic phrase: "I want to separate sin from crime. You may have to ask forgiveness for your sins from God, but not from the minister of justice. *There's no place for the state in the bedrooms of the nation.*"

This verity—borrowed from a *Globe and Mail* editorial—was hardly a startling proposition, but it made a disproportionate impact on an electorate numbed by generations of politicians blowing through their moustaches about the gross domestic product and federal-provincial relations. It was the first intimation that Trudeau could excite public opinion.

If Pierre Trudeau's subsequent conquest of the Liberal party appeared in retrospect to have been predestined, with the other leadership contenders serving as spear carriers, in the bleak chill of December 1967, just after Pearson's resignation, Trudeau's victory seemed far from inevitable. In fact, it was scarcely credible. To most Liberals Trudeau was an untested outsider, an upsetting left-wing presence not easily encompassed by the collective middle-of-the-road party mentality, still stuck in times past when Canadian politics were brokered by a dozen Liberal bigwigs.

The denizens of Ottawa's Rideau Club, where these power adjudicators met, were fond of telling each other the story about the time Trudeau turned up on a Saturday morning at the Privy Council Office dressed in desert boots and a boiler suit. The commissionaire on duty, convinced he was a plumber who had his worksheets jumbled, turned him away at the door. When his name was mentioned casually in early speculative talk about possible candidates, it was dismissed as a joke. ("How could anybody who combs his hair forward like that be a Canadian prime minister?")

During his leadership campaign, riding a chartered jet and wearing his signature leather coat, Trudeau travelled twenty thousand miles, making thirty stops. Every appearance produced hysterical ovations. He seemed able, without strain, to establish personal contact with his audiences, operating on a private wavelength the other candidates couldn't jam.

By 1968 television had taken over political conventions. Because TV screens can accommodate only one image at a time and tend to give all events equal significance, Trudeau gained most from the coverage. From the moment he entered the race, the electronic media's managers made an instinctive decision that he would be the winner and assigned full-time camera crews to his candidacy. Their message was not lost on the delegates. Throughout the convention eight cameras constantly clustered around the justice minister—recording Trudeau's wisecracks and outrageous body language. That blanket coverage gave him the advantage of built-in excitement, bathing the dancing man in a constant halo of artificial light. There was about him an indefinable intensity, the suggestion of pent-up power and hidden dimensions that fascinated the nation's TV viewers, impressed the delegates and frightened his rivals.

His emotional impact was demonstrated most forcefully when he arrived at the Ottawa leadership convention by train: women of all ages celebrated his appearance. The girls threw wedding rice, waved Valentines and squeaked in delight, gasping at the sight of him. The ecstasy extended to the next generation, particulary the women. "Something happens to people's faces when they see Trudeau," Ron Haggart wrote in the *Toronto Star.* "You can manufacture noise and screaming kids, but you cannot manufacture that excitement in the eyes. It's not madness, not in these excited matrons and lawyers. It is belief."

Recruiting delegates, Trudeau was completely at ease with himself and his audiences. He did again what he had done for so many years as a University of Montreal lecturer—combined theoretical musings with leaps of intuition, classical references and colloquial quips. To the familiar posture of a seasoned academic were added the touches of a cabaret entertainer. This involved run-on jokes and calculated mannerisms—putting a hand in his watchpocket, sipping water whenever he wanted a moment to think, raising his eyebrows to indicate that he and the questioner didn't need to add to the complexities of human existence by creating new ones. And—always—the exaggerated shrugs. These and other tricks of stagecraft, adroitly exploited, were combined with repartee:

Trudeau: "I hope to be a prime minister who doesn't resemble in every way the Pierre Elliott Trudeau of up to now."

Question: "And how will you change?"

Trudeau: "I'll have more regular hours."

Trudeau not so much captured people's hearts or minds as, in some mysterious way, connected subliminally with their nervous systems. No Canadian politician had ever come close to the collective madness that trailed this Phantom of this Opera. The colourful Ontario MPP Elmer Sopha astutely noted his effect on the swarms of young women: "They're transformed into a strange state. Their eyes are transfixed and they seem to be breathing through their toe nails. You'd think they all had asthma." It was a perfectly accurate description. The day before the Liberals' 1968 leadership convention, I found myself at a Château Laurier hotel reception, standing beside a middle-aged farming couple from Manitoba. As Trudeau made his way down the receiving line toward them, the wife visibly stiffened, turned to her huge block of a sideburned husband and moaned, "What if I faint when he comes in?" The husband smoothed down his Brylcreemed locks, rolled his eyes heavenward and gave her a look of calculated disgust. Just then Trudeau loped by and happened to shake the man's hand. It was a moment out of time, but even though they didn't speak, a visible connection had been made. Trudeau moved on, but the farmer stood there transfixed. His eyes glazed over, he hugged his wife and quietly began to cry. It was as though Trudeau was performing what Norman Mailer described as "the indispensable psychic act of a leader, who takes national anxieties so long buried and releases them to the surface where they belong." This was the mystery that made him the source of such fascination, the trick that the professionals running competing campaigns could not duplicate.

The climax came with his appearance on the convention floor. The candidates outdid one another by the size and noise of their marching bands, led by their most enthusiastic supporters waving placards and shouting their candidates' names. The Trudeau entry was exactly the opposite. He sat there during the speeches, trying to eat a bunch of grapes. He would throw one up in the air and catch it in his mouth. The TV cameras kept prompting him to do it again. ("Could we hear the crunch, please?")

Then it was his turn. As if pulled by a single string, Trudeau banners were silently lifted in every part of the crowded arena. The delegates, instead of applauding, let out a collective "AAAHH," a salute to a daring trapeze artist doing his star turn. The silent demonstration had been carefully planned, even if it looked spontaneous, as though the Liberal party had reached its pro-Trudeau consensus at that exact moment. Trudeau waited in the stands for precisely five minutes, then moved toward the platform. He talked about a Just Society, about strife in the world, about Canada's internal divisions, about each man's share of the eternal burden and confirmed his belief in the triumph of reason over passion. This was the sober, not the witty, Pierre, softly blowing his own horn. At the end of his speech, responding to the waves of applause, he bowed slightly, smiling, in his rounded Edwardian collar, a daffodil in his buttonhole. The candidate seemed assured of victory—in fact, the delegates underreacted to his charms: he barely won on the fourth ballot. It was a reminder that the Liberal party was still smug enough to believe that its mandate had little to do with magic.

———

THE ELECTION CAMPAIGN that followed was a combination of coronation and Beatles tour. Teeny boppers with manes of streaming hair gripped their machine-autographed photos of Pierre-baby to their chests and shrieked whenever he deigned to kiss one of their swarming numbers. Bemused toddlers borne on their parents' shoulders were admonished to "remember him" as excitement surged across the country. Press cameras clicked like hungry insects every time Trudeau stepped from his chartered jet, Caesar haircut intact, to make his triumphant way from one shopping plaza to the next.

I particularly recall landing in Dartmouth, Nova Scotia. We trudged down the plane's slippery steps into a cold, drizzly night. That was wall-to-wall Tory country at the time, but along the route from the airport, as if by a prearranged signal, people spontaneously came out on their porches to wave. Many had backed their cars into driveways so they could flash their headlights in silent salute to the Phantom in the darkened, closed limousine. At the other end of the country, in Victoria, where the monarchy was still an important issue, local Liberals questioned Trudeau closely on a topic he had previously dismissed as irrelevant. He won the crowd over with a shrug and the comment: "I was in Saskatoon last night and crowned a lovely queen, so I feel warm toward the monarchy." For a self-appointed philosopher-king, the campaign hardly qualified as a discourse out of Aristotle. In Winnipeg, to yet another horde of screeching supporters, Trudeau carefully explained, "I do not feel myself bound by any doctrine or rigid approaches. I am a pragmatist." His response was summed up in the yell of a fellow lapsed philosopher-king, who had quaffed too many Molsons. "Yeah, you tell 'em, Pierre-baby!"

There was a certain shock value in his appearance. Voters came prepared to be fascinated and scandalized by a wild man in sandals spouting socialist slogans. Instead they found an immaculate, demure professor delivering proposals that he made sound exciting but would not have been out of place in any Canadian Manufacturers' Association rally. Unable to classify him as a man of either the political right or the political left, most of Trudeau's listeners seemed happy to regard him as a man of the future. Awarded a conclusive majority (155 of 264 seats), Trudeau set out to govern a country which had, in effect, given him a blank cheque.

Trudeau saw himself as being in the tradition of Jean-Paul Sartre, the existentialist French philosopher who claimed that each individual is what he makes of himself—that "man invents himself through exercising his freedom of choice." This was a welcome notion to "Lucky Pierre," especially during his early years in power, when he became familiar with the mystical entity that is Canada for the first time and responded through authentic political acts; he imagined he could create

a workable political creed by revealing the character of the
nation to itself.

————

THERE HAD TO BE A GAP between his promise and his
performance. But that didn't explain why he almost overnight
became such a lightning rod for populist frustration. I remember watching with fascination a burly trucker at a motel near
Red Deer who had lost two quarters in a vending machine. He
stood back and kicked the thing. Nothing happened. He shook
it nearly off the hinges. No luck. Then he stepped back, took a
deep breath, glared at the offending contraption and cursed,
"God *damn* Trudeau anyway!"

Trudeau could never grasp the fundamental animating spirit
of Canadian democracy: that political parties are not ideological
armies but temporary coalitions of disparate men and women,
in it not for glory or monetary gain—but mostly as a divertisse-
ment. To him, politics existed to provide intellectual stimulation.
He could not grasp the idea that bored housewives from the
Soo became Liberals because party functions transmogrified
them into vaguely officious charmers or that unkempt carousers
from St. Boniface belonged to the party because they saw themselves as heavy-duty prime-time guys at political picnics. The very
notion that anyone would go into politics except as an act of
duty to the state or an exercise in ideological expression baffled
and escaped the leader's ken. As a result, during the first part of

his run, Trudeau almost invariably picked the wrong advisors—earnest clones who transmitted to him no sense of country, since their intuitions echoed his own.

Only four years after he had swept the nation's hearts and polls, Pierre Trudeau sat in a bedroom of the Château Laurier Hotel on election night, calculating the knife-edge margin of the 1972 campaign that would barely retain him in office. Turning to a sweating aide, he whispered: "I'll tell you one thing for certain: from now on, no more philosopher-king."

From then on, there was much innovation in Trudeau's approach, with most but not all of his agenda being limited to a perpetuation of the good old Liberal ethic, which held that the chief function of the party is to stay in power by defining and refining bureaucratic initiatives. The legions of academic enthusiasts who had enlisted early in the Trudeau crusade and organized campus clubs on his behalf were not misguided in viewing him as the first Canadian prime minister who had gone into politics with a recognizable set of beliefs. But he faced the insoluble dilemma of every professor who dares enter the political arena: intellectuals hunt truth, politicians seek power—and the twin quests operate in contrary orbits.

Most of Trudeau's ministers qualified as the Canadian equivalent of Whigs, a British political movement described by A.R.M. Lower, the Queen's University historian, as "people who in general were on the side of righteousness, took a benevolent attitude toward it, but felt no urge to advance interests other than their own or those with which they identified." In the subsequent process of travel and observation, he realized what all perceptive Canadian prime ministers have come to know: that the country is just too damn big and much too diverse to be effectively governed; that even the man who occupies the nation's highest political office is there not to seek historical vindication or to champion a New Jerusalem, but mostly to preside over the choice of available options—cross his fingers and hope for the best. In an interview shortly after gaining office, he told me: "We need to tell the people, 'Okay—if you want to have portable fridges on the beaches and portable television sets and so on, that's fine, but maybe we can't swim in the water because it's polluted. But if we want clean water, we'll have to pay higher taxes, which means we don't have our portable television sets. Now what will people choose? Perhaps they'll choose television sets. But at least they won't say then that the government can't do anything about pollution. I'm suggesting we have to explain this to people. Explain that they must have choices . . . It's a sense of helplessness which destroys society. It's the feeling that everything is out of control. But government can't really solve the problems by itself. What preserves free societies is the facing of difficulties by all its citizens."

———

TRUDEAU'S REIGN REMAINED an anomaly because within Official Ottawa, lucidity and frankness had always been in short supply. His deliberate vulgarisms and unwillingness to fudge the accepted quota of issues left a legacy of aphorisms, if not swift action:

Campaigning for the Liberal leadership on March 10, 1968, in Victoria: "An exciting Party should have both blondes and brunettes."

To a bull, at an artificial insemination centre at Milton, Ontario, on June 19, 1970: "It must be a good life."

In an interview, when asked about his prime ministerial duties: "I'm not going to let this job louse up my private life. And I don't wear sandals around 24 Sussex Drive. I go barefoot."

In Winnipeg on December 13, 1968, at a time of poor markets: "Why should I sell the Canadian farmers' wheat?"

When asked in April 1970 about Canada's indifferent policy to a starving Biafra: "Where's Biafra?"

That last quotation—used more frequently than any other to demonstrate Trudeau's arrogance—illustrated how even the most offhand of his comments had a deeper meaning. Unlike 99.9 percent of Canadians, Trudeau knew precisely where Biafra was, having visited that region of Nigeria during a world tour in the 1950s. His government's policy was to recognize Nigeria as a nation but not its breakaway province of Biafra. Since Quebec was pushing for separate international status, Trudeau was trying to underline his view that, legally, Biafra did not have a separate existence and should not be treated as a separate entity.

A faint Orwellian air hung over the nation's capital during the Trudeau years as the leader patrolled the ranks of his followers like an unblinking shark. Despite his shimmering intellect and resoluteness of purpose, Trudeau operated from a profound fallacy by attempting to stifle any signs of disagreement. Tolerating dissent is an essential means by which a society comes to terms with change, but the prime minister and his inner circle believed they could impose logic on events, that they could govern the country through legalism and reshape events to fit those legalisms. But events are never logical; history is born out of harsh realities and even harsher emotions, which cannot be cut to fit a leader's wishes or noble intentions. The Trudeau court lived and worked in an environment as cloistered as a high-walled Gobi Desert treasure city before Marco Polo came by. What they forgot was that in a democracy, minority's dissent is just as important and significant as majority's assent; that thoughts and feelings, however untidy, must be gathered from diverse sources, not among the gossip spreaders of the parliamentary cafeteria. Caught between militant demands and moderate possibilities, Trudeau occasionally retreated into petulance.

For their part, most of his colleagues were quite content to let Trudeau handle parliamentary matters. They tried to copy his air of elegant disdain in the House of Commons but could rarely carry it off. Eric Kierans, the most enlightened intellect at the Trudeau cabinet table, once complained to me about the nature of its deliberations. "It was like a papal procession. When the pope steps from the altar at St. Peter's and walks down the aisle," he confided, "the one thing you know is that he's going to get to the other end. You can argue and argue but, ultimately, the procession goes on its way. In cabinet, you were always listened to with great respect, but nothing would ever happen." Around the cabinet table, Trudeau's ministers were reduced to a league of awed men and women, not so much afraid to challenge his views as uncertain of their own in the face of his intellectual agility and strength of purpose.

I recall the time I was discussing the PM with Gordon Fairweather (later named the first chairman of Canada's Human Rights Commission but then a Conservative MP from New Brunswick), who commanded enormous respect and affection. When the Trudeaus had given birth to one of their December 25 babies, Fairweather was delighted. In a burst of bonhomie, he went down to his local post office on Boxing Day to send a congratulatory wire. In the post office the telegrapher, a true-blue Tory, refused to transmit the message. She tried to get Fairweather to give up on it. He wouldn't—and found the whole episode quite amusing, a vignette of his riding's unchangeable Tory ethic. When the House session opened in January, Fairweather went up to Trudeau at the Speaker's cocktail party and tried to tell him what had happened, thinking Trudeau might find it amusing. Trudeau sternly stared back at him, with no interest, and said—as though he thought Fairweather was fishing for a thank you for the telegram—"Oh, I never saw it. There were so many hundreds of them we decided not to be bothered." Fairweather later commented that he felt not so much hurt as punctured—as though he had been punched in the chest, hard.

And yet there were moments when Trudeau *did* show his feelings. On November 21, 1979, when he walked into the Liberal caucus, only Marc Lalonde knew what was about to

happen. Former health minister Monique Bégin, sensing something was up, whispered to a colleague: "*Il y a le malheur à la
porte*" ("Misfortune is at the door"). Trudeau pulled several
sheets of paper out of his pocket and in a flat voice started to
read: "I am announcing today that after spending nearly twelve
years as leader of the Liberal party, I am stepping down from
the leadership . . . ," then broke into tears, weeping too hard
to finish.

WHAT HAD REALLY HAPPENED during the Trudeau years
was that the very nature of Canada—a country agonizingly settled and developed in an east-west direction—swung around on
its north-south axis. Nearly everything that moved—air traffic,
long-distance calls, computer hookups, trade, taste, ideas and
ambitions—started to flow "up and down," rather than *across*
the continent. And yet the feds, who for generations had been
hypnotized by the Ottawa-Montreal-Toronto golden triangle,
still regarded Canada as an extension of Donald Creighton's
"Empire of the St. Lawrence."

After the troubles of the 1970 Quebec Revolution were largely
over, I had a long talk with Trudeau about the War Measures
Act and its imposition; what I remember most about that session
was his reaction when I suggested that, if he had not gone into
politics and stayed as a lecturer at the University of Montreal
pursuing his reform causes, he would surely have been arrested

and had his books seized in the October police roundup. "Let me answer you in theory," he replied. "If I had been on the side of those who were challenging the authority of the duly elected representatives—then I bloody well would have deserved to be in the risk of being arrested. You can't have anarchy without somebody getting a boot in the ass at the hands of the duly elected government. So, if I'd been on the side of the anarchists, I hope I would have been mature enough to say, 'Well, I personally didn't deserve it, but I can understand the state not lying down and letting the anarchists take over.'"

Terminally cool, Pierre Trudeau finally took leave of his office in 1984 after a turbulent sixteen years, with elegance and grace, happy not to linger merely as macho proof of his longevity or self-importance. More than any of his predecessors, he had made tough, unpopular decisions and challenged the voters to love him or lump him. They did both. By that winter the political terrain had become either a graveyard (the West) or a minefield (the rest of the country) for the embattled Grits, and the electorate was lying in wait to humble their leader. In his novel *The Deer Park*, Norman Mailer postulated a law of life: "that one must grow, or else pay more for remaining the same." On that basis Trudeau had overdrawn his psychic account. He decided to quit because he couldn't think of a reason to stay. The constitution was home; bilingualism was permanently in place; the deficit was out of control; his peace initiative was stalled; the economy seemed beyond salvation. There was no fun in the nation's business anymore, half the provincial premiers were acting like reactionary duds and the Tory Opposition had a respectable leader.

Trudeau kept his blue mood private except for one curious occasion in mid-October 1983, when he interrupted a political speech he was giving at Strathroy to deliver a soliloquy on his thoughts as he was being driven through the Ontario heartland. He spoke of his bewilderment about the country he administered but had never truly understood: "There was acre upon acre of farmland, and all we could see—though I pressed my forehead against the cold window—all we could see were little lights here and there. And I was wondering: what kind of people lived in those houses? And what kind of people lived, loved and worked in this part of Canada . . . ?"

The reason so many Canadians were so ambivalent about their leader was that they remained ambivalent about their country. Trudeau provided a catharsis from the outdated ennui of his nineteenth-century predecessors. He exposed our collective prejudices, regional jealousies and general stuffiness, so that when his term expired, instead of completion, there remained the feeling that somehow we had let *him* down, that his challenge to make us a little less grey, and play it a little less safe, had gone unanswered. His departure was a mixed blessing. This dichotomy of sorrow and jubilation was best caught in an old quote from the French essayist Jean de La Bruyère, commenting on the demise of a literary rival: "It is rumoured that Piso is dead. It is a great loss. He was a good man and deserved a longer life. He was talented, reliable, resolute and courageous, faithful and generous—provided, of course, that he really is dead."

He left office with one consoling thought. Pierre Elliott Trudeau, the constitutional lawyer turned phantom prime minister, had broadened his universe and made the world his stage, never for a moment forgetting to uphold his ultimate civil liberty: the right to be himself.

———

UNLIKE MOST RETIRED PRIME MINISTERS, who retreat into corporate sinecures, Trudeau experienced an active afterlife. Even if he was no longer running the country, he could still sway its perceptions. This exquisitely stubborn man never yielded. Age had permanently set his face into the carved alabaster mask of some distant crusader, but he emerged from his political grave to scuttle the twin constitutional accords—Meech Lake and Charlottetown—which would have revolutionized the country's constitution but not in the manner approved by the man in the leather coat. Trudeau had gone underground for three years after leaving power, never saying a public word. Then he emerged, rhetorical guns blazing, vigorously undermining support for Brian Mulroney's constitutional initiatives. A member of the French-Canadian Establishment by birth, upbringing and bank account, Trudeau became the embodiment of populist defiance. He adopted the guerrilla tactics of a Che Guevara on poutine, husbanding his resources for dramatic confrontations, using the elements of propaganda and surprise to make up for his non-existent constituency.

Determined to scuttle the referendum on the ultimate version of the Charlottetown agreement, on October 1, 1992, the former prime minister spoke passionately for fifty minutes to a gathering of cronies about the perfidies of the Mulroney initiative. The venue he chose was La Maison du Egg Roll, a Chinese joint in Montreal's working-class St. Henri district that offered all-you-can-eat buffets for $6.95. His intervention prompted nearly half of undecided Canadians to weigh in against the deal. He was not bothered by the fact that his criticism was unacceptable to most Quebeckers. As with his implementation of the War Measures Act a generation earlier, his intervention would heighten Quebec nationalist sentiment, but in his lexicon of values, that was worth no more than an emphatic shrug. John Ciaccia, a Quebec cabinet minister, accused him of "fanning the flames of bigotry," while Jean Paré, editor of *L'Actualité,* wrote, "Outside Quebec, Trudeau has found himself in the company, amongst others, of marginals and extremists to whom he gives not leadership, but a justification for their prejudices."

Long past his prime and with no tasks left undone except to defend the history he had made, he cast himself in the role of the country's beleaguered conscience. He was listened to partly because his beguiling appearance as the Phantom of the Canadian Opera was so convincing and partly because he was willing to rattle Brian Mulroney's chains but mostly because he played to the prejudices of English Canada. He brought out the worst in English-speaking Canadians, exposing their anti-French and anti-Catholic biases and regional jealousies. Outside Quebec Trudeau was hailed for putting down Quebeckers and their nationalist aspirations; inside Quebec he was reviled for, as *Le Devoir* columnist Lise Bissonnette put it, "being unreal, pathetic, a sore loser. One is nevertheless moved by this powerful man's raging and sad look at his vanishing dreams."

His activity was not limited to constitutional troublemaking. Trudeau consulted almost daily with his former deputy prime minister, Senator Allan MacEachen, who regularly brought parliamentary business to a halt by rallying the seventy-three Liberal members of the Upper Chamber to vote against the government. The Senate constituted Trudeau's government-in-exile, where such warlocks as Jack Austin, Keith Davey, Jerahmiel Grafstein, Michael Kirby, Leo Kolber, Colin Kenny, Joyce Fairbairn and Royce Frith obstructed pivotal Tory legislation, including free trade, the Goods and Services Tax and the drug patent bill. (The Trudeau-appointed constitutional whiz Senator Eugene Forsey bizarrely explained, "It's because I'm a John A. Macdonald Conservative that I sit in the Senate as a Pierre Trudeau Liberal.") At the same time Trudeau indirectly controlled what was happening inside the Liberal party by undermining John Turner's leadership, especially after the Bay Street lawyer jumped aboard the Meech Lake submarine. Jean Chrétien later admitted that, when he took over the party, he checked his speeches with Trudeau before delivering them.

Particularly galling to Mulroney, then in office, were the public opinion polls from 1988 onward that showed Trudeau, long retired, was consistently running ahead of him in popularity (55 percent to 14 percent in April of 1991), even though he was by then into his seventies and seldom budged from his art deco mansion on Montreal's Pine Avenue. Mulroney comforted himself with a witty bit of sarcasm. "I suppose if you're Pierre Trudeau," he said, "it must be kind of difficult to get up in the morning and look in the mirror and know you've seen perfection for the last time all day." Mila was more direct. "I want to know," she once asked me, "why people keep saying Trudeau is such a great intellect. Because he quotes Nietzsche? I could train Nicolas to quote Nietzsche if I wanted to. This doesn't make someone brilliant. The two keys that can unlock any door are intelligence and good judgement. Trudeau had no judgement. In sixteen years he took a strong country and damaged it. Also, I don't understand how this short, little, ugly, pock-marked man became a sex symbol. And here's Brian, with his wonderful, deep voice, those beautiful blue eyes, his generous nature and wonderful sense of humour . . ."

To Mulroney it seemed that his predecessor had not so much elevated the office of prime minister as crippled anyone bold enough to occupy it after him. To Trudeau battling the constitutional accords was only half the fun. He continued to influence social policy as well, possibly on the grounds that phantoms have to keep busy or they vanish. At a private Ottawa dinner party on April 6, 1988, held to mark the twentieth anniversary of his assumption of power, the former prime minister laid out a political agenda for the 1990s. "For too long," he proclaimed, "we have experimented with the dark side of excellence. For too long this

country has suffered from politics that stresses economic efficiency instead of social fairness—and it's in that direction our
party must make its next policy thrust."

Trudeau was criticized for being a man of the past, but in
response to such accusations, he would shrug and say, "I suppose Pythagoras was yesterday's man also, but two and two still
equals four." He was an equal opportunity political assassin, criti-
cizing Jean Chrétien ("he knew his limitations") with the same
throwaway arrogance he applied to Joe Clark ("headwaiter of
the provinces") or Brian Mulroney ("a sniveller, a constitutional
pyromaniac").

Whatever his faults, Trudeau understood the cold grammar of
power and refused to succumb to—or even recognize—the pressures and pulls of a country in turmoil. Like the Phantom he staked
out his ground and dominated the stage. His charter permanently
transformed the relationship of Canadians to their governments;
his reckless budgets left the country in such dire debt that only a
wave of political reactionaries, the style of leaders he hated most,
could rescue it. His pivotal contribution to the defeat of the Meech
Lake and Charlottetown accords was a flash triumph that could in
retrospect turn out to have been a national tragedy.

He was insensitive to the consequences of his political intru-
sions. "I'm quite prepared to die politically—when the people
think I should," he ruminated on one of the final occasions
we had together. "Politicians should be like Trappists, who go
around in monasteries and the only words they can say to each
other are: 'Brother, we must die one day.' I think this is true of

politicians. The world is so full of a number of things, I'm sure we could all be as happy as kings."

The last time I saw him was at a Montreal reception in the spring of 1995. Looking at Pierre a generation later, the only connection to his charismatic past was the gorgeous young woman sensuously draped over his arm. He seemed less feisty, more introverted—a philosopher-king without a kingdom.

As in the third act of *The Phantom of the Opera,* when the protagonist is brought to ground and his magical powers desert him, Lucky Pierre was eventually abandoned by most of his groupies and disciples. He had not changed; the country had.

Then I remembered my fantasy about Pierre Trudeau as the star in *The Phantom of the Opera* and realized that the fat lady hadn't sung yet. I turned to tell him. But he was gone.

Once a Phantom, always a Phantom.

—1995

Lester Pearson: A Good Man in a Wicked Time

THE POLITICAL DEEDS and misdeeds that account for a prime minister's legacy flow as much from luck as from his character. Lester Pearson came to office at a parlous moment in his country's history. A good man in a wicked time, he refused to subvert his decent instincts or abandon his quest for world peace and Canadian unity. He was not a politician corrupted by power, if only because he so seldom used it, except in the most subtle and unobtrusive ways.

Pearson's vacillation in office accurately personified the confused state of the country he was trying to govern, a Canada grown uncertain of its domestic and external purposes in a rapidly changing world. Although most of the economic, social, cultural and political forces that burst into the open during the mid-sixties were already in train before he came to office in 1963, their impact accelerated so swiftly that his world blew up under him.

If there was a unifying theme to Lester Pearson's productive stewardship, it was his fatalistic approach to history—not as an orderly progression of events, but as an accumulation of tumbling paradoxes in the midst of which anything might happen and almost nothing was foreseeable. He regarded politics as the formidable mission of trying to control that chaos, a province of infinite contingencies that no doctrine could encompass and no grand design could subjugate. At the same time he recognized that the essential issues would always remain insoluble (that's why they were essential) and saw himself as a creative improviser, possessed by the capacity to put disappointments aside, place them in new perspective and move on. All that a sensible man could do, he realized, was to try to work through his destiny with as little unpleasantness to himself as possible. To Mike "The Diplomat" Pearson, there was nothing wrong, and much that was right, in the Canadian tradition of muddling through. "We'll jump off that bridge when we come to it," he'd comfort assistants frustrated by his indecision.

It was no accident that the most memorable aspect of the Pearson style was a wry, self-deprecating sense of humour that flourished under stress. On November 25, 1964, when the Lucien Rivard scandal was breaking in the House of Commons and it looked as if his administration might be swept out of office on the pointed allegations of Tory prosecutor Erik Nielsen, Pearson was due to make a speech to a municipal banquet in the Prairie city of Lloydminster. This was his first public appearance since the serious charges had been raised against his government, but Pearson defused the situation with this opening: "I am grateful, Mr. Mayor, for your welcome, because in your local weekly paper—which was kindly sent to me in Ottawa by air mail before I came here so I could get into the atmosphere of the community before arrival—I noticed the headline on the front page. The headline read, and I took it down, WELCOME PRIME MINISTER and then underneath, another headline SEWER INSTALLATIONS PROGRESSING . . . Well, I warn you, I don't intend to go down the drain yet."

A politician, like a clergyman, is wise not to jest too freely about his vocation, but Pearson could make his puns work for him, both as a way of puncturing his opponents' rages and to help maintain his own equilibrium. During a question-and-answer period at a Canadian University Liberal Federation convention on February 2, 1967, he used an Adlai Stevenson story to illustrate his point. It was about the Indian fighter who crawled into the frontier fort with three arrows in his back and was asked whether it hurt. He answered: "Only when I laugh." Stevenson would tell the story and quip: "My job only hurts me when I *don't* laugh." Pearson added: "I sometimes feel the same way."

His amiable and irreverent lack of pretension was noticeable even in the trivia of his office arrangements. John Diefenbaker, his predecessor, had always kept in full view, as a symbol of his power, the red NORAD emergency telephone that connected him directly to the president of the United States. "I can get Ike any time," he would boast to visitors. Pearson not only removed the instrument from his desk, but hid it so well that one morning during the winter of 1964 when it rang, he couldn't find it. Paul Martin, the external affairs secretary, was in the PM's office at the time. The two men heard the NORAD phone buzzing, couldn't locate it and began to chase each other around the room like a pair of Keystone Kops.

"My God, Mike," said Martin, "do you realize this could mean war?"

"No," Pearson puffed, "they can't start a war if we don't answer that phone."

The instrument was finally located behind a curtain, and the caller—who wanted to know if "Charlie" was there—turned out, by incredible coincidence, to have both the wrong number and accidental access to one of the world's most private hotlines. (Pearson used the phone only once. On April 21, 1967, while he was being driven to his summer residence at Harrington Lake, his car struck a rock and broke its transmission. The hotline was the only telephone available, so Pearson called Washington to arrange for a tow truck to be sent out from Aylmer to get him moving again.)

———

PEARSON WAS FUSSY about personal matters, sometimes displaying a cranky peevishness toward the small errors or omissions committed by his staff. On one occasion during the Centennial summer of 1967, he got into a snit over a glorified portrait of himself done by the Vancouver artist Joyce Devlin. After he had criticized her work, he finally told her that his likeness didn't appear to make him look strong and decisive enough. "Who do you think you are?" the artist demanded in exasperation, "Winston Churchill?" Pearson never took delivery of her canvas.

Such displays of temper were rare, and if Pearson brought little grandeur to his office, neither did he occupy it with any sense of pompous pretension. In fact, becoming prime minister changed him very little. His personal tastes remained simple and surprisingly unsophisticated, considering the number of years he had spent in the supercivilized environment of the diplomatic circuit. The Pearsons rarely attended (or gave) cocktail parties, and when they did go, they usually lingered briefly, sipping weak rye and ginger ales. The rivalry between Pearson and John Diefenbaker even intruded into sport. They both enjoyed fishing, but neither had much luck at Harrington Lake, the PMs' official summer residence. Pearson kept hearing rumours that Diefenbaker had caught a four-and-a-half-pound trout and was unable to match this record. When he tracked the story down by talking to a farmer who lived nearby, he was delighted to discover that, while Diefenbaker had indeed hooked such a fish, he'd never got it into his boat.

Pearson's passion for baseball, hockey and football was intense. On one occasion, when he met two Ottawa Rough Riders in their civilian clothes, walking along a Château Laurier corridor, he not only recognized them, but also knew what positions they played and what their records were. After a crucial game in the 1965 Stanley Cup playoffs, he was taken to visit the

Maple Leafs' dressing room. Even though the exhausted players were sitting around in sweaty underwear with their numbers off, he knew each man's name and could discuss his statistics. Earlier, during a dismal political journey into rural Saskatchewan in 1958, Pearson was slumped in the back of a car, listening to the rasping tones of an old political colleague, Jimmy Gardiner, as he held forth on the iniquities of Tory agricultural policies. Pearson said nothing for mile after dusty mile, but as they drove through a small elevator town, he suddenly came to life and interrupted Gardiner by abruptly exclaiming, "Hey, that was Floral we just passed through. That's where Gordie Howe was born."

He followed the World Series with fascination, no matter what crisis might be claiming his attention, and could name the starting line-ups and batting averages of most American teams. On May 10, 1963, during his first official call on President John F. Kennedy at Hyannis Port, his knowledge was put to the test by Dave Powers, the resident White House baseball expert. While Kennedy listened, the two men traded managers' names, World Series statistics and other diamond lore. It was Powers, not Pearson, who tripped up on some southpaw's 1926 earned-run average. "He'll do," Kennedy remarked, and the two leaders proceeded to equip Canada with nuclear warheads.

Invariably charming in private conversation or intimate gatherings, Pearson often came across as disdainful and remote on the hustings, where the effectiveness of a democratic politician must be tested. Whenever he led the Liberals into electoral battle, he marched them backwards, snatching near defeat from the jaws of victory. Denied a parliamentary majority, Pearson was deprived of any political leader's most valuable asset: a clear mandate from his people. The reason he stirred so little mass emotion at election time was due to a basic shyness. There was about him an air of reserve, a feeling that he should not be drawn into situations where his prestige would be risked in routine encounters. He confessed to close friends that he just couldn't walk up to strangers and pump their hands without being afraid of either invading their privacy or compromising his dignity. He acted always within the consciousness of his limitations and of the voters' awareness of them. The simple fact was that he didn't like people in large groups because he thought they didn't like him.

At the start of the 1963 election, party organizers had worked hard to mount a successful campaign kickoff in London, Ontario, traditionally a poor territory for the Liberals. They succeeded so well that they not only filled the city's largest arena, but were also left with an overflow of two thousand potential supporters outside the hall. When Pearson drove up, David Greenspan, a bright young Toronto lawyer who had headed the local organization drive, pushed his way toward the limousine, shoved his head through the car window and shouted: "Mr. Pearson! These people outside can't get in. They've been waiting for two hours in the cold. Here's a bullhorn; you have to say something to them." Pearson shrank back and, with an emphatic head shake, said: "I can't do that." Finally, Gordon Edick, then the Ontario Liberal party's assistant director, physically barred Pearson's way into the arena until he had grasped the bullhorn to mutter an awkward acknowledgement of the crowd's enthusiasm.

This absence of communicable political passion confirmed him in the public mind as a curiously disengaged politician who could not be brought to bay by the urgencies of the moment. Although he had the advantage of great national issues to make the country hang upon his words, on few occasions did passion— or anger—burst through to reveal the extent of his emotional commitment to his own policies. In an age of image politics, when inspiration was replacing identity as the link between voter and candidate, Lester Pearson seldom projected any sense of personal commitment.

This feeling was reinforced by the fact that, during the first three years of his time in office while his government reeled from mishap to misfortune, few, if any, of the Liberals' legislative measures resembled the original proposals on which they were based. The Canada Pension Plan went through at least four mutations; the 1963 compromise with the provinces over the municipal loan fund made it into something very different from what had initially been put forward. Pearson's method of government often seemed to consist of engaging the nation in a horrendous rescue operation, made necessary by the Liberal leader's precipitate tackling of some hitherto insoluble national problem. Each time, Pearson's own political backtracking raised national frustration to such a peak that public opinion finally solidified behind him in order to help the government find some way out of its self-generated crisis. Almost as a side effect,

the issue itself would have been reduced to reconcilable pro-
portions. While this method achieved some impressive results,
Pearson's personal credibility diminished in the process.

The most spectacular example of the method's success was
Pearson's crusade for the adoption of a distinctive Canadian
flag. When he abruptly produced a red, white and blue pen-
nant with three maple leaves in May of 1964, only a few
Canadians felt particularly involved in the flag issue. Seven
months later, so much public pressure had been built up that a
majority of Canadians were hotly in favour of resolving the flag
debate one way or another, and when the Liberal government
applied parliamentary closure to cut off the Conservative anti-
flag filibuster, there was hardly a ripple of resentment. The
fact that the flag adopted had one less colour and two fewer
maple leaves than the initial design didn't really matter—
least of all to Pearson, who regarded adoption of a distinctive
Canadian flag (no matter what its detailed design) as his greatest accomplishment.

———————

WHILE HE ALWAYS APPEARED to be conciliatory, most of
Pearson's achievements came about through a procession of
crises that precipitated their own solutions, like thunderclouds
that send down rain to clear the sultry air. He was at his best in
times of great stress when his diplomatic training allowed him to
underreact to the torrent of events threatening to engulf him.

"That's blood under the bridge," he would airily say to nervous aides as they fretted about the next catastrophe that could befall the government. Grant Dexter, editor of the *Winnipeg Free Press* and a reporter of wisdom and tender conscience, once wrote about his close friend: "Mike is happiest when he's clinging to a precipice and just about to fall off."

During the crunch of a crisis, Pearson would launch himself on two or three different courses of action at the same time, agreeing with advisers who offered conflicting opinions, reserving his own decision until everyone else had shown their hand. His government's legislative proposals were treated like position papers presented at the beginning of international conferences, statements of basic intent open to revision as negotiations proceeded. He would allow events to play over possibilities, forcing the outlook now one way, now another. Then, just as the conflicting sets of options seemed about to collide, he would move in with a compromise that left all those involved free to claim partial victory. As the quintessential diplomat-politician, he was always more concerned with the consequences of failure than the rewards of success.

Because Mike Pearson felt certain that his inelegant fumblings at the negotiating table would be proved irrelevant by the long sweep of history, he was never overly concerned with press and public criticism of his style. But to a nation in trouble, the *appearance* of poised, responsible political leadership was not a factor of marginal consequence. To look wise was nearly as essential as being wise. Television had made the average citizen more aware of process; the mastering of technique had become the mark of modern man.

Even if it achieved most of his objectives, the Pearson method was undignified, creating the impression of a bumbling administration making the worst of each bad situation. Pearson's manner left the unfair impression of a prime minister who could not grip events on the move and was continually sprinting toward greatness only to stumble over self-erected barriers.

Yet it was the great paradox of the Pearson stewardship that, even if his government was not as good as it should have been, it was much better than it appeared to be. Although Pearson's achievement seemed limited to the civilizing of the *status quo,* an impressive stream of useful reforms were somehow squeezed through the minority parliaments.

As well as the new flag, Pearson's remarkably long legislative record included important reforms in parliamentary rules and the committee system; a reorganization of government departments; the foundations of a bilingual federal civil service; the redistribution of constituency boundaries by an independent commission; important changes in federal-provincial relations; the beginnings of constitutional reform; a new bank act; new regulatory agencies for transportation and broadcasting; a new labour code; the Canada Pension Plan; the Canada Assistance Plan; a guaranteed minimum income plan for old age pensioners; medicare legislation; the setting up of a health resources fund; youth allowances; the liberalization of divorce laws; industrial research incentives; provision for technical and vocational training schemes; a doubling in the External Aid program; the abolition of capital punishment for a trial period of five years; new bankruptcy, company and consumer legislation; the unification of the armed forces; collective bargaining for the civil service; establishment of the Order of Canada; new feed grain and crop insurance legislation; a fund for rural economic development; a new immigration act; and the setting up of several important new agencies, including the Economic Council of Canada, the Science Council, a corporation to encourage the Canadian film industry, the Company of Young Canadians and a corporation to manage and phase out the Cape Breton coal industry.

Prompted by the progressive activists who were his main advisers, Pearson let loose a torrent of new forces and pressures. By setting in train a series of fundamental social changes but failing to explain them or to channel them into some rational sequence of priorities, Pearson missed the political advantages that might have accrued to him and eventually lost control of the society he was trying to govern. Actually, Pearson was my favourite politician, not because of his diplomatic skills, his honesty or his many accomplishments, but because his cabinet leaked like the *Titanic*. I had broken so many of his government's secrets in my Ottawa columns that he began one 1966 cabinet meeting by forbidding any of his ministers ever to speak to me again. One of them, possessed by more wit and nerve than the others, responded with a straight face that since I was probably hiding under the cabinet table, it might improve my temper if I was given a chair. Even Pearson burst out laughing when two ministers surreptitiously looked under the table to see if I was really there.

———————

PEARSON'S MAIN POLICY PREOCCUPATION was his attempt to sponsor some kind of accommodation between Quebec and the rest of the country, a task to which he brought more sympathy and comprehension than any previous politician on the federal scene. Only the unfolding of history can pronounce the final verdict on Pearson's efforts to meet the potentially explosive aspirations of French Canada, but certainly it was on this crucial issue that he expended the most concern. Always the nimble-footed diplomat trying to find some political base to stand on, Pearson never really had any root constituency of his own. His views reflected the aspirations of no particular region or group, except perhaps the narrow horizons of the Ottawa Establishment. This alienation included even Pearson's own riding of Algoma East, for although he won re-election with easy majorities, he was not *of* it. It seemed perfectly natural to call John Diefenbaker "The Man from Prince Albert," but it would have been patently absurd to label Lester Pearson "The Man from Algoma East."

Diplomats live in an artificial cocoon of ritualistic exchanges, into which real people and their mundane problems seldom intrude. "His External Affairs experience, his years abroad, and his association with Mackenzie King combined in quite a consistent way to put Pearson out of touch with the realities of Canada," wrote

Professor Denis Smith of Trent University. "Some of his views were intelligent and tolerant and compassionate but they were often views held in a vacuum, hardly related to the real passions and complexities of the Canadian character, either English or French."

Although he loved the idea of Canada, Pearson remained something of a foreigner in his own country, a man without permanent roots who had lived in eighteen different houses on two continents during his period of public service. Having spent the wrong years in the faith, he came to the nation's highest political office too late in life to feel that vital rapport with the average citizen that nourishes successful politicians. As a result, the image of him imprinted on the public mind remained confused and vague.

The fact that the many blurred pictures the public had of Pearson as PM sometimes didn't even add up to the simple act of recognition was amusingly illustrated by a minor incident that occurred at the time of the royal visit to Prince Edward Island in the fall of 1964. Pearson and his entourage, including Jim Coutts, his appointments secretary, were quartered overnight at the official residence of the province's lieutenant-governor in Charlottetown. When a phone call for Coutts came from Ottawa, a local waiter, brought in to act as a manservant for the occasion, put down the phone, went upstairs and interrupted Pearson, demanding: "Are you Mr. Coutts?" When he heard the emphatically negative reply, the man, still unaware that he was addressing the prime minister, persisted: "Well, look, fella, you've got to help me find him. This is important." The anecdote may have reflected as much on the lack of formality among Charlottetown waiters as on the vagueness of Pearson's public image, but it was not an incident that could conceivably have happened to John Diefenbaker, Louis St-Laurent or even Mackenzie King.

Lester Pearson was probably the first man to serve as prime minister of Canada whose public and private personalities were one and the same. Unlike most of his thirteen predecessors, he wasn't noticeably enlarged by his arrival at the peak of Canada's political system. Pearson inspired familiarity without the under-current of mystery and excitement that people yearn for in their leaders. The office of prime minister demands of its occupant some special quality, a dimension of unrealized potential, to maintain a distance between himself and the people. Pearson's personality was fatal to any sense of awe. At the core of his perfor-mance, which produced astonishing results but very little majesty, was the fact that, during his time in power, he behaved as if he would rather be himself than a memorable prime minister. His tragedy was that he could not be both.

—1968

Walter Gordon: The Troubled Canadian

THE MOST CONTROVERSIAL member of the Liberal ministry—both at the beginning of the Pearson period, when his abilities were grossly inflated, and at the end, when they were cruelly debased—was that eccentric pursuer of lost dreams and gallant advocate of unlikely causes, Walter Lockhart Gordon.

It was Gordon's influence on federal government policy between 1963 and 1968 that marked the real difference between the St-Laurent and Pearson brands of Liberalism. Even his enemies were willing to admit that his role in revitalizing the Liberal party after its defeats in the late fifties was crucial; certainly, the influence he had on Lester Pearson in the early years of his administration was hard to overestimate. As the key left-wing member of a mildly reformist government, he stood for policies that made his less committed colleagues feel vaguely guilty, and despite the steady decline of his prestige after the disaster of his first budget, Gordon managed to maintain the moral leadership of the Pearson administration almost to the conclusion of its tenure. In fact, for most of the decade from 1958 to 1968, Gordon was so inextricably linked with Pearson that it was difficult to discuss one without the other. It was as though the two men absorbed from each other the initiative and strength they lacked separately.

At the beginning, their mutual dependence was based on a common lack of political experience and a friendship of more than twenty-five years' duration. They had met first in January 1935, when Pearson was serving as secretary of the Inquiry into Price Spreads and Mass Buying and Gordon was brought in to do a research study for the inquiry. At the time Gordon was twenty-nine, a partner in his family's Toronto accountancy firm by birth and training (if not by temperament), a charter member of Toronto's powerful financial establishment. The son of Harry Gordon, who had commanded a Canadian unit at Vimy Ridge, he had been educated at Upper Canada College and the Royal Military College.

He could easily have spent his life in the languid pursuits of the very rich, but an intrusive social conscience, which was activated by the discussions he had with farmers when he toured the Depression-ravaged Prairies during the winter of 1935, led to his involvement in public affairs. He soon became a roving ambassador of efficiency, moving from one public sector reform to the next with imperturbable ease and widely admired results.

Gordon came to Ottawa in 1939 to serve as a dollar-a-year man to help establish the Foreign Exchange Control Board and stayed on to become special assistant to the deputy minister of finance. He played a key role in negotiating the 1942 dominion-provincial tax agreement and was a co-author on the first wartime budget. When Walter Harris, in his 1955 budget speech, suggested that a major royal commission be set up to inquire into the nation's economic future, Pearson recommended Walter Gordon for the chairmanship. The project had been bitterly opposed by C.D. Howe, who regarded any inquiry into the Canadian economy as an investigation of C.D. Howe.

In the fall of 1957, when Pearson still had grave doubts about whether or not he should contest the Liberal leadership, he turned to Gordon for advice. His friend not only urged him to run, but also became his campaign manager for the 1958 leadership convention. Not quite three months later, when an election was called, Pearson suffered the most shattering electoral defeat a Canadian Liberal leader ever faced (down to forty-eight seats) and Gordon, feeling partly responsible, turned his energies to the rebuilding of the moribund party machine. "Walter was the real architect of our party's renaissance," Keith Davey, the Liberals' national organizer brought in by Gordon, said afterwards. "He was the man who made all the tough decisions."

IN 1961 GORDON PUBLISHED *Troubled Canada,* in which he outlined the essence of the Liberal platforms for the 1962 and 1963 elections. In the first campaign, he moved into active politics by contesting and winning the Davenport seat in downtown Toronto.

Pearson and Gordon grew ever closer in this period not only because they were brothers-in-arms, but also because Gordon was Pearson's kind of guy—civilized, not essentially political, a man one could talk to. His very closeness to the leader left him open to charges of Machiavellian intent and scarcely endeared him to old-line Liberal politicians either before or after the victory of 1963. They may have reluctantly accepted him as a political organizer, but they never approved his policies, particularly the economic nationalism that was his most urgent concern. When he got into trouble, as he did so spectacularly so often, many long-time Liberals were secretly glad, or at least openly amused. Walter Gordon co-opted the Liberal party without ever convincing it.

He never did conquer the Canadian people, in part because the kind of man he seemed to be tended to obscure the kind of man hewas. Witty, intelligent, contemporary and humanitarian, he looked merely overprivileged, the very model of an upper-middle-class WASP in pin-striped suit and regimental tie. He also suffered from the rich man's disease: a painful case of gout. To most people he seemed to be a dilettante, forever playing at politics, a crackpot millionaire with mischievous aims and obscure resources. It was true that he liked good food, vintage wines, paintings, antiques, travel and the company of his peers. He could be warm and amusing with close friends but remained an intensely private person, who abhorred the little arts of popularity that are the touchstones of politics in Western democracies. His language was that of his class—cool, reasonable, passionless. He could never transform himself from an ideologue into a revolutionary, and in the conduct of his nationalistic crusades, he remained a Garibaldi without a horse. Even his books, with their revolutionary implications for Canadian society, read like dry texts on beekeeping.

The emotions that move most politicians to spend their waking hours mouthing platitudes had no place in his makeup. "If you have too highly developed a sense of the ridiculous," he once told me, "you can't get through daily political life in Ottawa without laughing, and that's not allowed." In a town where ministers seldom made even minor observations without first taking a *tour d'horizon* of all the rumours they'd heard in the previous twenty-four hours, Gordon stood out as a man incapable of diversionary small talk. He made lists of what he wanted to discuss with the people in his appointment book and expected them to do the same. A typical opening move was to lay the appropriate power-point list in front of himself and ask his visitor, "Who'll go first?" The traits that isolated him most from his fellow politicians were his decisiveness ("I think in straight lines") and his willingness to delegate power to people he trusted.

————

WHENEVER HE APPEARED in public, Gordon diluted his impact by invariably assuming one of two facial expressions: mild boredom or intense boredom. Though his manner was rooted more in shyness than in arrogance, his offhand behaviour left a feeling of aloofness and failed to impress most of the visitors to his office. He never even tried to give the appearance of appreciating the advice constantly poured onto his desk by lobbies of angry, often frantic, businessmen.

A skeptical man with a highly developed sense of individual responsibility and accountability, he abhorred pretence of any kind. As minister of finance, he often had to fly to Washington, but he would invariably have his assistants phone ahead to request that no official representative of the Canadian Embassy meet his plane. He especially enjoyed such freedom when there was another minister on the incoming plane and he could watch the flunkies bowing to, say, Paul Martin, while he would climb off the aircraft, zippered overnight case in hand, unattended and carefree. His dislike for empty formalities was also apparent in his refusal to allow his aides to insert into his budget speeches the two or three perfunctory French sentences that English-speaking finance ministers normally mangle. He did not speak French and considered it an insult to French Canadians to pretend that he could take a run at it.

He was indifferent to the procedural rituals of the House of Commons and was always getting it wrong. In May of 1963, as he walked down a parliamentary corridor with Pat Carney, then business columnist for the *Vancouver Sun,* he pointed to the Commons chamber and confided: "I find this terribly time consuming." During one debate on federal-provincial relations, when he began by staunchly defending the government's record, he was interrupted by Michael Starr of the Conservatives, who shouted: "Cut out the politics, Walter!" Gordon disarmed Starr by replying: "Well, I had to have *some* sort of introduction . . ."

Gordon always expected the worst from his encounters with the public and was seldom disappointed. During a visit to England on July 1, 1964, he addressed the London Canada Club to mark the ninety-seventh anniversary of Confederation. The flag debate was just beginning in Canada at the time, with Lester Pearson still committed to his original three-colour, three-maple-leaf design. But Gordon, who had little patience with symbols, had forgotten the colours and kept referring to the new Canadian flag as being "red, white and gold." Every time he made the mistake and said "gold," a few voices in the audience would shout back, "Blue." Gordon thought they were yelling "boo," and the fifth time he was interrupted, he smiled sadly to himself and said, "I was afraid of that."

His friendship was hard to win, but once gained it was enduring, even in the most trying of circumstances, and his unheralded kindnesses to friends in good times and in bad were legend. His personal popularity with the progressive elements in the parliamentary caucus was always high. He was the only minister who tried to encourage and bring along new cabinet talent (particularly Ben Benson, Larry Pennell and Joe Greene) and was always forthcoming in his dealings with backbenchers.

Gordon had felt a warm sense of rapport with Guy Favreau because they were both dedicated amateurs in politics and knew the feeling of having to wipe egg off their faces. On November 26, 1964, in the bear pit of the debate over the Rivard scandal, Gordon was the only minister who came to Favreau's defence in the strongest possible terms. "I can only say," he told the Commons, "that if a man like my honourable colleague, the minister of justice, were ever forced to resign for the kind of political reasons suggested, I for one would not be happy to remain in this House." (What no one knew at the time was that a few hours before the debate, Gordon had received word that his son, John, a student at Ridley College in St. Catharines, had been struck in the eye by a flying puck and that his sight might not be saved.) The weather had grounded all planes that afternoon, so Liz Gordon set off for St. Catharines by bus. But her husband, who wanted to accompany her, stayed behind to defend his friend Guy Favreau. The boy recovered, and Favreau was never even told of the accident.

WALTER GORDON'S MAIN PROBLEM as a politician was his impatience. He could never wait until public opinion crystallized or until the full implications of a complex political issue were clear. He preferred to put forward alternatives to be tested in the crucible of actual experience. "My inclination is to ask, 'Why not?' if I hear what sounds like a good suggestion."

His work habits were acquired during the twenty-five years he spent as the moving spirit of Woods, Gordon and Company, Canada's best-known firm of management consultants. It may be significant that he practised a profession in which a man earns his living by recommending alternative solutions to corporate problems, with the understanding that the client will reject those ideas that prove impractical. He was never satisfied with things as they were and liked to experiment. "Neither governments nor individuals," he maintained, "should ever be satisfied with conditions as they are. They should strive continually to improve things and to give a lead in the introduction of reforms. It is well to remember that all changes and all reforms are likely to provoke opposition to begin with. Perhaps unfortunately, that is a natural reaction of human beings to anything that is new. But once people become used to some new measure, especially in the sphere of social security, they will complain even more loudly if it is discontinued."

In contradiction to the classic economists of the past, Gordon didn't recognize the free marketplace as the most appropriate mechanism for allocating national assets. He believed instead that the central government should be charged with a vital role in deciding how Canadian resources ought most fairly to be exploited. In effect, he did not consider successful businessmen as necessarily possessing the best brains or being the best company. He saw them as a faction to be placated, not a force to be followed. Because he was personally rich, Gordon was not afraid of tackling established power blocs. Politics to him was an end in itself only insofar as it could translate human necessities and moral obligations into legislative accomplishments.

In many important ways, his attitudes ran directly counter to the view of Liberalism prevailing during the St-Laurent–C.D. Howe period, which held that corporate capitalism was at the very centre of Canada's social order. "The Liberal party," Gordon told a meeting of the Hamilton and District Liberal Labour Group on April 14, 1967, "must always stand for the average Canadian, for the unorganized and the inarticulate, and not for special occupational groups or social classes." Such an approach implied that the major share of the benefits flowing from economic growth should not go to the investors, risk takers and corporate managers but should be distributed to less privileged individuals. It was this philosophy that made Gordon a very unusual minister of finance. Instead of deliberately casting himself as the villain of the cabinet—the man who traditionally holds up the spending estimates of his colleagues until they prove to him that their pet schemes are really essential—Gordon was the chief advocate of bold spending proposals. Since this left no minister in the role of defender of the public purse, the Pearson government's growing budgetary deficits and serious overspending eventually led to a fiscal crisis. The Canadian cabinet system makes no provision for a minister of finance who happens also to be an evangelist.

ALL OF GORDON'S PECULIAR passions for causes and all
the paradoxes in his character were illuminated by the way he
went about mounting the major crusade of his public career:
his fight to repatriate the Canadian economy. Like the Northern
Vision of the Diefenbaker years, his economic nationalism provided the Pearson administration with its most imaginative,
and most disappointing, policy venture—imaginative because,
like the Diefenbaker vision, it had the potential of endowing
Canadian life with a sense of shared national purpose; disappointing because, as in the case of the Northern Vision, intentions far
outran accomplishments.

The economic benefits of American investment in Canada
were so overwhelming that any appeal to stop—or in any way
control—the influx of such funds ran squarely against the self-
interest of many influential citizens, particularly members of the
business community. They brought down on Gordon's head one
of the most vicious personal campaigns ever mounted against a
Canadian cabinet minister. The businessmen were all the more
enraged because they regarded Gordon as a traitor to his class.

Because Gordon was obsessed with formulating solutions
to the problem of foreign ownership, rather than trying to
persuade Canadians that a problem existed, economic independence remained an abstract issue. He never effectively replied
to those who saw nationalism as an anachronistic evil, and failed
to make clear his firm conviction that nationalism is an expression at a group level of the very essence of humanity, its belief in
individualism.

His theories for the economic repatriation of his country had about them a dampening air of calculated vagueness that left much of their originator's intent to the beholder's imagination. "We can do the things that are necessary to retain control of our economy and thus maintain our independence," he insisted. "Or we can acquiesce in becoming a colonial dependency of the United States, with no future except the hope of eventual absorption." He believed that this was the central issue of our time and that it should be acted on without equivocation or emotion. His aim was statesmanlike: to alter the Canadian economic setting and gradually draw the people behind him in an attempt to recapture control over the nation's economic destiny. But he could never get enough cabinet ministers on his side to make economic independence a plank in his own party's platform and was constantly haunted by the fear that if the issue were once rejected by voters, American business corporations would interpret the result as giving them a permanent mandate to expand their Canadian operations.

Gordon's policy demands were not extravagant. No developed nation in the world had set fewer limits and regulations on foreign investment than Canada. Gordon only wanted to begin the repatriation process so that at some future date, more stringent measures might not be needed to protect what was left of Canada's vanishing independence. He believed, with President John F. Kennedy, that "those who make peaceful revolution impossible—make violent revolution inevitable."

Boldly, if at times superficially, Gordon challenged accepted beliefs about the place of the nation-state in an increasingly interdependent world. He attempted to head off criticism of his thesis by equating nationalism with patriotism. "In wanting to retain our independence," he emphasized, "we are no different from the British, the French, the Swiss or the people of other countries, including the United States. Some may call this nationalism, and so it is. It amounts to a proper respect, loyalty and enthusiasm for one's country, and a legitimate optimism and confidence about its future."

Gordon's suggested cure was a strong dose of government intervention. He wanted to pit the authority of the Canadian state against the power of foreign capital. What gave the issue its cutting edge was Gordon's awareness that the essence of national independence had become economic power, which in the sixties consisted not only of capital investment, but also of control over new technology. "Gordon had intuitively perceived the import of the new political landscape," wrote Professor Abraham Rotstein, an astute University of Toronto political economist, in the *Tamarack Review*. "The age of affluence is only another name for the technological society which is the source of our abundance. The economy is the home of this new technology and what goes on in corporate board rooms has a public significance far exceeding the fate of each individual enterprise. The politics of the new technological society increasingly turns on the question of who makes these crucial corporate decisions." What Rotstein meant (and Gordon realized) was that the effect of the new technology was to upgrade economic life to the level of a vital national interest and that to lose control over corporate decision making (as Canada was rapidly doing) implied loss of the nation's ability to exist in meaningful independence. Gordon could not reconcile the two main strains of Canadian Liberalism: the party's concern over social reform and its barely suppressed desire for economic integration with the United States. The saturating force of the cultural, political and economic compulsions of American civilization was the dominant factor in world politics during the sixties. The Pearson government's response to this pressure, which could be felt in Canada more than in any other country, was always to avoid trouble, even if the national psyche was damaged in the process.

American tax laws made it difficult for Americans to give up a significant share of their stock holdings to Canadians. Losses on Canadian operations, for example, could be consolidated with American income for tax purposes only if the parent company retained at least 80 percent ownership of the subsidiary. In the oil and mining industries, U.S. depletion allowances were granted for foreign, as well as domestic, operations, providing full corporate control was maintained. The antitrust laws also put pressure on American firms to maintain a total hold over their Canadian operations. At least one important prosecution under these laws (the Timken Roller Bearing case) had established the precedent that if a U.S. company attempted to direct the production and sales policies of a subsidiary in Canada that was not wholly owned, it would be acting "in restraint of trade." The simplest protection against such charges was to turn the subsidiary into an outright branch because no firm can conspire with itself. Similarly, the Antitrust Division of the United States Department of Justice did not hesitate to prosecute American companies when their Canadian subsidiaries entered into agreements, perfectly legal under Canadian law, that offended its view of American law.

The most obvious extraterritorial application of United States laws in Canada was the Trading with the Enemy Act, which prohibited the subsidiaries of American firms abroad from selling any goods or services to Cuba, mainland China or North Korea, even though these sales were perfectly legal under Canadian law. The American regulations employed powerful sanctions: the executives of a parent corporation whose foreign subsidiaries engaged in such trade were held directly responsible and liable to hefty fines and/or ten years in jail. When the late U.S. secretary of state John Foster Dulles was asked just who would qualify as an "enemy" within the context of this law, he replied: "An enemy is anybody the State Department says is."

————

THE HARSHEST OPPOSITION to Gordon's nationalistic ideas came from the cabinet's right-wing ministers and its western members plus another group of non-ideological ministers, who simply regarded Gordon as an irresponsible dilettante whose ideas were jeopardizing party support across the country.

Outside the cabinet, he was constantly being attacked by Liberals as the man most responsible for the party's inability to attain a parliamentary majority. Because of his economic nationalism, he was referred to at party meetings in British Columbia as "that tab-collar Castro," and Stuart Keate, publisher of the Liberal *Vancouver Sun,* told a meeting of American businessmen: "It's true that we have some economic nationalists, but any country that can survive three wars, floods, rock slides and other natural disasters, can survive Walter Gordon." Ross Thatcher, the Liberal premier of Saskatchewan, labelled Gordon "the worst and most dangerous Socialist in Canada." His very name produced a flush of anger in most businessmen, who privately went beyond the socialist label and seriously debated among themselves whether he might not be "some kind of Commie nut." E.P. Taylor, speaking from Lyford Cay in the Bahamas, labelled Gordon's insistence that subsidiaries be forced to sell 25 percent of their equity stock to Canadians as "absolute nonsense, contrary to good business principles, unnatural and monstrous."

Throughout the West and to a lesser degree in the Maritimes, Walter Gordon's theories of economic nationalism were regarded as a thinly disguised cover-up for Toronto protectionism. The influx of foreign capital had done much to free the citizens in both extremes of the country from the detested yoke of the Bay and St. James Streets brand of capitalism. In Gordon they thought they recognized the grip of the Toronto-Montreal industrial establishment, which through its tariff and price-fixing policies, had long exploited the resources of their areas, with minimal returns to the inhabitants, and which was now attempting to reassert its dominance.

Neither was there any significant support for Gordon's policies in French Canada. The Quebec nationalist tradition, with its cultural and social roots, was not compatible with Gordon's economic thesis. The target of French-Canadian nationalists had never been American investment but the economic influence of Montreal's English-speaking managers. In fact, American dollars were welcomed in Quebec to offset the power of the province's own English-speaking community. Most of the Quebec ministers in Ottawa, particularly Pierre Elliott Trudeau and Maurice Sauvé, had been fighting Quebec nationalism all their political lives. They could not do battle against one kind of nationalism in their home province without at the same time opposing the Canadian nationalism implied in Gordon's economic doctrine.

Walter Gordon's inability to move the nation in his direction was due to the historic accident that Canada matured into nationhood at a time when the human race was moving, as the eminent critic Northrop Frye pointed out, "towards a post-national world." In the long jostling of their history, Canadians had never been able to settle the nagging question of whether their northern subcontinent could retain its political sovereignty while espousing only indistinct and not always compatible brands of nationalism. Still, despite the limited success of his nationalistic crusades, Walter Gordon's time in public life enlarged not just his party, but the nation as a whole. He had three qualities rare in politicians—courage, simplicity and selflessness; they made him for a time the conscience of his country.

—1968

Frank Underhill: A Liberal for All Seasons

THERE CAME A meaningful moment last night during a dinner given at Ottawa's Rideau Club in honour of Frank Underhill's eightieth birthday when he said, "I simply cannot understand the view prevalent today that there is something vicious about the Liberal establishment." Looking around at the smug adherents of that elitist conclave, sitting comfortably in the club's red leather chairs, peering at their guru through the cigar smoke and nodding their heads, it was hard not to agree.

However far they may have strayed from Underhill's ideals, these were the paladins who made this country what it was. The good things and the bad things about it were all their doing. They sold it to the Americans (in order to retrieve it from the British, they were at pains to point out), but they also put into practice their ideal of a humane and relatively progressive society.

The Underhill dinner was a cozy and very Canadian occasion, with a hundred or so of his friends gathered to pay tribute to one of the most influential thinkers this country had produced. But what was meant as a salute to a great man seemed at times more like a self-congratulatory farewell to a political generation.

They were all there, the big-L and small-l liberals (Lester Pearson, Frank Scott, Eugene Forsey, Bob Bryce, Escott Reid and Graham Spry among them) all moving out of public life now and watching their ideology being assaulted—on the outside by the radicals and on the inside by the technocrats. It was a cerebral faith in the power of intellect, a kind of unshakable trust in the reasonableness of man that held this group together and allowed it to transform the country.

But intellect and good intentions were no longer enough, and Canada was moving out from under them. Pierre Trudeau (who was not included in Underhill's personal invitation list) was cast in a very different tradition.

Of all the people there, Frank Underhill himself seemed to be most aware of the fundamental shift in the power structure that was taking place, and with the effortless erudition of a great classical scholar, he delivered the class valedictory. He recounted how, as a young student from Stouffville, Ontario, he had gone to the University of Toronto and discovered the writings of Thomas Hobbes: "I'd give anything if I could open the magic pages of Hobbes again for the first time. It was a genuine conversion. I had seen a new heaven and a new earth. It dawned on me then that I could spend the rest of my life studying politics, and that's what I've done. When I look at all the permanent adolescents in the universities now—the undergraduates, postgraduate students and young staff members who are seeking their identities in confrontation and protest instead of getting down to the tough clarity of books—I can't be thankful enough that I was born in 1889."

In solid Establishment tradition, Underhill gently chided Pearson for having attended the wrong college at Oxford. "If Mike had only gone to Balliol instead of St. John's, he would never have allowed that loud, rowdy demagogue from Saskatchewan to get going" because, as he reminded all those present, "the mark of a Balliol man is the serene assurance of an effortless superiority." While at Balliol himself, from 1911 to 1914, Underhill joined the Fabian Society and came under the influence of George Bernard Shaw and H.G. Wells. After spending the war as an officer with the British infantry, he came back to Canada and became a history professor at the University of Saskatchewan, later moving to the University of Toronto. "I returned from the war to find the Prairies on fire with progressivism, and that, in turn, swept me off my feet."

Along with half a dozen colleagues who attended the celebratory dinner, Underhill drafted the original Regina Manifesto, which launched the CCF. He broke with socialism twenty-five years later and became a reluctant Liberal. ("At times I have had to hold my nose while marking the ballot.")

Though Underhill has written hundreds of provocative articles and reviews, the comment of his which caused the most controversy was an offhand remark he made to the 1940 Couchiching conference. "We now have two loyalties," he said, "one to Britain and the other to North America. I venture to say that it is the second that is going to be supreme now. The relative importance of Britain is going to sink no matter what happens." This mild downgrading of the "mother country" caused such an eruption that the university board of governors nearly fired him and the Ontario legislature talked of cutting the university's provincial grants. (One MPP called him "a rat trying to scuttle our ship of state.")

The case blew itself out when no one could find a stenographic record of Underhill's remarks. Twenty-two years later, the University of Toronto exonerated him by awarding him an honorary degree. At eighty, Frank Underhill looked back at some of these incidents, and his conclusion was that while his generation accomplished much, it failed to live up to its own ambitions. "We men of the 1930s," he said, "put too much faith in politics. You can't have a great politics without a great culture at its base, and we were attempting a great politics with a colonial culture."

What he didn't say is that you also can't have a great politics without great minds. Frank Underhill is certainly one of them.

—1970

Judy LaMarsh: The Gutsy Charmer with Class

THE QUALITY THAT allows most federal politicians to survive their grimy trade is a profound sense of detachment. Issues and principles dissolve into cynical responses to the call of each passing hour; private lives are relegated to an incidental distraction. Eventually, their souls leak out of them, mixing with the comatose decor of the House of Commons' neutral walls.

Judy was different.

Julia Verlyn LaMarsh had that rare and terrible gift of natural rudeness. Loyal to her friends, merciless to her enemies, generous with herself, above all she was gloriously gutsy, governed by the unvarnished dictates of her feelings. She never tried to hide anything, least of all her emotions, existing within the tumult of her own making, as vulnerable as an open wound. She elevated honesty to a profound moral option. While some of her fellow female politicians insisted that their formal photographs be taken through so many layers of cheesecloth they were made to appear like mummies behind mosquito netting, Judy just stuck out her chins and told them to click away. When she landed at Eskimo Point in the Northwest Territories during the Centennial celebrations, she introduced herself to a group of Inuit by patting her ample hips and exclaiming, "See, I brought my own supply of blubber!" After her helicopter landed on Steele Glacier in the Yukon, she just stood there and yodelled.

She lost her temper easily, once threw an ashtray at Senator Keith Davey (even though he was one of her most ardent supporters) and resigned from the Pearson cabinet (for two days at a time) on at least a dozen occasions. Her legislative achievements were considerable, but her behaviour in office often shocked the fastidious and discomfited the established. "She was very democratic," recalled George Loranger, one of her former aides. "She treated the office boy and her deputy minister exactly alike—she constantly gave them hell."

The novels she wrote were her final passion, but she just couldn't get the sex scenes right. "When you're engaged in a sexual act," she would explain, "no one's there getting a bird's eye view. When I was trying to describe it, I kept giggling." It was typical that when she was awarded the Order of Canada on her deathbed, as a farewell gesture by a nation that had rewarded her contributions with remarkable stinginess, Judy's main reaction was to bitch about some of the people she thought were fools who had been similarly decorated.

She died with the raw courage and primitive dignity that exemplified her life, deciding late on the afternoon of Friday, October 24, 1980, "Okay, no more medication. That's it."

The reason Judy's death touched so many Canadians is that so few celebrities manage to preserve their real selves inside their public masks. Judy LaMarsh endowed each of her many careers with energy, intellect and commitment. To the end, she never for a minute gave up her essential, gutsy humanity.

—1980

PART 3
Business

Peter Munk: The Man for All Seasons

IAN DELANEY, Fidel Castro's favourite capitalist, won his corporate spurs working for Peter Munk. He was for a time second in command of Munk's formidable empire as president and chief executive officer of Horsham Corporation, its central holding and management arm.

He got to know his boss well. "There aren't too many people I've worked for who I am prepared to admit have altered my view of business," he acknowledges, "but Peter Munk is certainly one of them. His style, his energy, his inability to ever stay down when he's been knocked over, the brilliant way he articulates objectives—both internally and externally—and changes them if necessary. He is absolutely undaunted by the size and scope of any project. He thinks on a scale that would stagger most people. His forbearance and his generosity, his judgment, his . . ."

Delaney goes on citing Munk's stellar qualities as if he were reciting some sort of pagan catechism about a long-departed hero or saint.

"But . . . ," I say.

"Oh, yeah, well, of course, he fired me," Delaney confesses. "He was the controlling shareholder, and I was the chief executive officer, and I wanted to have things my way. Obviously, we were incompatible. So he fired me."

Hasn't that made Delaney bitter?

"Frankly," he says, "I would have fired me a year and a half before he did."

A small taste of the Munk magic.

Simone Signoret, the French film star, once observed that trying to explain the secrets of acting was impossible. "You shouldn't try to explain the mystery inside you," she mused. "You either have it or you don't."

Peter Munk has it. It's the perfect analogy, since Munk is an actor. He has a dozen faces. His expression seldom changes, but his appearance shifts with his moods. One moment he looks as confused as an usher at a shotgun wedding, so uncertain of his cause that he stutters and stumbles. Ten seconds later, he has the magisterial bearing of a pope presuming worship. Same guy; different mood. Those who know him most intimately—all three of them—swear that he is a false extrovert, aggressive and demonstrative when the occasion requires visible strength. But more often, he is remote and private, a man whose countenance betrays the fact that he has travelled some lonely terrains in his time. He has been at the top and he has been at the bottom—and has successfully confronted and absorbed both experiences.

Out of that catharsis has emerged the hard core of the man's character. It took most of three decades for Munk to acquire the self-esteem that now fuels his ventures that have included the realized ambition to own more of the world's gold mines and, at one time, urban real estate than anybody before him, and if possible, after him.

His motives aren't as innocent or as complicated as making money. It's restitution, redemption and revenge that drive him—the three great Rs in Peter Munk's life. It's about giving the finger to all those snotty guys who never waved goodbye as he snuck away to his twelve-year exile in the South Pacific after the Clairtone fiasco back in 1967—and didn't welcome him back with a ticker parade down Bay Street.

That's the essence of the Peter Munk story. All else is detail.

"If personality is a series of unbroken, successful gestures, then there was something gorgeous about him," F. Scott Fitzgerald wrote about his best known antagonist, Jay Gatsby, "some heightened sensitivity to the promise of life, as if he were related to one of those intricate machines that register earthquakes ten miles away." Peter Munk can claim similar credentials. He, too, is possessed by a heightened sensitivity that endows him with the power of second sight so he can see through people and events to unexpected realities.

Munk is not physically beautiful, but he is daring—and that makes him charismatic. When he gets excited he becomes an emotional hang glider, talking so fast that you can hardly follow his thoughts. Yet when he's sharing hopes or secrets, he dramatically lowers his voice, as if he were a Cold War spy confiding the address of his East Berlin safe house.

Spending time with him is exhilarating but exhausting. Munk doesn't treat visitors merely as listeners. They must turn themselves into co-conspirators in whatever crusade is occupying his attention or their stay is brief. Those callers who come bearing new deals or supportive messages are rewarded with rapt attention. He welcomes old friends with a smile you could auction at Sotheby's.

The once widely circulated comic strip *Li'l Abner* featured a sad character named Joe Btfsplk. Whenever Joe appeared, trouble was sure to follow. His gloomy approach to life poisoned the mood of anyone unfortunate enough to be in his presence. To signify that misanthropic outlook, Al Capp, the strip's creator, always painted Joe with a black rain cloud hovering over his head. If there were a comic-strip creation with the opposite characteristics, its inspiration would be Peter Munk. He creates an intense, yet festive, atmosphere wherever he goes. The ingredients that allow Munk to light up a room with the grace of his presence are not easy to isolate. Maybe it's his air of ingenuousness, those beseeching eyes and mock sighs, the way he rolls words and favourite phrases around his tongue as if they were chocolate-dipped maraschinos.

———

MUNK'S MESSIANIC SIDE is seldom on public display. But at least twice a year at the annual meetings of his two companies, when he rises to address his shareholders, he lets go. His appearance is preceded by executives from Barrick (his gold-mining company) who flood the room with so many upbeat statistics that by the time Munk stands up to speak, the shareholders seem to be holding themselves back from shaking their butts, waving their hands in the air and shouting, "Hallelujah!" At the 1996 Barrick annual meeting Munk made news by unreservedly praising the record of Chilean general Augusto Pinochet for his economic reforms, glossing over his bloody human rights record (his assassins murdered at least three hundred thousand innocent people) and the millions he stole from his government's treasury. Munk is unrepentant. After not very convincingly explaining to the crowd how truly humble all this success has made him feel, Munk confesses, as he did at the 1992 annual meeting, "Barrick is my life. It's something I created, I conceived, I conceptualized, I lived. It's a miracle not to be repeated. It will go down in the annals of business history."

Within twenty months of that oration, Munk had diversified by moving into real estate, acquiring the near-bankrupt property empire of Peter Bronfman's Trizec Corporation and turning it into a bonanza. "The goddamn real estate business," he complained in pretend anger. "It's the graveyard of the human ego."

Since Munk bought Trizec and turned it into TrizecHahn, he expanded its downtown holdings in North America by acquiring properties worth US$3 billion. The company bought such high-profile structures as Toronto's CN Tower; Mann's Chinese Theatre in Hollywood (which was turned into a $200 million entertainment centre); Desert Passage on the Las Vegas Strip; the WestEnd City Center in Hungary, next to Budapest's main train station; and Chicago's mighty Sears Tower, the world's second-tallest office building.

"Euphoria is so common in real estate, because the more you win, the bigger bets you place," explains Munk, sounding appropriately euphoric. "But I don't see this as a gamble. Gambling is when you roll the dice and double your assets if you win—and if you don't win, the banks and shareholders lose. But I don't confuse gambling with doing business. Gambling is when you roll the dice; business is when you control the dice. When I decided to buy Trizec, there wasn't a Canadian real estate company that could raise a buck. Half my board, led by Jim Tory, threatened to walk out on me when I suggested doing it, because they thought real estate was dead forever after the Campeau and Reichmann disasters. We injected some serious money and had almost unlimited access to capital in that low-interest-rate environment.

"Why am I not staying only in gold?" he demands. "We're still the world's most profitable gold company, but gold, by definition, is a limited commodity. We've built up a $14 billion mining company in a business that has total market capitalization of $110 billion—that's less than Microsoft. In real estate, at $10 billion, we haven't scratched the surface. It's the world's biggest business. It's been around since the days of Cleopatra. At $100 billion, you're a factor."

Whatever he does, Munk will move TrizecHahn's emphasis outside his home continent: "Why would I fight for the North American market, which is overbuilt and overmailed, with nearly zero growth of people's disposable incomes, especially at a time of rapidly rising Internet and catalogue sales? I'm going to concentrate on Prague, Budapest, London and other great European cities where the populations—and car ownership—are doubling every four years and the kids have spent their lives sucking on a giant hind tit, not able to buy what they see on TV. That's changing. Now they want to visit Planet Hollywood, buy Nikes and Big Macs, shop at the Gap and Ralph Lauren. Where are they going to go? Those old dusty streets where you can't even park a car? Most of these historic cities are ossified, remaining just like they were fifty years ago. We're the only ones who can put it all together, turn shopping into an entertainment and vice versa. I come from an international background, speak other languages and, thank God, haven't been spoiled yet . . . Anyway, don't let me get carried away." (I won't.)

Since he can spout with equal, volcanic enthusiasm on gold and real estate, is he in the gold business or the real estate business? Neither. Peter Munk's business is business. His personality is the opposite of Donald Trump's—he is introspective, moody, intellectual, something of a dreamer in the land of hard sell. Yet the two men have one thing in common: both are obsessed by the art of the deal. Munk has been deeply involved in at least four unrelated lines of work: consumer electronics, hotel ownership, gold mining and real estate. While the detailed technical knowledge required in each industry only bored him, he has, with one or two exceptions, negotiated deals that have taken his competitors' breath away. He operates at the very top levels of the international business world with the skill of a champion swordsman, a Zorro who knows precisely when to feint and when to thrust.

He has a deserved reputation for lightning megadeals that turn industries on their heads, but he is really surprisingly conservative, only *appearing* to be bold. Every step of each corporate foray is planned to the last detail. And if he does make a mistake, as he did with Clairtone by allowing governments to control his destiny, he never makes it again. "I look at every business like skiing a very steep new hill," he says. "The key is to look down, laugh and tell yourself it's just like any other hill. You use the same techniques. The moment you panic—the moment you think, Oh God, this is broken powder, there are rocks—you aren't going to make it. I don't make a deal a minute; I have long-term objectives. I do *business* deals, not deals per se. Some people are deal junkies—they carry fifteen pieces of paper around, each with a different proposition. I never do that. I know where I want to go because I'm convinced that I'm right."

Such certainty is based not on phoney self-confidence that towers over his tallest buildings, but on his record of buying when an industry, such as gold mining or commercial real estate, is bottoming out, then surfing the crest of its comeback. "I'm not one of these guys with a super IQ," he says. "I don't sit around working out mathematical formulas. I'm not a workaholic. I never miss four weeks' skiing in the winter or going to my island on Georgian Bay in the summer. I love women. I love good food. I love great wine. I love good friends. I am so focused, so consumed, so excited about what I do. I love my family. I love my wife." (Don't you envy such simple Men of God who have gone uptown?)

———————

PETER MET HIS WIFE, the former Melanie Bosanquet, while skiing in Gstaad, where she operated a boutique in the Palace Hotel. He had gone in to buy something for his then-wife, Linda, and took Melanie out for a drink. They lived together for a few years and were married in 1973. It's a happy partnership. "Melanie," he exults, "is a super girl. Great wife. Fun. Good partner. Likeable. Worldly. Not pretentious. Warm. Thoughtful. She is very important to me." They have two daughters, Cheyne and Natalie; Peter also had two children—Anthony and Nina—with his former wife, Linda.

Munk lives well but not as ostentatiously as his friend the late Sir James Goldsmith, who owned six houses, including an estate called Cuixmala on the west coast of Mexico, sixteen kilometres north of Careyes. It consisted of eighteen thousand acres of jungle and wetlands—filled with wild zebras, monkeys and big cats, as well as four hundred crocodiles—plus two thousand acres, enclosed with barbed wire, where the main house was situated. He employed a hundred servants and at least the same number of gardeners. The main house had a golden dome and enough rooms to comfortably accommodate fifty guests, or a hundred in a pinch. That's the kind of luxury Munk could afford if he wanted to. Munk's attitude to money is as nonchalant as that of most inordinately wealthy individuals. "I'm worth more than $100 million, but that doesn't particularly turn me on," he says. "To me, money is like the points you win in tennis. If I hadn't earned that first $5 million long ago, I probably wouldn't feel that way, but I did that when my Southern Pacific Hotel chain went public thirty years ago, and I haven't changed my lifestyle since."

The year he received $32 million in personal compensation from Barrick (because he cashed in some of his stock options), Munk was attacked by an angry shareholder at the company's annual meeting, who thought it was "wicked and wrong." Munk paused for thirty seconds before he responded. "Well, I'll tell you what I think," he shot back. "I did make $32 million, and I deserved it, and here's the reason why: I've created $12 billion worth of value, and so from that I took a small piece." Then he had an afterthought. "You know," he said, "as I think about it, what this country needs is more Peter Munks, not less." The objecting shareholder sat down, and the room burst into prolonged applause.

Munk maintains a house (with tennis court and pool) in Toronto's Forest Hill Village; a farm in the Caledon Hills; an apartment in Paris; and a chalet at Klosters, Switzerland, as well as the island on Georgian Bay. This is his favourite sanctuary.

It's an old, many-times-expanded cottage (originally built for $9,000) that now covers most of his private island, bought for $1,200 in 1958. "That's been my real link to Canada," he says. But it's at Klosters that he comes into his own. One of the world's premier ski resorts, which draws both social and mountain climbers, Klosters' nearby Parsenn region has the world's most dangerous alpine ski runs. One of the Parsenn runs is in the *Guinness Book of World Records* as the world's longest (at fourteen kilometres) and toughest ski slope. It is his daredevil approach to the most hazardous of these suicide trails that prompts some of his friends to inquire, after a few drinks, why he is trying so hard to kill himself. "I do take risks," he admits. "It's one way of fooling myself that I possess eternal youth. We all like to believe that we're forever in our thirties, whether we chase girls—which I don't do anymore because I am happily married—or chase mountains. Skiing is the only thing in life I do well, apart from business. I can still power-ski with any twenty-five-year-old. I can get through any trees, can handle anything. So can Melanie. I know I could have a major accident, but life is full of risks. That's the exciting part. After a day on the slopes, I feel elevated, youthful, sexually invigorated, physically rejuvenated, intellectually ready to tackle anything."

Klosters is the winter residence of the kings of Sweden and Norway, as well as Prince Charles, who has become a Munk intimate. Munk subsidized a hardcover publication of Charles's collection of his own watercolours and offered to hire David Wynne-Morgan of Hill and Knowlton, one of England's most astute public relations experts, to help the bumbling prince regain public confidence, but the prince chose to flounder on his own.

In 1993, after the episode in which Charles was overheard in a tapped telephone conversation, telling his beloved Camilla that he wanted to be reincarnated as her Tampax, Munk spent four days with the depressed heir to the throne. "I was very sad," he recalls. "The man was being hounded. If my cleaning lady had her phoned tapped and her conversation recorded and given to the newspapers, the whole world would back her up in claiming that she had a right to privacy and no one, but no one, could invade her fundamental rights. Prince Charles wasn't even given the chance to defend himself because he's unable to sue. He tried six different ways but wasn't allowed by Buckingham Palace. I know the conversation was quite shocking. Okay, but I asked this of a hundred friends of mine and people in Klosters: you name me a normal man who, at one time or another, when he is totally assured of the privacy of a single one-on-one affair, in a moment of passion, did not say things which, taken out of context and put into a newspaper, would be highly embarrassing. Why, then, are we so hypocritical in the late twentieth century, when we're protecting every goddamn minority group, imagined or otherwise, but Prince Charles, we don't give him the same kind of courtesy? I did everything to try and build up his ego, and I kept on telling him that he represents an institution in whose name people died or sacrificed their lives and ultimately, because of those sacrifices, defeated Hitler. I mean, you've got to stand back and think of those concepts. I tried really hard. He became so emotional, smashed the table with his fists, spilled our wine. Then I couriered him a long letter, and he sent me back a handwritten note six pages long. But nothing worked. He can't recapture people's confidence until he regains his self-confidence."

————————

ONE OF MUNK'S FAVOURITE VISITORS to his place at Klosters was Conrad Black, who dropped by annually while attending the Davos conference nearby. "I adored him," Munk exclaims. "I know he's pompous. When he was thirty, he behaved as if he was sixty-five. He is outrageous in every respect, a snob, right-wing, aggressive—all the wonderful things that we Canadians have given up being." Munk was a guest at Black's wedding to Barbara Amiel in London and decided to give them a grand present: their honeymoon. He knew they were flying to Australia anyway, where Conrad then owned newspapers, and Munk's original partner, the elegant David Gilmour, ran a luxury private resort, called Wakaya, on one of the Fiji islands. Gilmour had lost his young daughter Erin (in an unsolved murder), who spent her last Christmas with him at Wakaya, and it was in her memory that he built the club. There are eight exquisitely designed and luxuriously appointed bureys (huts), one per couple, on the island's beaches. Wakaya features four chefs to cater to the guests, fourteen sporting activities and every other imaginable luxury. Munk gave the newlyweds a week's holiday there, but they almost didn't make it.

When the blissful couple got to the Fiji airport, after a gruelling twenty-hour flight, Conrad headed for the local VIP lounge,
which didn't exist, Fiji's airport being furnished mainly with a
few plastic chairs and squadrons of buzzing flies. "Conrad was
angry," Munk recalls, "because he had never not been treated
as a VIP. The Fiji airport is no Heathrow. It's a big room with
natives trying to hustle you to buy candies. It was over a hundred
degrees, and there was no air conditioning." Finally, Gilmour's
plane arrived to take them to the resort, but it was a bumpy ride,
and all that anyone remembered was Black muttering, "I'll kill
Munk." But then the plane landed, the newlyweds got out and
Conrad, though absolutely frazzled, spotted a familiar-looking
figure leaning against a nearby palm tree. "There," he said to
Barbara. "That looks like a better-looking Tarzan version of
Michael Heseltine!" (A leading British Conservative, Heseltine
was then trade minister and rival for the succession of Margaret
Thatcher.)

"Well, it is," Barbara replied, and Conrad felt that at last he
was back in civilized company.

"Conrad was a sight," Gilmour recalls. "I couldn't imagine
him in short pants, but by the fourth day, he looked like he totally
belonged. Actually, he looked like he owned the island. He went
from totally cynical to totally happy, and though he and Barbara
came for a week, they stayed twenty-two days."

———————

ONE ATTRIBUTE MUNK prizes, with Black, is the ability to formulate long-term strategies and then stick to them. "Peter can pick up on his mental radar screen the essential priority, then identify and analyze it as the tip of the iceberg—or once, of the pyramid," says his partner Gilmour. "His ability to think originally stems from the composition of the business experiences of his life."

Munk's Hungarian background as the son of wealthy and divorced Jewish parents and the story of how he escaped the Nazi invasion when his grandfather bought a place on the last train out of Budapest bound for Switzerland have become familiar territory, best told in the highly evocative *Kasztner's Train* by Anna Porter. "I don't really consider myself Hungarian; I feel much closer to being Swiss," he says. After the end of the Second World War, he followed two of his relatives to Toronto and studied electrical engineering at the University of Toronto's postwar Ajax campus. The details of how he and his friend David Gilmour launched Clairtone (with $3,000 of borrowed money) as North America's first manufacturer of top-quality, solid-state radio/record player consoles have been told many times. Less familiar is the profound psychological impact that venture had on his future. "It was my first love, my first infatuation with the romance of business," he recalls. "It was unrequited, it was immensely uncompleted, and maybe that's why it made such a major impression on me. But it was an experience that formed the foundation for everything that I have accomplished in my life."

Clairtone went from making four high-fidelity sets in 1958 to selling a hundred thousand units a decade later, winning worldwide recognition along the way. Frank Sinatra ordered a unit, as did Hugh Hefner, Sean Connery and Dizzy Gillespie. "Listen to Sinatra on Clairtone stereo. Sinatra does," went the ads. The most fashionable New York department stores sold the units, while sound-conscious Japanese and German consumers recognized the sets as the world's best. Clairtone was hailed by the Canadian government as the leading example of what imaginative industrialists could accomplish in a country then better known for its fur, lumber and iron-ore exports.

As their company grew, the partners were so determined to keep expanding ahead of the market that they decided to establish a new, modern factory to manufacture all the components of their sets under one roof. They were too severely undercapitalized to finance a plant on their own, so they applied for a grant from the government of the job-hungry province of Nova Scotia to subsidize its construction. The inexperience of the local labour force resulted in heavy cost overruns, but worst of all, the government insisted that the firm move quickly into the colour-television market, which was then supposed to be opening up. The expected boom was premature, and most consumers held off buying their sets until prices dropped, while the Clairtone units suffered crippling technical and marketing problems. When losses mounted to unacceptable levels, the Nova Scotian politicians fired Munk and Gilmour. The government took over the operation, and in two short years, ran it into the ground.

Meanwhile, the two young entrepreneurs had lost their money and their reputations. They settled an insider-trading charge out of court and felt they had to leave the country.

"It was the classic impossible dream," Munk later recalled. "Everything I've done afterward has been child's play compared with Clairtone. My ego was destroyed. What I learned was never to give away your destiny. Don't put control into the hands of a body that doesn't have interests aligned with your own."

That searing experience is still never far from Munk's thoughts. In 1996, for example, when both Barrick and Horsham, the holding company that had recently bought Trizec, were resounding successes, the *Wall Street Journal* decided to publish a Munk profile.

"Hello, Mr. Munk. Some analysts say that they don't fully trust Horsham," the *Journal* reporter started off her interview.

"What would you like me to say, madam?"

"Well, what is your comment?"

"I have no comment. If they don't trust it, they must not buy it. Only those who trust it should buy it."

"Well, some people talk about your record in Clairtone."

"Madam, you know I was fired from Clairtone in 1967. That is a generation ago. In the meantime, I started Barrick, which has been the best-performing stock on the New York Stock Exchange for two of the past five years."

"But how do you feel about Clairtone?"

"I'm exceptionally proud of it. For nine years Clairtone represented a unique Canadian achievement. Both in design and in technology, we won the highest accolades. Never have Canadians produced a product with such sophistication as this. It failed, and to the extent that I was the founder and CEO, I accept all the responsibility, but you know, I hope I have learned from my mistakes. That's all I have to say to you."

———

FOLLOWING THE CLAIRTONE DISASTER, Munk and Gilmour went into purgatory halfway around the world and spent the next decade in Fiji, where they built up Southern Pacific Hotel Corporation, a remarkable chain of fifty-four resorts that fetched an impressive $128 million when they sold it in 1981. Along the way, Munk had picked up another partner, the Arab arms dealer Adnan Khashoggi. At first he was a welcome source of investment funds, but his personal habits soon got on Munk's nerves. There were reports of his cavorting simultaneously with ten prostitutes and of his regularly ferrying Playboy centrefolds to his Spanish villa aboard one of his four private jets. He had just taken delivery of the largest and most luxurious private yacht ever built when Munk visited him in Monaco. The ship had every imaginable luxury, including a computerized deep freeze, with frozen animal carcasses hanging from hooks. Depending on the number of guests Khashoggi was bringing home, the chef could punch, say, A-32 into his computer, which would produce an eighty-pound lamb, or B-41, which would provide half a side of beef. "I sat with Adnan and Melanie at the ship's launching party, and as he took us into his bedroom, which was four times bigger than my living room at home, I noticed on his coffee table a glass box, and inside was a model of a huge yacht.

"'Is this a model of the *Nabila?*'—which is the boat we were on, I asked him.

"'No,' he said, 'it's my new one!' (That yacht turned out to be half the length of the QE2.)

"'But you've just finished paying \$35 million for this one. Adnan, why do you need a new boat? Is there something wrong with this one?'

"'No, but you know I like growing.'

"'Adnan, you've got the world's biggest yacht. You just took possession, you just paid for it. Why on earth would you spend your time on designing a bigger boat?'

"When his helicopter took us away, I said to Melanie, 'There's going to be big trouble' because this was sheer insanity." (Khashoggi later ended up in a Swiss jail, and Munk paid his bail.)

But Khashoggi remained a partner for one more venture. In 1974 Munk and Gilmour decided to erect the ultimate luxury resort. With a projected final price of US\$400 million, it was to stretch over ten thousand acres and be built on the banks of the Nile in the shadow of the great pyramids. These elaborate plans were enthusiastically approved by Egypt's then-president, Anwar Sadat, who later backed away from his commitment. It took nearly twenty years before the courts vindicated Munk and Gilmour with appropriate payment of damages.

When Munk and Melanie arrived back in Canada in the fall of 1979, they were not exactly welcomed. He went, brown fedora in hand, calling on the Canadian Establishment, but they turned up their noses. "Most of Bay Street," he recalls, "treated me like a fugitive and a loser. Not a word of my achievements, which had been forgotten by all except the very few who had been a part of them. I had made it big in the South Pacific, but back home I was still a pariah. I remember being invited to have lunch in the boardroom of McLeod Young Weir, and on the appointed morning, they phoned and said the directors were all busy and couldn't do it. Despite my requests, Wood Gundy never did talk to me. I knew that if I wanted to be at peace with myself and build an international business presence, my home port must be Toronto. That was where I had to clear my name."

———

AFTER A FALSE START in the oil business, he decided to go into gold mining and established Barrick. His first major purchase was the Camflo gold mine, which had a tiny producing shaft thirteen kilometres west of Val d'Or in northern Quebec. The cost of the acquisition was to pay off the $100 million loan Camflo's former proprietors owed the Royal Bank. The Royal, then headquartered in Montreal, wouldn't even talk to Munk about it, after letting him wait for an hour past his appointment time. He had to get his friend Joe Rotman to fly to Montreal to vouch for him before they agreed and gave him only a year to repay what then seemed like an enormous amount. (In 1989, after Munk agreed to include the Royal Bank in the largest single gold loan ever— US$420 million—senior vice-president Brian Gregson gave a lunch for Monk at the bank's headquarters. The visitor took all of twenty seconds to remind the Royal executive of the Camflo incident, an admonition to which Gregson replied, "We know what you're talking about, but I just want to tell you that we would love to do this business with you; we would like to be amongst your lead bankers. We checked on the behaviour of the bank and you in connection with the Camflo deal and would like to say that, despite the fact that we work here for the Royal Bank, between the two of us, you were much more of a gentleman.")

How Munk raised these funds from a standing start—allowing him to move into the big time—may well have been his greatest achievement. Camflo was insolvent at the time, though its stock was still listed on the TSE at $1.75. By persuading fifty investors to pay $2.10 each for Camflo treasury shares, which they could have bought for 35¢ less on the open market, he closed the deal and bought the company. Even in retrospect, that seems the most questionable of bargains, but those investors—and the lucky few who bought Barrick shares from its modest beginnings—exhibited blind faith in Munk, which was generously repaid.

Along with Camflo's modest cash flow, Munk obtained the services of its three most important executives, mine manager Bob Smith and geologists Brian Meikle and Alan Hill. They became his key executives in the drive for gold. Smith, a compact, muscular, hard-rock miner (who insisted that his favourite girlfriends were Lady Luck and Mother Nature) became president of Barrick in 1985 and was the mining brains of the outfit. The industry was then in deep trouble, but Munk was convinced that European pension-fund managers, who always maintained some gold shares in their portfolios, would have to switch to North America because of mounting political unrest in their previous favourite investment region, South Africa.

One of the benefits of buying Camflo was its 26 percent interest in the Pinson mine, just east of Reno, which led the Barrick team to Nevada. The saga of the Goldstrike deposit, which was the luckiest break that transformed Munk into a financial powerhouse, had none of the romance usually associated with mining. There was no grizzled prospector, fluent in authentic western gibberish, who struck it rich, no platoon of hardy miners drilling some dimly lit mine slope to seek the motherlode. The discovery of Goldstrike took place not in a blinding flash of recognition, but in a slow, thirty-year process of advance and retreat, faith and doubt, opportunities seized and missed, careful diamond drilling and meticulous assaying. Barrick—the ultimate winner—had nothing to do with discovering the property, but everything to do with making it economically feasible and fully exploiting its potential. Located on 6,870 acres at the north end of the Tuscarora Spur in Nevada's Eureka County, an hour's drive from Elko, Goldstrike turned out to be North America's richest gold deposit.

Although the first serious exploration of the site dated back to 1962—it had been staked by several companies, and there was a small producing mine on the site—it wasn't until Smith and his Barrick crew arrived in 1987 that the full dimensions of its deposit became clear. Barrick had purchased the mine for US$62 million, mainly on the hunch of the Camflo trio. The great strike occurred on March 24, 1987. Smith was in Florida on holiday when Meikle telephoned with some unbelievable news. "Bob," he said, "we've pulled a hell of a hole. It's 600 feet, averaging 0.36 ounces of gold per ton!"

"Brian, that's bullshit," Smith replied. "Some son of a bitch salted the core. We better go back, resample the whole damn thing and drill another hole." Smith didn't dare tell Munk because the news seemed too good to be true. The second hole showed even better results. Eventually, eleven diamond drills were honeycombing Goldstrike's bottom layers, and one 450-foot length of core averaged 1.089 ounces of gold per ton. For an amazing fifteen months, the drill crews were confirming a million ounces of new gold every thirty days. Even after more than a decade of mining, the property (with 10 million ounces already sold) still contains gold reserves of 29.3 million ounces, the largest gold cache in North America.

The Barrick miracle won the acceptance on Bay Street that had eluded Munk for such a torturously long time. "For years," wrote Ira Gluskin in the *Financial Times*, "I used to hear that there was a Peter Munk discount. It was only four years ago that Barrick was at a discount to its peers because of the alleged moral deficiencies of Mr. Munk, incurred in the year 8 B.C. Today, Barrick sells at a premium, and the very same Peter Munk is a national hero and credit to his race, creed and lineage."

Munk's other contribution to the industry was hedging. Because he had put all his own money into Barrick and couldn't afford to lose it, he devised a scheme that made gold mining independent of gold prices. It involved selling the shiny stuff three years forward to banks willing to be locked into their loan positions. In the summer of 1998, when gold was selling under US$300 an ounce, Munk was getting more than $400 and had reduced costs to below $150, except at his Pierina mine in Peru, which was getting ready to pour gold at an unbelievable $50 an ounce. That prospect, originally owned by Arequipa Resources, was purchased in 1996 for $1.1 billion from Catherine McLeod, a young Vancouver mine finder, who personally made $19 million on the deal. Two years earlier, Munk paid $2.1 billion for Lac Minerals, which included some underdeveloped mines in Chile. And he bought the sad remnants of Calgary's Trizec Corporation, once Canada's prime commercial real estate company.

———

GREG WILKINS, a former racing-car driver who was named company president, insists that he's not trying to collect marquee properties for publicity or ego reasons. No question, the Munk company's marquee building in Canada is Place Ville Marie, architect I.M. Pei's famous crucifix-shaped skyscraper in downtown Montreal. Built in 1962 on a vacant lot owned by the CNR, the forty-three-storey building, which comprises three million square feet of prime office space, became the head office of the Royal Bank and many other firms. Built on top of the city's main commuter railways, it pioneered the construction of the underground shopping malls that now spread below most of the downtowns of North America. Trizec floated a $250 million debenture to refinance the debt of Place Ville Marie and upgraded the building, including construction of Pei's original lobby ceiling, which was specified but never completed.

In 1994, when Munk had just closed his bid for Trizec, he flew into Montreal with some of his senior executives to do a presentation on behalf of Barrick for his intended takeover of Lac Minerals, then in play. The group was driven from the airport to the Ritz-Carlton Hotel in an airport limousine, Munk riding shotgun in the front seat.

"Hey, how is Montreal doing?" he asked the driver.

"Nothing's doing," was the glum reply.

"Any exceptions?"

"Yeah, Place Ville Marie. It's rented."

At that point, Munk wasn't quite sure what he owned in Montreal as part of his new Trizec acquisition, but he knew that Place Ville Marie was top prize of his local portfolio, so he asked the driver why it was the exception. Why was it rented when every other building was in trouble?

"Look," the driver pointed, "it's right there. You can see it sticking up. It's the biggest building in Montreal."

"But why is it full?" Munk repeated.

"Well," the driver confided, "it's the ownership. You see, Place Ville Marie is owned half by the pope and half by Paul Desmarais.

So what would you expect?" Montreal's two popes. You couldn't do much better than that.

I was *Maclean's* business editor when Place Ville Marie was first proposed, and I interviewed Bill Zeckendorf, the legendary New York developer who won the building contract. Zeckendorf worked in a huge, round office on the top of one of his downtown skyscrapers, and while we were talking, he was carrying on two telephone conversations simultaneously and giving his secretary instructions about a future lunch date. At the end of my visit, I couldn't resist asking the harried tycoon if he got ulcers working at such a frantic pace.

"No," Zeckendorf replied. "I *give* them." But the New York developer met his match in James Muir, the no-nonsense Scotsman, then chairman of the Royal Bank, which was financing the Montreal project. "Jim keeps things simple," Zeckendorf told me. "If you're his friend, you can do no wrong; if you're his enemy, you can do no right. And if you're worth considering at all, you're in one category or the other."

The many differences between the two titans were resolved only when Muir agreed to become Place Ville Marie's lead tenant for a then-unheard-of annual rental of $2.6 million. The bank chairman was persuaded to move in partly because Zeckendorf assured him that by using a telescope from his top-floor office, he would be able to peer into the private dining room of the rival Bank of Montreal headquarters, so he could identify the clients its chairman, Arnold Hart, was wooing by entertaining them for lunch. And that's how Place Ville Marie was born.

IN 1996, BEFORE BRE-X was discovered to be a fraud, Munk felt that Barrick was the obvious company to go after the so-called world's greatest gold deposit and did his best to negotiate a deal.

"I had a handshake with David Walsh and J.P. Morgan [the Bre-X advisers], who recommended our deal," Munk said. "All the controversy would not have happened because their [Bre-X's] investment bankers gave them the full go-ahead, and this would have been a beautifully done, smooth deal." But, for once, Munk somehow couldn't make it stick.

"I wasted months and months of time, and I was very disappointed, heartbroken, because it just didn't make sense that we couldn't make a deal. Our field engineers, our drilling rigs were on the ground in December, because J.P. Morgan and the government had agreed. But Felderhof shut the door on us, sent our people back and abused Bob Smith, our president.

"It wasn't until that morning when it was announced on BBC radio that it was a fraud that I jumped for joy. Suddenly, the whole thing became crystal clear." He couldn't buy a gold mine because there was no gold mine to buy. "I had been in bed with depression when I lost the deal in February. I had never tried so hard, and I just couldn't understand it. Nothing worked, and suddenly, the moment it was announced as a fraud, I went from a deep depression and a psychosomatically induced flu to great good health in fifteen minutes. It was like someone opening up a window on a totally dark tunnel. Everything—all the meetings, all the delays,

all the incompatible little details—everything totally made sense."
Thus the sad ending of the Bre-X saga.

———

MUNK IS NOT in retirement mode. "I feel more energized," he
says, "more enthusiastic. This is not a time to worry about bio-
logical age or chronological age. It's a time to enjoy life and do
things better than you have before. I've got the experience and
the ability—the best of both worlds." Except for his son Anthony,
who has been a director of Horsham, none of his children are
involved in his business, and they will not inherit his companies.
His fortune will be left mostly to the foundation he has set up to
encourage the spread of "liberty, freedom and free enterprise."

Munk won the acceptance he so treasured long ago, but somehow it's never enough. In the spring of 1993, he was appointed
an officer of the Order of Canada [in 2009 he was promoted to
Companion] and cried through most of the ceremony. "Peter
Munk is well respected because of the super jobs he did with
Barrick and Trizec, and nobody can take that away from him,"
says Bill Wilder, the former head of Wood Gundy and one of
Bay Street's High Establishment figures. "But he's never going
to be one of the boys playing poker at the Toronto Club. He's
a cold-blooded, tough Hungarian who is going to paddle his
own canoe." Munk has since not only joined the Toronto Club,
but was also the first Jew to become its president, though he still
doesn't linger for the afternoon poker jousts.

What separates Peter Munk from the usual run of successful tycoons is his hard-won self-knowledge. "Whenever we complete a large deal," he once told me, "I always tell my people not to get too euphoric and remind them not to get caught up in the deadly sin of hubris. I keep drumming into them—and make them repeat it back to me, so I'm sure they've got it—that we're still the same human beings we were fifteen years ago when we were struggling. Balance sheets may change, but people don't. We'll never get too big for our britches."

—1998

For the Love of Andy (Sarlos): Of Casinos and Markets

DURING THE THREE decades Andy Sarlos dominated Canada's financial markets—as the leading Canadian financial guru of his generation—he operated according to his own rules and his own priorities. There was no one remotely like him. He paid more attention to the long arc of history than to the spurts and pulse of the Dow and valued friendship above profit.

"His contacts were phenomenal," recalls Max Yamada, who worked for him. "Before joining his firm, I had run the largest U.S. dollar account in Canada for fourteen years and always got the first call from Wall Street. But after a week in Andy's office, I realized how business was really done. He could call literally anybody, and they'd always call back. Fast."

Sarlos was not the richest investor in the country because he was a born gambler and enjoyed losing as much as winning. "If I was right all the time," he once told me, "it wouldn't be any fun. It's the risk that makes the market an exciting place to be." But he knew how to play the odds, and in 1977 alone, the value of stock in his investment trust, HCI Holdings Ltd., more than tripled. At one point so many people wanted to buy shares in his firm that trading on the TSE had to be halted for four hours. During much of the 1980s, his trades accounted for 10 percent of the TSE's daily totals. By then he was spending $8 million annually in brokerage fees, which made him the largest individual source of commissions on the Street. He seemed to be in on every important deal. In one transaction involving the Hiram Walker–Consumers Gas merger, he and his partners walked away with a $19 million profit.

He hypnotized his peers. "What's Andy up to?" everybody wanted to know. In the wine bars and private clubs that ring Toronto's brokerage houses, where the senior analysts go to trade lies and fables, the talk was often about the source of his market magic. Why was this diminutive Hungarian, whose Establishment credentials were zilch, consulted by just about every big player in the country? Why did the likes of Peter Munk, Peter Bronfman, the Reichmanns in their day, Trevor Eyton and many others of equal rank scarcely make a major move without seeking his input?

The answer was simple. He gave advice the way a priest grants absolution—freely, and with no hidden agenda. That was unheard of on Bay Street, where contacts at his level usually mean leverage that can yield fat fees. Sarlos never marketed his friendships or his wisdom. "He was a giant of a man," Munk said of him, after his death in 1997. "A real prince who never said an evil word about anybody and was more interested in making money for others than for himself. He was also very shrewd—on a human level, twice as shrewd as George Soros. I can't even say how much I'll miss him, personally and in business."

To know him was to trust him. "Andy is Numero Uno with me," declared Gus Van Wielingen, one of Calgary's oil million-aires. "I don't mind giving Andy my chequebook any time. I'll even show him how to sign my name." As his network widened, Sarlos became an active philanthropist, and after the fall of Hungary's Communist regime in 1956, he contributed much time and money to help revive the economy of his former home-land, including the financing of a bank, a department store, a newspaper and the country's first modern shopping centre.

Playing the market, he always went to the source, whether it meant visiting rigs in the field and talking to the roughnecks actually drilling for oil or studying the sulphur market, because its supply-demand curve determined steel-manufacturing sched-ules six months in advance.

He was a student of power and knew, for example, that CEOs of companies under threat of takeovers often act on the basis not of their disposable power, but of their disposable psychic energies. That trait made them vulnerable at pivotal moments, and despite his gentle manner, Sarlos knew when to move in for the kill. "Good traders," he maintained, "rely on what they hear; great traders assimilate the available facts, then act on the basis of their gut instincts and sheer nerve. Balls are as important as brains."

A Hungarian by birth and persuasion, Sarlos shared the national trait of being impossible to stop, once moving in a desired direction. (It's a well-documented fact that Hungarians will follow you into a revolving door, yet emerge ahead of you.)

The son of a Budapest grain trader, he was drafted into the Hungarian air force and arrested by the occupying Communists for plotting to defect to Yugoslavia. His subsequent imprisonment changed his life. "Death seemed a better alternative than life," he recalled, "because for a year, the guards always made you believe you'd be executed the next morning, and many of us were."

Sarlos later fought with distinction in the 1956 Hungarian Revolution, fled to Austria and eventually landed in Canada. After taking an accounting degree, he spent ten years in Labrador with the Canadian branch of Bechtel, the giant U.S. engineering and construction firm then building the Churchill Falls power project. On Bay Street his first venture was to buy out the failing Hand Chemical Industries, a small Milton, Ontario, firm which was going broke making fireworks, but had the advantage of a TSE listing and $1 million in its treasury. In the next five years, he parlayed that seed money into $200 million.

But it wasn't uphill all the way. In the 1982 market crash, his company's stock fell from a high of $45 to 47 cents. He ended up with debts of $150 million. It was Sarlos's proud boast that he paid back every cent, instead of escaping, like most firms in his positions, into a "restructuring" mode, which would have saved him millions. He believed in the stock market, but when I once railed at him that it was just a goddamn casino, he gently corrected me. "No," he chided. "Never compare the stock market to gambling. Casinos have rules."

During the past decade or so, Sarlos continued to trade, but his role was more advisory. "Check it out with Andy," became the Street's war cry whenever a big deal was coming down. He never let up, though he suffered from increasingly serious heart trouble, undergoing three major operations, and was twice declared clinically dead.

The dignified and superbly organized way he died was typical of the man. On April 24, 1997, as he was leaving his office, he asked his chief assistant, Hal Jones, to close all his future positions. He was so weak he could hardly stand but insisted on taking part that evening in a conference-call board meeting of Peter Munk's TrizecHahn real estate company via his bedside telephone. Two days later he lapsed into a coma from which he never emerged.

The previous week Andy Sarlos had dined out one last time with Peter Munk at the Toronto Club and told him, "I am totally at peace with myself. I have had more lives than I deserved."

Perhaps, but Bay Street without Andy Sarlos will be an infinitely less interesting and much less compassionate place.

—1997

"Young Ken" Thomson:
The World's Shyest Multi-Billionaire

HE MOVES THROUGH life with studied gracelessness, doing few of the things one would expect from a man of his means and opportunities to venture and enjoy. Deferential to the point of absurdity—and parsimonious to a point far beyond that—Ken Thomson has turned self-effacement into an art form. Yet he is the leading philanthropist of his day, and if being gentle, generous and family oriented is a crime, he is guilty as charged.

His astonishing communications empire swirls about him, throwing off $4.4 million a week into his personal dividend account, employing 105,000 on four continents—on the way to becoming the world's largest multimedia oligarchy. It already ranks fourth—after Germany's Bertelsmann, Capital Cities/ABC and Time Warner Inc.—and has circulated or sold an incredible forty thousand editorial products. Thomson owns a real estate arm (Markborough, with assets of $2.3 billion) and an overseas travel subsidiary that operates 40 percent of England's package tour business and five hundred Lunn Poly "holiday shops." "Young Ken," as everyone calls him, is also the sole proprietor of Britannia Airways, the United Kingdom's second-largest airline, which carries six million passengers aboard fifty-six jumbo jets. Because the Thomson companies' debt ratios were unusually low and their credit lines were virtually unlimited, Thomson was in the enviable position of being able to buy any $5 billion property that came along. And did.

By mid-1991 Thomson's personal equity holdings were worth $7.7 billion, which, according to *Forbes,* ranked him as the world's eighth-richest individual. The listing placed Thomson well ahead of Gerald Grosvenor, sixth Duke of Westminster, who was England's richest man, and such celebrated moneybags as Italy's Giovanni Agnelli, Hong Kong's Li Ka-Shing, the Gettys, the Rothschilds and the Bronfmans. He also happened to be— by quite a wide margin—the wealthiest Canadian.

Unlike these and other worldly figures who have qualified as rich and famous—and behaved as if they were—Thomson acts as if he were ordinary enough not to be noticed. There are few public clues to his private thoughts or personal motivations. Compulsively shy of personal publicity and seldom interviewed except about his art, he would much prefer to be invisible, and in fact almost is. "The lowest profile," he contends, "is the very best to have."

Although he seems scarcely aware of it, Thomson is caught in a time warp between the high-tech world of his communications conglomerate and the unbending Baptist ethic of rural Ontario, where he simmered up. "We were raised on the principle that you kept yourself to yourself and that only the members of your close family were your true friends," recalls his niece Sherry Brydson, who grew up with Ken. "You played it close to your chest and believed that only with family could you let your hair down. Ken has taken it a step further. He's got to the point where he doesn't let his hair down with anybody."

Even in his dealings with long-time business colleagues, Thomson demonstrates an air of impenetrable reserve. It is entirely in character that his office, on the top floor of the Thomson Building at the corner of Queen and Bay streets in downtown Toronto, has a vertical moat. Public elevators run to the twenty-fourth floor, but only prescreened and thoroughly vouched-for visitors are allowed into the private lift that ascends to the twenty-fifth level shared by Thomson and John Tory, his chief corporate strategist.

———

THOMSON'S OFFICE HOUSES part of his art collection, including most of the 204 canvases by the Dutch-Canadian artist Cornelius Krieghoff that he owns—hanging there, looking as uncomfortable as nuns in a discotheque. Gathering Krieghoffs has been Young Ken's most visible passion, but his real cultural hero is a somewhat less exalted artist in a very different art form: It is Clarence Eugene "Hank" Snow, the Nova Scotia–born country singer. Thomson regularly visited Hank at the Grand Ole Opry in Nashville, owns all his records, has been to Snow's house in Tennessee and presented him with a gold Hamilton pocket watch that was a family heirloom.

———————

KEN THOMSON'S PSYCHE is so difficult to penetrate because he behaves like a superb actor, able to detach himself from whatever crisis might be occupying his mind. Occasionally, very occasionally, an emotion will flicker across his shuttered face, only to be withdrawn quickly, like a turtle's head popping back into its protective shell. Exceptions to such closed-end reticence come unexpectedly.

A few seasons ago, Posy Chisholm, a sophisticated and vivacious Toronto socialite, who looks smashing in hats, has a profoundly developed sense of the absurd and possesses a remarkable memory, found herself at London's Heathrow Airport, about to board British Airways Flight 93 to Toronto. When she spotted Ken, the two acquaintances decided to travel together, though Chisholm first had to trade down a class, wondering why Thomson was too cheap to travel in style and comfort.

"You know why I'm flying home?" Thomson asked when they were settled in their narrow seats.

"No, I don't, not really," Posy replied.

"To give Gonzo his evening meal," the press lord matter-of-factly explained. "I've been away from my dog for five days now, and I miss him so terribly. We were half an hour late leaving London, and I'm really nervous because we had a late takeoff that they might give him dinner without me."

"Oh, Ken," Chisholm tried to reassure her agitated companion, "they'll make up time across the ocean."

"Gonzo is crazy in many ways but very, very lovable," Thomson went on as Posy, crammed into a steerage seat beside the fretting billionaire, began looking longingly down at the heaving Atlantic. "Gonzo is the sweetest dog. He's everybody's pal, especially mine. He's a Wheaton terrier, the colour of wheat, off-white. Actually, he's got a little apricot."

"How about some champagne, Ken? No? Oh, well . . ."

"Gonzo leads a good life. I plan my trips abroad around him. I never go to annual meetings unless I've got him covered. I couldn't put him in a kennel; he's a member of the family. He seems to have an understanding of what's happening all the time. We communicate. We know what the other is thinking. We love each other."

"I suppose you take him walking . . ."

"Oh, I take him out all the time. Early in the morning, late at night and every time I can in between. If I can't get home for lunch, my man goes up and walks him. He might be there right this minute. Gonzo's got to have his exercise."

"Doesn't he have a garden?" asked Posy, grasping for relevance.

"He doesn't want to stay out all day. Gonzo's a people dog. He likes walking in the park, and then he wants to come back inside."

It was going to be a long flight.

Chisholm remembered a friend joking that if she was ever reincarnated, she wanted to come back as Ken Thomson's dog. So Posy told him, hoping the idea might amuse the single-minded tycoon.

"Well, she'd be well looked after," was the earnest reply. "I tell you, Gonzo is a big part of my life. I know that sounds awfully funny. But it's a fact. I think of him all the time. I look after him like a baby."

"What about your wife—does Marilyn love Gonzo too?"

"One time, I was looking at Gonzo, and I said to Marilyn, 'Geez, he wants something.'

"She said, 'We all want something.'

"'Yes, but he can't go to the refrigerator and open the door. Gonzo can't tell you he's got a pain in his tummy. We've got to look after him, anticipate everything he wants. It might be a bit of food he needs, maybe to go out or just a show of affection.'"

At this point Thomson leaned forward to emphasize the significance of what he was about to reveal. "I tried to figure what Gonzo was really after," he confided. "It's a game we play."

"So, what did Gonzo end up wanting?" Posy Chisholm half-heartedly inquired—purposefully fumbling under her seat, hoping that was where they kept the parachutes.

"A *bikkie!*" exclaimed the world's eighth-richest man. "That's what Gonzo wanted—a bikkie!"

There followed a lengthy silence. Thomson seemed satisfied there was little point trying to top that remarkable bit of canine mind reading.

About half an hour out of Toronto, the tycoon started to get restless because the 747 had been unable to make up its original delay and was not going to arrive at 17:35, as scheduled. He put on his coat and complained so bitterly about the possibility of getting home late for his dog's feeding that Chisolm suggested she take his luggage through customs and drop it off at his house—while he dashed through the terminal, bound for Gonzo.

———

KEN THOMSON SIGHTINGS are like that. If he knows and trusts the person he is with, he will talk about his dog or his art collection, but that's it. Unlike nearly every other rich and powerful individual of even a tenth his wealth and influence, he creates few contrails. "The smartest thing those who have more than anybody else can do is not to flaunt it," he says. "It's resented and it's in terribly bad taste. It shows a poor sense of priority.

"Everybody has their own ways of doing things," he allows. "It's all a matter of temperament. A lot of people who make money fast spend it fast. It's very difficult to live a simple life and love your dog as much as I do. I spend as much time as I can with my family, walking Gonzo, watching a fair bit of television. I like to get in my car and fill it up with gas. So if you add up running the business with all the personal things I do, there's not an awful lot of time and energy left after that. I am as happy as can be."

Walking your dog and filling your car with gas may well be the path to eternal happiness, but those who know Thomson best insist that he is not as content as he claims. "He's not a man doing his choice of things," his niece has emphasized. "If he'd had two or three brothers, he would never have chosen—or been chosen—to run the family empire. I get the impression of someone doing his duty. He is intensely loyal and was very attached to his father, so when my grandfather said, 'I'm going to start a dynasty and you're going to carry it on,' Ken said, 'Right.' It didn't really matter that he might have preferred to be the curator of an art museum—and now he's training his son David to take over, just as his father wished. He's doing it with goodwill but not much joy. Every morning when he wakes up, he must say to himself, 'I'm unhappy being a businessman, but wait a minute, it's bringing me all this other stuff like my art collection that I couldn't otherwise have—so it's a trade-off.'"

Everything Ken Thomson says and does underlines that he's fundamentally decent, that he would be quite happy to have his epitaph read: "What a Nice Guy." He really *is* a nice guy, but he is much more than that—and despite his pose as the ultimate *innocent,* his self-assurance can be devastating. For instance, he readily conceded to a *New York Times* reporter in early 1980 that "there is a limit to how many papers one man, or company, should own," insisting that his own firm had yet to grow to such "ludicrous" extremes. "We will know ourselves, if and when we do," he reassured the dubious commissioners on the 1980 Royal Commission on Newspapers. Thomson then owned forty daily and twelve weekly Canadian newspapers, one of the largest concentrations of press ownership anywhere.

The best evidence of Ken Thomson's success in perpetuating his anonymity is that most Canadians, even fairly sophisticated businessmen, still regard him as the youthful and untried inheritor of the publishing empire built up by his father, Roy Thomson. They dismiss the current press lord as "Young Ken," an immature figurehead, whose main accomplishment is to have been his father's only son.

"Young Ken," in fact, is seventy-four years old.

"I'm not young anymore, but I don't really mind being called 'Young Ken,'" says he. "My dad was such an unusual individual that nobody can expect to be anywhere near a carbon copy of him. He was one of a kind. He channelled his ambition in a single direction and everything emanated from that. Now it's a different world we live in."

———

YOUNG KEN he may be, but his record in office has been nothing short of spectacular. He force-fed his father's business empire from annual revenues of $725 million in 1976, when he took over, to $11.5 billion a decade and a half later. The total equity value of the companies he controls has sky-rocketed from less than $1 billion to more than $11 billion, exponentially surpassing Roy Thomson's impressive rate of annual growth and ranking second only to Bell Canada in terms of market capitalization of Canadian corporations.

In 1989, following the sale of the Thomson Group's North Sea oil holdings for $670 million, its publishing assets were combined into an umbrella organization (the Thomson Corporation). Ken uncharacteristically boasted that it would allow him to set his sights on any target. "I can't imagine any publishing company anywhere in the world that would be beyond our ability to acquire," he proudly pointed out.

Ken Thomson leads a double life and enjoys both. In Canada, he is a mega-wealthy commoner. In England—and most of non–North America, where titles still mean something—he is Baron Thomson of Fleet of Northbridge in the City of Edinburgh, the hereditary peerage bestowed on his father on January 1, 1964, two days before he lost his Canadian citizenship for accepting a British title. "I regret giving up Canadian citizenship," Roy Thomson said at the time, "but I had no choice. I didn't give it up. They took it away from me. They gave me the same reward you give a traitor. If I had betrayed my country, that's the reward I would get—taking away my citizenship. Canada should allow titles. If you get a title from the pope, there's no trouble accepting that."

What happened was that Roy Thomson turned down Prime Minister John Diefenbaker's 1959 offer to appoint him governor general of Canada. "It wouldn't have suited me very well because I'm too much of an extrovert for that," Roy declared at the time. "I can't conceal my feelings very easily. I talk too much, everybody says, but I talked myself into more deals than I ever talked myself out of, so I'm still ahead of the game. At any rate, it worked out for the best. Since then, I've got a hereditary peerage. And I'm a Knight Grand Cross of the Order of the British Empire, that's a GBE, which is the highest degree of the Order of the British Empire. That entitles you to be 'Sir.' If I hadn't got a peerage, I'd be Sir Roy, so I'm right at the top of the heap."

During their visits to England, the present Lord and Lady Thomson roost in a four-bedroom flat (purchased for $180,000 in 1967) in Kensington Palace Gardens, off Bayswater Road, which was used for interrogating high-ranking Nazi officers captured during the Second World War. A secluded street with extra police protection, this is where many of the ambassadors to the Court of St. James have their residences. While abroad, the introverted Ken and Marilyn Thomson of Toronto are transformed into the introverted Lord and Lady Thomson of Fleet, using their titles, with two sets of clothing and accessories as well as stationery and visiting cards. "I lead a dual life and I'm getting away with it!" Thomson delights. "It actually works."

One place it hasn't worked is in the House of Lords. Ken has never taken up his father's seat in Westminster's august Upper Chamber. The older Thomson glowed with pride the day he received his title. After celebrating by queuing up at Burberry's for a cashmere coat reduced from the British equivalent of $150 to $80, he had his official coat of arms carved on his office door (it featured the bizarre image of a beaver blowing a hunting horn under the motto "Never a Backward Step"). When one elderly London dowager persisted in calling him "Mr. Thomson," he barked: "Madam, I've paid enough for this goddamn title. You might have the good grace to use it."

Having been elevated to the House of Lords, Thomson seldom attended its sessions and didn't particularly enjoy himself
when he did. "I've made a lot of money, but I'm not the brightest
guy in the world, by a hell of a long ways," he once commented.
"I've found that out since I've been in the House of Lords. About
90 percent of the things they discuss there, I'm a complete ignor-
amus about. I've got a one-track mind, but I bloody well know my
own business."

"For Dad, the title symbolized what he had achieved from
nothing, and he made me promise I wouldn't give it up," Ken
recalls. "He told me he'd like to see me carry it on because he
rightly suspected I was the type of person who might not want
to. I remember telling him, 'Well, Dad, I think you're a little
naughty to ask me to do that because everybody should have
the right to make his own decisions in this world. But after what
you've done for me, if you really want me to, I'll make you that
promise.' Now, I didn't promise him I'd use the title in Canada
or that I'd take up my seat in the House of Lords. So now I'm
happy to have it both ways."

————————

ANOTHER OF THE INHERITANCES from his father was
the attitude that while making money was holy, spending it was
evil. The Thomson style of penny pinching—father and son—
goes well beyond sensible parsimony. "Nobody has any sympathy
for a rich man except somebody that's richer again," Roy once

ruminated. "I mean, hell, I eat three meals a day and I shouldn't. I should probably eat two. And I only have so many suits of clothes, and I'm not very particular about my dress anyway, and I can't spend, oh, not a small fraction of what I make, so what the hell am I doing? I'm not doing it for money. It's a game. But I enjoy myself. I love work. I like to be successful. I like to look at another paper and think, Jesus, if only that was mine. Let's have a look at the balance sheet."

Roy Thomson's approach to spending was on exhibit in the marathon bargaining sessions he staged when he was renting space for his Canadian head office at 425 University Avenue in downtown Toronto. The landlord, a hyperactive promoter who had a tight-fisted reputation of his own to uphold, despaired of reaching any reasonable rental agreement because Thomson's offer was so far below rates charged for comparable space elsewhere. When the press lord finally wore him down, the building's owner gasped in reluctant admiration, "Mr. Thomson, you really are cheap!" To which an indignant Roy Thomson responded, "I'm not cheap! You're cheap! I'm cheap *cheap!*"

The photographs of the original Lord Thomson weighing his baggage so he wouldn't have to pay extra on his economy flights across the Atlantic, going to work on London's Underground or lining up for cafeteria lunches created a comic mask that somehow took the hard edge off his business deals. His outrigger spectacles, with lenses as thick as Coke-bottle bottoms, magnified his glinting blue eyes as he peered at the world with Mister Magoo–like good humour. Seated next to Princess Margaret at a fashion show, he spotted a lamé gown on one of the models. "My favourite colour," he told the princess. "Gold!" During Thomson's 1963 encounter with Nikita Khrushchev, the Russian dictator teasingly asked what use his money was to him. "You can't take it with you," Khrushchev reminded him. "Then I'm not going," Thomson shot back.

Young Ken's scrimping habits are equally mingy, if less well known. Although he is a member of six of Toronto's most exclusive clubs—the York, Toronto, National, York Downs, Granite and Toronto Hunt—he prefers to lunch by himself at a downtown yogourt bar. He does most of his shopping on department store bargain days.

Murray Turner, a former Hudson's Bay Company executive who knew Thomson slightly, was shopping in the Loblaws store at Moore and Bayview when he heard a shout, "Murray! Murray!" and saw Thomson beckoning to him. As he reached the side of the world's eighth-richest man, it was obvious that Thomson could hardly contain himself. "Lookit," he exclaimed. "Lookit this! They have hamburger buns on special today. Only $1.89! You must get some." Turner looked in disbelief at Thomson's shopping cart, and sure enough, there were six packages of buns, presumably for freezing against a rainy day. "I'd walk a block to save a dime at a discount store," Thomson readily admitted.

The press lord appears to dress well (his shoes are handmade by Wildsmith's on London's swank Duke Street), but his suits are made for him by a cut-rate tailor in Toronto's Chinatown at $200 a piece from the discounted ends of bolts he picks up during his journeys to Britain. In Toronto he lives in a twenty-three-room mansion behind a set of handsome gates at the top of Rosedale's Castle Frank Road, built in 1926 by Salada Tea Company president Gerald Larkin. A prime example of Ontario Georgian-style architecture, the dwelling is rundown, its curtains left over from its first owner. The Thomsons (Marilyn's parents live with them in a coach house) usually eat in the kitchen to save electricity, and the family has been unable to retain housekeepers because of the low pay. Even the help's food is rationed. Cookies are kept in a box with the Thomson name lettered on it. A strict allocation of two of Mr. Christie's best is placed on a separate plate to feed the rotating parade of cleaning women.

Besides the London flat, the only other Thomson residence is in Barbados, where he owns the Southern Palms Hotel. To maximize profits, Ken and Marilyn stay in a third-floor walk-up apartment whenever they visit instead of occupying one of the luxurious main-floor suites. Toronto travel impresario Sam Blyth occasionally books them aboard West Indies cruises on a travel agent's discount.

Thomson owns a Mercedes 300-E but usually drives his ancient Oldsmobile ("it clunks around, but it's the car that Gonzo prefers"). He once purchased a red Porsche turbo. ("Honestly, not one of my more practical expenditures. I was thrilled at first, but I hardly use it—I've probably driven not more than twenty-five miles in it this summer.") The Thomsons seldom entertain and seldom go out. When they do, preparations include discreet calls to find out precisely what other guests have been invited, whether anyone will be smoking or drinking and how soon they might comfortably leave.

There has been much argument among his headquarters staff over how much cash Ken Thomson actually spends per week. Some insiders claim it's twenty dollars; others insist it's at least forty. No one bids any higher. He has credit cards but seldom, if ever, uses them. "It's an idiosyncrasy," says John Tory, his chief confidant. "It's just very difficult for Ken to put his hand in his pocket and spend money. Yet he's extremely kind and generous. When we're rushing to a meeting and we're late, if he sees a blind man, he'll stop, miss a couple of lights and help him cross the street." Tory didn't need to add that the blind man got no money. Thomson wouldn't discuss his spending habits. "I agree with my father that you should use only a small portion of your money on yourself and that you have some kind of obligation to do something useful with the balance. He thought the most beneficial thing you could do with money was to invest and reinvest it, to keep it growing—and so do I."

————

ROY HERBERT THOMSON, whose father was a Toronto barber, quit school at fourteen to become a five-dollar-a-week clerk, and in 1931 purchased a fifty-watt radio station in North Bay, Ontario, and another later at Timmins—so he could sell the radio sets he was lugging along country roads—is one of the sustaining legends of Canadian capitalism. Less well known is the way the hardships of the Great Depression permanently imprinted themselves on generations of the Thomson clan. "I'm still horrified by people who don't make soup stock out of meat scraps," says Ken's niece Sherry, who spent her youth in the communal Thomson home at Port Credit, just west of Toronto. "And if you were making a custard with three egg yolks, you could have knocked me over with a feather the first time I saw a woman throw the egg whites down the drain. That just wouldn't occur to me; the whites are tomorrow's dessert. You used everything and got into the rhythm of making your own jam and freezing your vegetables." (At about that time, Roy's daughter Irma had to canvass funds from neighbours to get the roof of the Thomson house fixed because Thomson refused to spend the money.)

The Port Credit household, which for a time included not only Ken, but also his sisters, Irma (Sherry's mother) and Phyllis Audrey, and most of their children, was run according to stern, puritanical precepts. "Granddad loved us very much," Sherry recalls, "but the affection was always very gruff. It was a staunch, didn't-come-from-much kind of family, so that signs of affection came out almost by accident, as asides." She remembers her mother being locked out by Roy, the family patriarch, if she ventured home after midnight. This was not when Irma was a confused teenager but a serious and intelligent adult well into her thirties, divorced, with a nine-year-old daughter, and dating again. Luckily, the family had German shepherds, and a dog porthole had been cut into the sunroom door. Irma's dating partners still recall having to push her, 1940s dirndl and all, through the dog door after their goodnights. "They could only do that in the summer," according to Sherry, "because in other seasons, the ground got too wet. When I became a teenager, I was locked out by my mother, in turn, and had to climb up the trellis."

———

YOUNG KEN ATTENDED elementary school in North Bay, where he worked summers as a disc jockey at his father's radio station, CFCH. His main assignment was to play background noises meant to evoke the crowd sounds and clinking glasses of a ballroom while big-band dance numbers were on the air, but he also fell in love with the music of Hank Snow and dreamed of actually meeting him someday. When the family moved to Toronto, young Ken was enrolled in Upper Canada College. After an unsuccessful year at the University of Toronto, he joined the Royal Canadian Air Force but was never promoted beyond Leading Aircraftman, the equivalent of a lance-corporal in the army, spending most of the war as an editorial assistant on *Wings Abroad,* a propaganda weekly. He took his discharge in London and spent two years at Cambridge, though the university had no discernible effect on him. After spending a year on the editorial staff of his father's Timmins *Daily Press,* he moved back to southern Ontario, where Roy Thomson had acquired the Galt *Evening Reporter.* His five-year apprenticeship there was an important formative influence, as were the weekends he spent at the Port Credit house.

Roy Thomson had moved to Scotland in 1954 but returned
to the family homestead in summer and at Christmas. The elder
Thomson held court while watching the TV set in front of him,
listening to the radio beside him, petting the Scottie dog at his
feet, eating fruit from a bowl with a little paring knife, all the
while reading a murder mystery.

Young Ken loved frightening his nieces and nephews, especially when they slept in garden tents during the summer. "He'd
put a sheet over his head and ghost us," Sherry recalls. "Or he'd
hide behind a bush and make fake owl noises. But we always
knew it was him and we'd yell, 'Oh, Kenny, stop it!' He was very
much the tease."

By the late 1950s, Roy Thomson had not only acquired the
prestigious *Scotsman,* but had also won control, in what was the
world's first reverse takeover bid, of the powerful Kemsley chain,
which included London's influential *Sunday Times.* Roy's lucky
streak broke in 1967, when he acquired the daily *Times,* Britain's
great journal of record. The *Times* did not lose its lustre under
Thomson, but it lost him bags of money.

Thomson had, by this time, become a fixture among British
press lords. He could always be depended upon to say something
mildly outrageous and to pose for yet one more photograph
showing off his skinflint habits. "They say business is the law of
the jungle" was a typical sally. "I think it's the law of life. If you
want to prosper, you've got to be ambitious. You've got to be
ready to sacrifice leisure and pleasure, and you've got to plan
ahead. I was forty years old before I had any money at all. But

these things don't happen overnight. Now, how many people are there that will wait that long to be successful and work all the time? Not very many. Maybe they're right. Maybe I'm a bloody fool. But I don't think I am."

American tycoons J. Paul Getty and Armand Hammer approached Thomson in 1973, offering a 20 percent share in their Occidental consortium, preparing to drill in the North Sea, where Phillips Petroleum had already found valuable indications. Roy bet his family's (as opposed to his company's) fortune on the play, though oil was then worth only $3.60 a barrel. When Occidental struck the giant Piper field and later the Claymore— and prices climbed to $14 a barrel—Thomson overnight earned an extra $500 million.

"Most people would say, 'I wouldn't want to do what you've done, even for your success,'" Roy reminisced in one of his last interviews. "They'd say, 'You've missed a lot out of life, and success hasn't made it all worthwhile.' But it has to me. It's just a matter of ambition and determination. You keep plugging away. I learn more from my failures than I learn from my successes because I learn bloody well not to do them again. Nothing has ever happened to me in my life that hasn't been for the best. Now I accept death. I lost my wife. I lost a daughter, but those things, I mean, you can't measure them in terms of happiness or success or failure. I'm a very imperfect individual, and I've done a lot of things I shouldn't have done, but I honestly am not a person who caused anybody any suffering if I could help it."

Henry Grunfeld, former chairman of S.G. Warburg, the

London merchant bankers who had helped finance Thomson, remembers his last conversation with Roy in the bank's Terrace Room at its Gresham Street headquarters. "It was about three weeks before his death, and we both knew it was the last time we would meet. He told me he was worth about $750 million, or whatever it was, and complained bitterly how much he wished he could have made a billion. 'Why, haven't you got enough, Roy?' I remember asking, especially since he was so obviously very ill. He looked surprised, as if he had never considered the question, and shrugged, 'Henry, it's just for the fun of it. . . . ' It was pathetic."

Thomson died on August 7, 1976, and Ken was suddenly in charge. His father had passed away both too soon, because the younger Thomson was not ready to take over, and too late—because Ken was by this time fifty-three years old and had spent most of his adult life following his father a tactful step behind—like a commercial version of Prince Philip. Inheriting a father's business is difficult; succeeding as powerful and articulate an individual as Roy Thomson—recognized as a folk hero of capitalism—was impossible. Ken tried valiantly to turn himself into an extrovert but quickly conceded that it was mission impossible. "The nice thing about my dad was that he was so unusual. No one in his right mind could expect me to be the same. I'd be happy to go unnoticed. I've tried to be a good, sound businessman in my quiet way, but I can't say I've been a slave to business. I've tried to strike more of a balance between my personal and business lives." His father's friend and adviser, Sidney F. Chapman, summed up the situation more succinctly: "When you live in the shadow of a legend, you don't go flashing mirrors."

————

KEN'S FIRST MAJOR DECISION was to cut family ties with the the *Sunday Times* and the *Times,* where union problems had forced suspension of publication for eleven months. During their twenty-one-year stewardship, the Thomsons, father and son, had poured at least $2 million into the properties without any significant return. Their loyalty to those great institutions without any apparent fiscal controls was totally out of charac-ter. Thomson sold the two papers for the value of the land and buildings to Rupert Murdoch and gradually moved his busi-nesses back to Canada.

The company owned forty-three daily and eleven weekly Canadian newspapers at the time. What they had in common, apart from ownership, was a blandness so pervasive that no self-respecting fish could bear being wrapped in their pages. "Disliking Ken Thomson, let alone detesting him, is wholly impossible," confessed Richard Gwyn, a leading Canadian commentator who once worked for him. "He radiates niceness from every pore, down to the holes in the sole of his shoes. He's self-effacing, shy, unpretentious, soft-spoken. He peppers his conversations with engaging archaisms, like 'golly' and 'gee whiz.' But then you stop feeling sympathetic because you realize that his innocence is just a synonym for timidity. And you realize at the same instant that the reason Thomson newspapers are bland is that they are led by the bland."

The Thomson operational code had been set down by Roy, and it didn't initially change much under Ken. Both Thomsons regarded editors as expendable eccentrics, and Clifford Pilkey, then president of the Ontario Federation of Labour, once called their company "a vicious organization, certainly not compatible with what I describe as decent, honourable labour relations." Reporters did not receive free copies of their own newspapers, and earnest bargaining went on to deprive delivery kids of half a cent in their meagre take-home pay. Most positions had fixed salary limits, so that anyone performing really well would inevitably work him- or herself out of a job. In pre-computer days, Thomson papers sold their used page mats to farmers as chicken-coop insulation, and Canadian Press teleprinters were adjusted from triple to double spacing to save paper. Each newsroom telephone had a pencil tied to it, so there would be no wasteful stubs floating around. "God help us if they ever realize there are two sides to a piece of toilet paper," one publisher was heard to whisper at a management cost-cutting meeting.

————

IN THE WINTER of 1980, Thomson had used some of his North Sea oil proceeds to purchase, for $130 million, a major Canadian newspaper chain, FP Publications Limited, but that

projected him into new and unfamiliar territory. FP had fielded
an impressive Ottawa news bureau under the capable direction
of Kevin Doyle (later the editor of *Maclean's*) that included
such stars of Canadian journalism as Allan Fotheringham,
Walter Stewart and Doug Small. The bureau regularly beat the
Parliamentary Press Gallery to the news, but it didn't fit in with
Thomson's usual barebones operation. When FP's Edmonton
bureau chief, Keith Woolhouse, who was working out of his
one-bedroom apartment, asked for a wastebasket, Thomson's
executive vice-president, Brian Slaight, wasn't going to stand
still for such an outrageous request. Doyle tried to diffuse the
situation by offering to send out an extra wastebasket from the
Ottawa office.

"Is it excess to the Ottawa bureau?" Slaight, ever the champion of independent editorial control, sternly demanded.

Doyle, about to break the news of Prime Minister Pierre
Trudeau's resignation, calmly replied, "Well, if you mean, do we
really need it, no, I guess we don't."

At last, a triumph for head office. Slaight could hardly contain
himself. "We have a truck that goes from Ottawa to Toronto to
Winnipeg, then on to Edmonton. If we put the wastebasket on the
truck, it will hardly take up any room, and won't cost us a cent!"

So the wastebasket jauntily journeyed across the country,
and it took only a week and a half to reach its destination. But
the Edmonton bureau's troubles were far from over. Woolhouse
wanted to rent an office and needed furniture. Slaight vetoed
the initial $1,600 estimate but later approved a bid of $1,100

from a local repossession centre. That didn't save Woolhouse. He permanently blotted his copybook by purchasing his pens and paper clips on the open market instead of from the repossession house. The Edmonton bureau was soon closed, as was the entire FP news operation.

On Thomson's sixtieth birthday, Roy Megarry, then in charge of the *Globe and Mail,* published a special one-copy issue that was substituted on Ken's doorstep for the real thing, that had a front page with his picture on it and several feature stories about Gonzo. "That morning, Ken did phone me," Megarry recalls, and said, "'What are you doing, you rascal?'—he frequently refers to me as a rascal—and admitted he had been stunned, because for a split second he thought it really was that day's *Globe.* 'It was a cute thing to do,' he later commented, 'but I hope it didn't cost the company too much money.'"

————

DURING THE LATE 1970s, Ken Thomson enjoyed a unique problem. With oil prices up to as much as $34 a barrel, his share in the North Sea fields purchased by his father was throwing off annual revenues of $200 million. That's not the kind of sum you keep in your mattress. Tax reasons, plus the wish to get into hard assets, dictated new acquisitions, but the chain had run out of cities, towns and even villages where they could maintain monopolies. Thomson went shopping for a safe, timeless investment for his family.

While on a flight to London, John Tory passed over to Ken an annual report of the Hudson's Bay Company, with the comment, "This is one you should think about." That struck Thomson as a weird coincidence because he *had* been thinking about the Bay, ever since Fred Eaton at a party had mentioned that the HBC was lucky because so much of its profit flowed from non-merchandising sources. "It was like mental telepathy," Thomson recalled of the airplane conversation. At first glance, the Hudson's Bay Company seemed a perfect takeover target. It certainly carried the kind of historic pedigree that would please a British-Canadian lord, it was widely held, with no control blocks that would have demanded premium prices, and it was a well and conservatively managed enterprise. It qualified for the Thomson methodology of acquiring companies that turned decent prof- its without requiring day-to-day involvement. (There is another theory why Thomson settled on the Bay. He walked Gonzo most often through Craigleigh Gardens, near his Rosedale home, and at night the most visible object from the shrubbery is the ochre neon sign at Yonge and Bloor, proclaiming "The Bay! The Bay!")

On March 1, 1979, Ken Thomson and John Tory called on Don McGiverin to announce they were bidding $31 a share—36 percent over market value—for 51 percent of the Hudson's Bay Company. At the Bay's board meeting two weeks later, Governor George Richardson reported that in a meeting with Thomson the previous Sunday evening, he had failed to persuade him to buy less than 51 percent. The board decided that the pre- mium offered for control was not high enough and that $37 to

$40 would have been a more appropriate amount. That consideration was aborted by the sudden entry into the bidding of grocery magnate Galen Weston, offering $40 for the same percentage, though part of it would have been payable in stock. Unlike Thomson, Weston hinted that he intended to fire most of the HBC executives, replacing them with his own.

The first telephone call Thomson received after word of his intended takeover leaked out was from Fred Eaton, "I wish you luck. Welcome to the world of merchandising." The second was from Galen Weston, advising him of the competing bid. By April 2, Thomson and Tory had raised their bid to $35 for 60 percent of the HBC stock. Weston countered with an improved offer ($40 for 60 percent), but once Thomson came in with an unconditional cash offer of $37 for 75 percent of the shares—$276 million more than he had originally been willing to pay—the bidding stopped. The Bay board met on April 4 to approve the takeover formally.

Ken Thomson did little to enjoy his position as the HBC's proprietor, neither becoming its governor nor taking part in any of its historic rituals. One exception was a summer journey he took to Baffin Island and Hudson Bay with his wife, Marilyn, two of their children, Lynne and Peter, and George Whitman, the company's vice-president of public affairs, an ace Second World War pilot who had fought in the Battle of Britain and had since earned a cross-Canada reputation as a social animator. They had just finished lunch at Ross Peyton's tiny hotel at Pangnirtung on Baffin Island, and Whitman was relaxing on a small rise overlooking the town when up puffed Marilyn and said, "George, I want to do some shopping at that co-op you told me about. You got any money? Here I am, married to the richest man in the country, and he won't allow me to have any credit cards or anything like that. Can I borrow a hundred dollars? But don't tell Ken about it."

Whitman peeled off the bills, and she skipped off down to the co-op. Just as she disappeared from view, as if on cue, the world's eighth-richest man came up the hill with the same request. "George, I want to go up to the Bay store and buy some fishing tackle. Can you lend me a hundred dollars?" Later that day, as they were fishing, Ken began to eye Whitman's down-filled vest so wistfully that the Bay man finally told him to take off his Eddie Bauer finery and slip it on. "If you like it, it's yours," Whitman offered, expecting to agree with Thomson's refusal. Instead, the press lord held out his hand and said: "Let's shake on it." And that was the last Whitman ever saw of the vest that had been his Linus blanket on many a northern expedition—or the money.

———

IF THERE IS ONE SANCTUARY where Ken Thomson can find peace, it's in the private world of his art objects. Within these hushed precincts, he can revel in his own aesthetic universe, indulging his whims without the budgetary problems that inhibit most collectors. He richly deserves his reputation as the premier collector of *habitant* scenes by Krieghoff (some selling for as high as $275,000), all of them magically revivified by one of England's best restorers. "He knows every picture the artist painted or attempted to paint and is constantly improving his collection," according to the Earl of Westmorland, the director of Sotheby's in London. "He's got a great eye and a passionate love of art," echoes Christina Orobetz, the president of Sotheby's Canadian company.

His collections include the only wood carving Michelangelo ever did, stunning boxwood and ivory carvings and some fabulous miniatures by Octavio Genelia. Death is a recurring theme of his collection, which includes any number of realistically rendered skulls—the carving of a sleeping child using a skull as a pillow, the tableau of a starving wolf being strangled by a skeleton and a pear-wood skull hinged to reveal a miniature Adam and Eve on one side and the crucifixion on the other. The most unusual—and most treasured—objects in his collection are the ship models carved by French prisoners in British jails during the Napoleonic era. They did the carvings to keep from going insane but had few tools or materials, so most of the hulls are fashioned out of the bones of their dead, the rigging braided out of their hair.

As with most of his enterprises, Ken Thomson's art collection is not exactly what it seems. Nearly all of it belongs to Thomson Works of Art Limited, a company owned by his three children so the increase in value of the collection will be exempted from taxes on his death. The Krieghoff paintings offer their owner an extra incentive: every Christmas, Ken lends one or two canvases to Hallmark, which sends him free Christmas cards bearing the imprint of his painting in return. "They give me a thousand cards free and another four hundred wholesale," he boasts. Naturally, the cards are mailed with unsealed flaps to qualify for the lowest postal rates.

—1997

David Thomson: Fortune's Child

SHORTLY AFTER I first met David Thomson, he invited me to his Rosedale mansion in Toronto. It was really an art gallery, with kitchen, bathroom and bedroom attached. Of all the many art objects he showed me that day, the most memorable was a magnificent depiction in gnarled, petrified wood of the crucifixion, with a near-life-size Jesus mounted on its original cross. The carving had been the worship point of an unidentified church in southern Germany during the last quarter of the twelfth century.

"The agony of Christ is pronounced with the hips slightly tilted," he explained. "The profile of Jesus' head is quite spectacular. In this piece one confronts the beginnings of Gothic carving and the tremendous expressionism of the northern world . . ."

He went on and on, praising the creative genius of the holy sculpture in his living room, speaking in a guttural monotone, his throat muscles stretched by the force of his concentration.

Overcome by the emotional intensity of the moment, I reacted with one of the great gaffes of uninformed art commentary.

"Look at those nails," I offered helpfully, "how honest and meretricious they are . . ."

"Yeah, well actually, I put them there myself," he shot back, looking at me as if I had just thrown up on his hand-woven Persian rug. "They're what the cross is hanging on."

Bad start.

I remembered that small incident of a decade ago as David Thomson moved into the top job of Thomson Corporation, a multinational electronic information provider, with annual revenues of more than $10 billion. Its stock, 73 percent of it owned by the Thomson family, is worth $48 billion, making David the richest Canadian and head of the country's largest privately controlled enterprise.

Burdened with an original mind, his brew of ideas constantly in ferment, the forty-four-year-old heir is starting out on the journey for which he has been training all of his precocious adult life. He will guide the world's most successful digital media empire, which operates in one hundred countries and is radically changing how business is done and how executives think.

It will be a fascinating spectacle. David Thomson may well be the prototype twenty-first-century global executive, a corporate space cadet who follows an existential path to highly profitable self-enlightenment. His thought process is a one-off. No head of a major Canadian firm behaves or acts like him.

A cerebral energy bunny on the loose in corporate North

America, he relies on a strictly instinctive approach to business decisions, which these days are based on the data that overheated computers spit out. "In the end," he confided, "judgment and instinct are still the elements of great success. One can have all of the numbers prepared, all the logistics, all the statistics run, but until one faces a human being or a corporate entity, one really has no sense of its service, let alone its potential. How can one quantify success or failure? Is it a failure if it revives a purpose, if it makes one move in another direction that is successful, that in fact is absolutely necessary as a learning curve? I really believe in that. I've experienced it."

There is a touch of extrasensory perception about the man and his postmodern gibberish, which reminds me of nothing so much as the evocative jazz solos of Miles Davis, improvising his way to melodic truth. It's the loosey-goosey character of jazz that allows it to regenerate itself. David Thomson understands that hip approach. He lives it. "I am absolutely compelled to follow my feelings," he told me, "or I forfeit the right to live."

Even before he took over, the youthful chairman had made a tough decision. Despite heavy pressure from within that his company's headquarters ought to be moved south of the border, where most of its business originated, The Thomson Corporation will remain in Canada. (Only one of its subsidiaries still has a Canadian address. The company is actually run on a day-to-day basis out of the Metro Center in Stamford, Connecticut.) "Absolutely, our head office is staying in Canada," Thomson insisted. "It feels good. It feels right. There is nothing more to say, really." At the same time, he refused to speculate on whether or not he will eventually take up his grandfather's hereditary title and join the British House of Lords.

He has climbed to the highest position within the Thomson Organization with no profile; has yet to grant his first newspaper, television or any other interview (except for the two occasions he talked to me); and is so circumspect that his 1988 marriage to Mary Lou La Prairie, a department store fashion buyer, was missed by Toronto's social columnists and went undetected even by the nosy Rosedale mavens whose mansions surrounded his home. They had two daughters, Thyra Nicole and Tessa Lyss. He has since been divorced and later married Laurie Ludwick, a bright and lively public relations consultant with whom he has a son. He spends much of his spare time joyfully raising his daughters by his first marriage.

Tall and wispy, with curly, sandy hair and penetrating blue eyes, David is light on both feet, betraying the easy grace born of his training in the martial arts. Intensity characterizes his thoughts and actions. Ask him the meaning of life or the time of day and the brows furrow into deep scars (the forehead is too youthful to show supporting wrinkles), the eyes grow reflective and the brain cells almost audibly start churning. There is no small talk. Ever.

––––––––––

EDUCATED AT THE HALL SCHOOL in England and Toronto's Upper Canada College, the youthful David painstakingly stayed away from the sports and military training in which both schools then specialized. "I never understood the emphasis on playing games as the only forum for exhibiting manliness," he recalled. "The Upper Canada College Battalion was an unnecessary and wasteful commitment, illustrating the shallow nature of so many contemporaries in early life. As a chore it was counter to the deep emotional issues which I sought to begin my journey." Not your average prom-date jock.

He read history at Cambridge, concentrating on studies of the civil service in India from the late eighteenth to the mid-nineteenth centuries. To lighten the academic load, Thomson played left wing on the 1976 Cambridge hockey team that beat Oxford for only the fourth time since 1930. "I like to think I was on the team because of my abilities," he laughed, "but I owned a Volvo station wagon which afforded me a constant place."

David's most significant formative influence was the time he spent with his grandfather, Lord Roy Thomson of Fleet, at his country manor house in Alderbourne Arches, Buckinghamshire. "He was very lonely and we conversed for hours about business and people," he reminisced. "His curious mind was always questioning why things were done in a particular way, seeking to understand the forces that affect people's judgments. He was an optimist with an uncanny ability to seize opportunities that others couldn't see. This approach was in complete parallel to my own nature." There was another parallel: Roy Thomson unleashed the random thoughts that he credited with helping him resolve the most complex of corporate problems by guessing the murderer in the dozen Agatha Christie and other whodunits he devoured every week. Those stories were for him what resolving the mysteries of the art world would become to his grandson: less an escape than a way to sharpen and exercise the mind for managing the exponential growth of the family fortune. (Every morning of every day David still puts on the copper bracelet his grandfather wore to ward off arthritis as a reminder of the old man's spirit.)

The trust set up by Roy Thomson, who died in 1976 after accumulating corporate assets worth at least $750 million, formally appointed David to succeed Young Ken as head of the Thomson Organization. "David, my grandson, will have to take his part in the running of the organization, and David's son, too," the dying Thomson wrote, spelling out the rules. "For the business is now all tied up in trusts for those future Thomsons, so that death duties will not tear it apart. The Thomson boys who come after Ken are not going to be able, even if they want to, to shrug off these responsibilities. The conditions of the trust ensure that control of the business will remain in Thomson hands for eighty years."

It was during the many "séances" with his grandfather that David first became seriously interested in art. It quickly became his obsession but has never been based on financial gain or social acceptance. Aware that any cultural hobby pursued by a rich kid was bound to be dismissed as dilettantish, he put in a long and arduous apprenticeship under Hermann Baer, an articulate expert in medieval art who ran a small shop on London's

Davies Street, which rented antique props to the film industry. His other significant mentor was his father, whose collection, David claims, "should be celebrated in its completeness; even the frame mouldings are harmonious." The relationship between the two men is close but not cloying, with the senior Thomson occasionally wondering if his son is tuned in to worldly realities. "David gets feelings that I never get from pictures," Ken admitted. "He never misses the technical aspect of art. He talks about the soul, the true message of a painting and can read what the artist had in mind when he did it. He gets signals that even I don't understand."

David's fealty is genuine and profound. "Given my passionate experience in so many realms, I have never felt more admiration for an individual. Father's contributions to the family and business have been absolute inspirations. Like sculpture it is the space that surrounds them, rather than the space they occupy that truly matters. My father's relationship with me has also been combustible, as you might expect.

"The art world has taught me harsh lessons about human nature," David confessed. "Money does not open every door. A real collector will rarely sell a work unless he can replace it with something even greater that has more personal meaning." Thomson's most valuable acquisition was J.M.W. Turner's magnificent *Seascape, Folkestone,* which Lord Clark, the former director of the National Gallery described as "the best picture in the world." David bought it at auction in 1984 for $14.6 million, outbidding the National Gallery of Scotland; five years later it was valued at $50 million, and he has sold it for more since. His most lasting dedication is to John Constable, the miller's son who, along with Turner, dominated English landscape painting in the nineteen century. David's first purchase, at nineteen, was a page out of the artist's 1835 Arundel sketchbook, and his collection of his major works, which now includes eighty-six of his drawings, ranks as the world's finest private representation of Constable's art. "His sensibility has had a strong influence on my personal philosophy, which I carry forward in all walks of life, including business," Thomson enthused. "So few people allow themselves to openly see and question scenes and events as he did. All too often subjects are viewed from a narrow perspective, with strong conclusions drawn in advance. Being possessed by imagination, curiosity and such dreamlike qualities doesn't mean one is incapable of pragmatism and tough decision making. Whenever you lose that sense of idealism, you lose your reason for being."

That sense of idealism has taken Thomson into the soggy pastures of existentialism, at least in the sense that he feels diminished unless he meets the challenges he sets for himself. Intensely attracted by war and danger, he has put together a London-based collection numbering three-quarters of a million letters documenting first-hand experiences of combat throughout history. He often imagines himself in battle. "I become excited at the thought of measuring myself in varied situations, alongside Wellington in India or being in a fighter, attacking a formation of bombers and being vastly outnumbered. It's an interesting way to test yourself because you set your own limits."

Among his favourite documents is one of the last letters written by Antarctic explorer Robert Falcon Scott, found beside his
frozen body in 1912, which Thomson regularly rereads as an
example of an undaunted spirit facing death. "The existential
idea of life's journey is very important," he contends. "It's all too
easy to become cynical and to forget that we are all children at
heart, that when you leave those youthful dreams behind, you
leave a great part of your being forever, you abandon your sense
of wonder and astonishment, the idea that you can be spiritually
moved by something or someone."

His artistic impulses have expanded to collecting "the northern school," featuring sixteenth-century Flemish canvases,
nineteenth-century Scandinavian art and twentieth-century
Canadian paintings, as well as photography. More important, he
is gradually moving away from his penchant of maintaining his
collections strictly for private pleasure. He is constantly lending
canvasses to public exhibitions, and his own collections will almost
certainly end up, as will his father's, at the Art Gallery of Ontario.

Thomson makes little effort to separate his passion for art
from his devotion to business. In his mind they are twin strands,
usefully entwined: "I take art so seriously because it's one of the
few pursuits in which I can totally unravel my soul. For me, the
act of creation comes through in a better appreciation of business." There is, according to the youthful inheritor, almost no
aspect of art that can't be related to some part of the Thomson
Organization's operational code. "If you look at Limoges and
Mosan, two of the great French workshops producing art in

the twelfth century, you might think, 'What the hell does that have to do with business?'" he points out. "Limoges in central France made fantastic reliquaries and chalices for churches and cathedrals with very few variables. But the Mosan craftsmen were different. They worked the market between Liège and Cologne. Their representatives sat down directly with the local bishop and asked what he wanted to see in the holy shrine. They were, in effect, forming the first customer focus groups and producing castings that were far superior to the Limoges enamels. You can't do anything well in publishing, electronic or print, without a highly developed sense of audience."

————

THE YOUNG THOMSON'S learning curve in business realities received its most valuable spurt during the 1980s. He spent most of that decade with the Hudson's Bay Company, then owned by his family, working as a full-time retailer, right down to selling socks at its Yorkdale department store. His most moving experience was his time at a fur-trading post at Prince Albert in northern Saskatchewan. "The juxtaposition was dramatic," he recalled. "On July 4, 1980, I bid successfully for a Munch woodblock; the following week I was in Prince Albert, being taken to the post's backyard, where ten bear claws were positioned on the cement floor, with fresh bloodstains and tissue intact. One fellow proceeded to demonstrate the various new traps and took me through the back room, where numerous shiny models were hanging. He hinged several in open positions and tossed a branch into the claw. I shall never forget the powerful crescendo of the folding pincers. For one of the first times, I enjoyed a completely unfettered response to life, isolated from big cities and the diversions of money. We drove along dirt roads, watched sunsets, merchandised the store, went fishing and talked of our childhoods. The experience was unforgettable, and I developed a deep respect and empathy towards those real people."

At the time, some of his co-workers accused him of grilling underlings about their superiors' performance, then attacking those in charge on the basis of what he'd heard. They claimed that he could operate at only two speeds, full throttle or total indifference, and recalled HBC management meetings where he would grow bored, slump at his desk and finally start reading a book. "David used to phone from Liechtenstein on a Sunday night and say, 'Hey boss, can I get Monday off?'" complained Marvin Tiller, then in charge of the HBC's Northern Stores, where the young Thomson put in some time. During his shift with the HBC, Thomson kept a private journal, recording his thoughts—among them: On display: "Spotlight the ring on a model's finger in a downtown window . . . use all senses, including the aroma of good cooking." On expansion: "To build a new shopping centre or store is an analytical decision with no feelings. Yet selling decisions are all feelings." On Zellers: "Slop it up. Far too clean." (He later had a brief but spectacular success running the Zellers chain, where he raised operating profit by 45 percent.)

Most Thomson employees who came in contact with David during his time with the HBC respected him but eventually overdosed on his intensity and rococo lingo. He told one dissatisfied staff member that perhaps he should consider leaving the firm because there were certain disadvantages and anxieties involved in working for someone like him. "But at the end of the day," he added, "you may say: 'You know, it's interesting working for David. Even if he's mad.' If that means I'm not normal, I'm perfectly happy with that. That's the type of dialogue I really enjoy because it not only gives me strength, but allows so many wonderful business initiatives to occur."

Hey, you had to be there.

Will his retail experience help him run a digital communications empire? "Absolutely," he replied. "The retail business requires constant interface with the market in terms of the ability to read and respond to reality. The electronic delivery system to which we have moved opens up a different customer segment with endless possibilities."

A useful guide to David's plans for the Thomson empire can be deduced from his favourite reading of the moment: *Good to Great,* a book that documents the road to corporate excellence by American business guru Jim Collins. Its main theme is that most successful organizations are led by eccentric individuals who feel passionately about their businesses and about the people who inhabit their companies. "For me that was not a revelation," emphasizes Thomson, "but it was really thrilling to have that reinforcement and to understand how basically unknown these individuals are, even today, and yet they charted new waters and perpetuated the strength of their organizations. Their experiences and passions outside the business define their promise within."

His private office, where David has been patiently waiting to take over his father's empire, features such incongruous objects as an original, dark green ejection seat from a Second World War Nazi Luftwaffe fighter and large canvasses by Patrick Heron, a contemporary British artist who specialized in jarring colour patterns. "The artist's courage was phenomenal," says Thomson. "He was like a father to me." Heron's work also decorates his house, hanging on either side of his vaulted living room. Every wall is crammed with paintings that include canvasses by Edvard Munch, Picasso, Mark Rothko, and Paul Klee. And then there are his art objects: facsimiles of the original texts of T.S. Eliot's "The Waste Land" and George Orwell's *1984* showing the authors' corrections in ink; a study of fences from the Middle Ages; an animation cell from Dr. Seuss's *The Grinch Who Stole Christmas;* an Ethiopian book of holy scriptures in hippopotamus-hide binding from 1500; an original Schulz cartoon of Charlie Brown; and a small woodcut from Lower Swabia, dated 1420.

In the past each new experience has provided the bounce that determined David Thomson's direction. Now there is no escape from ultimate responsibility. "I feel that I have enough platforms in my life that level me," he maintained, "whether it's my little girls or my other passions. I hope I am able to balance all of these emotional forces for the good of all." He is not a man who nurtures doubts about his past performances or future prospects. But a shadow hangs over him: can he channel all his high-fizz intensity and passion into corporate pursuits or will he one day quietly implode? He recognized that dilemma early, in 1975, when he chose the quote to place under his graduating picture from Upper Canada College: "We are never so much the victims of another as we are the victims of ourselves."

—2002

The Immaculate Passions of Nelson Davis

ANY JOURNEY OF exploration deep into the land of Canada's super-rich at one time led the traveller to the unusual driveway of a Federal-style mansion overlooking the Rosedale Golf Club in outlying Toronto. Running off at right angles from one of those fashionable cul-de-sacs that lattice the city's northern reaches, the driveway had been carefully designed, with sharp twists that slowed a car down precisely to the speed at which it would glide to a noiseless stop before the front door of this museum-quality, multi-million-dollar house.

What really set off this driveway—and gave a clue as to both the wealth and the character of its owner—was that the crunch beneath the tires of the visitor's car was strangely muted. Even on the driest day, the slightly yellowed "gravel" yielded not a speck of dust. And for good reason. When Nelson Davis, who was this country's most unusual and certainly least visible multi-millionaire, was building this house, he covered the driveway with the only rock that produces no dust: meteorite. It is chemically inert, so hard that it's occasionally used to polish stainless steel. After a long search, Davis discovered an available cache of the rare substance that had plummeted to earth thirty miles southeast of Cleveland, Ohio. He paid $10,000 to have it crushed and brought to Toronto. Then he had no dust in his living room. Or so the story goes.

Nelson Morgan Davis ("Nels" to his friends) looked and acted like a character straight out of a late John O'Hara novel. Yet he stood out among the super-rich Canadians of his generation as a man with unique ideas about money and its uses. Most of the Canadian wealthy are obsessed with the sheer "moneyness" of money—their fascination is in watching their investments reproduce themselves through sometimes more and often less immaculate financial transactions. They are much more interested in *making* money than in spending it.

Not Nelson Davis. He sought all his life not so much the fact of becoming personally wealthy as the *sensation* of enrichment. The only validation of your fortune, he believed, was to spend it through an endless pursuit of perfection in its many forms. "Every time I make a dollar," he explained, "I spend a quarter of it on myself. There's nothing wrong with that." (Nelson Davis's gross personal income ran to at least $12 million a year.)

Striving for perfection in all things was an obsession with Davis: the perfect houses (he had four); the perfect cars (he had six); the perfect servants (he employed eighteen); the perfect boats (he owned twenty); and the perfect golf course.

A long-time member of the Rosedale Golf Club, Davis had second thoughts about belonging in the early fifties when a duffer's ball nicked his nose. "I'll build my own," he vowed. (Nelson is a man of few words.) He promptly bought a 350-acre tract near Markham, north of Toronto, dammed up streams, moved trees, threw up hills and built himself Box Grove, one of the best eighteen-hole golf courses in the country. Davis was the club's only member and he employed his own pro (Jimmy Johnstone). Arnold Palmer flew up frequently to join them. Box Grove was sold for $3 million to IBM Canada in 1966 for use as the company's private country club. Davis now plays most of his golf at the Laurel Valley Golf Club on the Mellon estate in Pennsylvania.

He owned a 1933 Alfa Romeo in mint condition, but his most valuable vehicle was a 1904 Royce, made before Charles Rolls joined the firm. Because it was one of only two such cars still in existence, a few years ago Rolls-Royce attempted to obtain it for the company museum. Never having heard of Nelson Davis and presuming him to be a not-very-well-informed colonial, the company wrote him a mildly condescending letter, suggesting he trade his ancient car in for a more contemporary model at their expense. Davis, who had three new Rolls-Royces at the time, replied with a one-line note that may be a classic of its kind: "What would I do with a new Rolls-Royce?" (Davis eventually donated the Royce to an American automotive museum.)

———

NEARLY AS POWERFUL as his passion for perfection was his yearning for anonymity. Men of great wealth are always shielded by unlisted telephones, family retainers, phalanxes of lawyers, as well as a species of hangers-on known as various counsellors. But Davis carried his insistence on privacy to breathtaking lengths. His Toronto house had *five* unlisted telephone numbers. His entry in the *Canadian Who's Who* gave no personal information whatever. Even inside the higher echelons of the business Establishment, he was a figure of speculation and mystery. "Nelson is an enigma," said Charlie Burns, Toronto's Establishment stockbroker. "I've known him a little all my life, but I really don't know very much about him." American journalists who occasionally stumbled across his name and glimpsed the extent of his fortune offered to place him on the covers of *Fortune, Time* or the *Saturday Evening Post* if he would only speak to them. But he refused to be interviewed. The only time his name appeared prominently in Canadian newspapers was in 1969, when he provided the $200,000 in cash demanded by the kidnappers of his niece, Mary Nelles. "I have always believed in keeping myself anonymous," he told me at the time, "and I don't want to change that policy now."

Davis was possessed of a strong sense of identity and did not require any public presence to remind himself of who he was and how far he had come. There are those rich men who need publicity so they can read about themselves and be comforted that they are indeed alive and doing swell. Nelson Davis was a keeper of distances. He viewed the world with the undistracted gaze of a sentinel scanning distant fields through the battlement of a castle wall and moat that keep strangers at a safe distance.

He had a slightly ruddy complexion and colourless eyes, the kind of appearance and bearing that made it difficult to pick him out in a crowd. Exquisitely mannered, precise to a fault, his formality was that of an Anglican deacon on Palm Sunday. He was a warm, honest and kind man, who placed great stock in friendships ("You're judged by the friends you have," he said). But at large parties, where men bear-hug each other and women air-kiss guests they barely know, his politeness could be cool. He wouldn't have alcohol consumed in any of his houses. When the late Eric Phillips, who loved a drink, was spending a weekend at Davis's large island home in Muskoka, the host insisted that the Argus Corporation partner climb aboard one of the many motorboats before "imbibing." Davis was never known to swear. His strongest oath was "The heck with it." His sense of perfection even intruded on his eating habits. One evening, when he was taking a group of guests to the Sunday night buffet at the Paradise Valley Country Club in Scottsdale, Arizona, he insisted on tackling the food precisely at the opening hour of six o'clock so they could all have the pick of the fare before anyone else had messed with it.

Davis belonged to a dozen of the most prestigious private clubs in North America and was proud of the fact that he was the first Canadian invited to join the Rolling Rock Country Club built on the great Mellon family preserve at Ligonier in Westmoreland County, Pennsylvania. He rarely used his other club memberships, preferring to entertain a few close friends in one of his homes. He divided his year approximately into thirds, spending four months each at his main houses in Arizona, Muskoka and Toronto.

Davis's showpiece remained his house on Toronto's Riverview Drive, a gallery of craftsmanship furnished with the sort of rarefied objects museums display behind stretched red velvet cords. Called Eagle House, and built exactly to Federal specifications (which was the American interpretation of Georgian architecture), it had model eagles perched everywhere—on walls and the back veranda, over the garage—and painted on car doors. The dwelling took seven years to finish—three years being researched, one year being planned and three years being built. It was decorated by John Gerald of New York, the garden and driveway planned by Stuart Ortloff, who executed most of the landscaping for the mansions lining the fashionable coast of Long Island.

Everything about the dwelling was the product of its owner's perfectionism. There were handmade mouldings from New York, entire fireplaces brought from England, gold door fittings taken out of Fifth Avenue mansions that had been pulled down. Glass cases lined the halls to display priceless collections of Georgian silver and Meissen china, which Davis took out and allowed guests to hold. The downstairs furniture was entirely English—some satinwood, some mahogany, all of museum quality—including a hefty Sheraton table in the dining room surrounded by Adam chairs. There were silk hangings framing the windows, in pale colours, with everything immaculate, somehow untouched and untouchable. Upstairs was a collection of American glass and furniture; the only Canadian objects in the house were two bedside tables in a guest room. Mrs. Davis's bedroom was all done in pink; his suite resembled the quarters of a battleship captain, with a ship's lantern, dark wood and small, flush drawers. One cupboard held thirty pairs of shoes, fashioned out of various reptile skins.

It took a staff of eighteen maids, gardeners, chauffeurs and cooks to operate Nelson Davis's various establishments. He had an easygoing relationship with his servants, despite the occasional strains. When his two children were growing up, their governess, a Miss Parker, who drove them to school and did the family shopping, felt she had to have a new car. Davis bought her a Buick station wagon. He was then asked for an audience by Warren, his chauffeur, who came in long-faced and said, "I may not have pleased you, sir, but what did I do that was so terrible that you would want to hurt me like this?" It emerged that he had been insulted, couldn't hold his head up with the other staff, because he had to drive an Oldsmobile 88 while the governess had the new Buick. Davis's wife, Eloise, said this was nonsense, that the chauffeur should be fired. But Davis decided that Warren was just too knowledgeable about the cars and the plumbing and wiring in the various households. Some time later, they were entertaining dinner guests when the cook sent word via the butler that the stove fuse was blown, so she couldn't do the vegetables. Warren was sent for and arrived in white tie and tails. That made Eloise angry all over again, but Nelson was adamant. Warren stayed.

————

NELSON MORGAN DAVIS grew up in Shaker Heights, Ohio, the son of a manufacturer who served as deacon of a Congregationalist assembly. Everything his family had was of the best quality. He recalled, for example, that the only recordings allowed into the house were luxury sets on the Victor Red Seal label. Young Nelson's main interest was mathematics. "When I went to high school in Cleveland," he remembered, "the assistant principal, who was a lady and an excellent mathematician, invited six of us to take a special course in higher mathematics, which involved trigonometry, spherical geometry, analytics and calculus. We were a fortunate group. In fact, I can remember my first year at Cornell University, when I took the three-hour final examination in trigonometry, handed in my paper to the professor in twenty minutes and left the room to good-natured boos and catcalls from my fellow students. Fortunately, I never missed a problem during the whole year. I also learned a trick way of addition so that I could add three columns of figures at one time."

Instead of attending the required sixteen hours of lectures a week, he went to thirty, and in his graduating year, could have taken a degree in mechanical engineering, general arts, civil engineering or honours science, depending on which set of exams he chose to write. He also earned considerable pocket money by selling off the catering contract for the senior prom to the highest bidder.

Family legend has it that after young Nelson left college, his father decided he should head for Canada, sending him on his way with fifty dollars, a railway ticket and his blessing. Nelson did arrive in Toronto just after the 1929 crash with few assets, but he came on a specific mission. His father-in-law owned Chainway Stores, a group of cut-rate variety outlets in southern Ontario that had been badly hit by the Depression. Davis restored their financial health and liked the country so much that he decided to stay. He began buying up middle-sized companies, financing his deals through loans from the old Imperial Bank. When he went to borrow his first $250,000, the bank manager had allotted Davis only a fifteen-minute appointment to state his case. He stayed three hours, outlining five different ways in which he could repay the money ("the sixth was up my sleeve") and ended up borrowing an eventual $13 million, all of which was paid back within seven years. He spent the profits from his expanding operations buying up blue-chip stocks at their Depression lows. These investments provided the main source of his fortune

Nelson Davis's empire consisted of about fifty companies engaged in paving highways; transporting new cars; lending money; and manufacturing paint, varnish and nylon stockings. The complex was held together by N.M. Davis Corporation, which produced an annual sales volume of more than $200 million, and he had no other shareholders. His after-tax net was about $4 million, and his biggest worry (as he explained it to me) was trying to find ways of spending the cash fast enough before another $4 million came rolling into his private coffers the following year. This was no easy task, but he did his valiant best. "We could be a lot bigger if we went public," he says. "But if you do, you live in a goldfish bowl, and I didn't want anybody chasing me."

Davis administered his unique conglomerate from yet another mansion (Penryn House) at the bottom of a dead-end street in Toronto's Bayview district. He worked in the Tudor dwelling's former living room near a fireplace with a hand-carved mantel, surrounded by precious furniture (there was the inevitable elephant-sized Sheraton table in the dining room) and walls hung with canvasses by English masters. There was not much evidence on the main floor that this was an office instead of a residence. Monthly and annual operating statements from each of the fifty companies he owned were kept behind a yellow curtain in a mahogany cabinet. The telephone seldom rang. "I get paid for what I know, not for what I do," he said.

When F. Scott Fitzgerald coined his famous aphorism "The rich are different from us," he could have had Nelson Davis in mind. For nearly forty years, he hunted perfection, placing few limits or conditions on its achievement. Only he knew how close he had come. His face was not the visage of a man much given to introspection or ecstasies. But neither did it bear the ravaged cast of misanthropy that distorted the countenance of so many men of his wealth and persuasion.

Yet somehow it seemed symbolic that with all their possessions, the Davises' favourite roosting place was their upstairs study. It was a modest bourgeois den—a television room, really, that wouldn't have looked out of place in any suburban bunga-low. Nelson and Eloise retired there after supper most evenings, watched a little TV, fetched each other some warm milk and retired early. Maybe Fitzgerald was wrong after all.

Unobtrusive and gentle in his demeanour, he had a perma-nent twinkle in his eye, but practical jokes were not his long suit. He remained vaguely puzzled and disturbed for thirty years after his friend Bud McDougald pulled a great stunt on him in 1949. Davis had visited Herbert Johnson, the famous London hatter, and with a typically grand gesture, purchased two dozen mod-els, one in every second shade the store had on display. When McDougald heard about Davis's buying spree, he promptly ordered the other twenty-four hats and asked for the bill to be sent to his friend Nels. Davis paid the account but seldom donned any of the forty-eight pieces of headgear and never men-tioned the receipt of the extra hats to his pal Bud.

Still, it is his role as the agent who made McDougald's posthumous wishes come true that may be Davis's most lasting legacy. Before his unexpected death, McDougald had often dis-cussed with Davis his intention of passing on the Argus reins to the Black brothers. He admired in particular the stretch of knowledge and ideological depth of Conrad, plus his record of turning the Sterling newspaper chain into a profitable enter-prise. The problem was that with the optimism and disdain of common mortality so typical of him, McDougald never really planned to die and made no provision to ensure the Black brothers' succession. It was during the crucial negotiations that followed Max Meighen's attempt to gain control of Argus that Davis stepped in to help persuade Maude McDougald and Doris Phillips (who owned 47.2 percent of the stock in Ravelston Corporation, the Argus holding instrument) that they should sign their shares over to the Blacks.

The death of Nelson Davis robbed Canadian business of one of its last titans. His old-fashioned chivalry was no match for the computer-trained whiz kids scrambling to the top of the corporate ladders. But he was a man to go tiger shooting with. Once you earned his respect, he never let you down.

—1979

Paul Desmarais: King of the Establishment

THE OLD TITAN reminisces as we sit on his front porch. "I had the great advantage of being born in Sudbury," he says, "which is a truly bilingual community. So I could speak English and understand the English mentality. I grew up hanging around garages, drugstores and pool halls, fighting to speak French, yet going to school and playing hockey with mostly English-speaking kids." Few Canadians are more smoothly bilingual and bicultural than Paul Desmarais. But he is French. His ancestors came to Canada from Paris in 1657 and settled in Verchères, on the south shore, close to Ville Marie at the foot of Mount Royal. In 1905 his grandfathers moved from Gatineau to northern Ontario as foremen for the CPR, supervising cuts of timber for railroad ties, and later owned a general store and a sawmill in the village of Noelville.

The assets Paul controls add up to $100 billion; his annual income is more than $33 million. The boy from Sudbury is very rich and very powerful—and something more: he is a key political player in the matter of Canada's survival as a nation. He is not only the dean of Canada's Establishment, but also a bold advocate for federalism.

His political convictions have long driven the radical nationalists wild. During the FLQ crisis, Paul Desmarais was regularly burned in effigy; he was threatened with assassination so often that the Quebec police bluntly informed him they could not guarantee his safety. None of it cowed Desmarais, who made it his business to gauge the characters of Pierre Trudeau, Daniel Johnson (Sr.), Robert Bourassa, René Lévesque and Lucien Bouchard.

Given that history, the "porch" on which Paul Desmarais and I are talking is aptly located. This is actually the marble terrace of a twelve-thousand-square-foot neoclassic manor house designed by the kid from Sudbury himself and modelled on Thomas Jefferson's magnificent Monticello. Desmarais built it nowhere near Sudbury, but in Palm Beach, Florida, where the climate, political and otherwise, is nothing like home. Desmarais controlled every detail, even throwing up an artificial hill precisely high enough to cut off views of the road, so that from the house, you may see, without distraction, straight out to the Atlantic Ocean.

All the better to contemplate Europe's gain and Canada's loss, for during those long years in which Paul Desmarais largely opted out of his native land's economy, he built instead a new business empire across the Atlantic. All the better to wonder, with Lucien Bouchard, the latest prophet of Quebec separation, why the boy from Sudbury, now in his seventies, has lately been bringing his money back home again, to Canada.

Among titans, Desmarais is in a class of his own. Over the years, I have enjoyed a stormy relationship with the man, whose aptly named Power Corporation ranks as the most remarkable example of how business power can be wielded and expanded. He seldom speaks to journalists, but Desmarais did open up to me when I was researching a book. After he heard that it was printed, but before he had seen its contents, he scribbled me a note: "If it's good, I'll buy five hundred copies. If it's no good, I'll buy all the copies."

He never made good on his promise, which was too bad because we were ready to keep the presses rolling. Instead, he decided to sue me. At issue was my description of one of his more intricate financial manoeuvres. He instructed his Toronto legal adviser, the formidable J.J. Robinette, to demand an injunction that would have prevented the book's publication.

Since the volume was already printed and awaiting distribution, the only way to deal with Desmarais's threat was to alter the text. To await litigation would have killed the entire project. So on a rainy October weekend in 1975, a dedicated group of McClelland & Stewart employees hand-pasted seventy-five thousand paper patches of ten lines of reset type, one by one, over the offending paragraph. Desmarais later accused me of using bad glue. When I objected that we had tested it to make sure the sticker couldn't be ripped off, he exultantly exclaimed:

"A friend of mine put your book in the freezer for two weeks, and the damn sticker just peeled off!"

Twenty years later, his dominant features seem ageless: the lively brown eyes disengaged from whatever may be occupying his mind; the long, sensitive fingers and the thumb that curves outward, signalling a hot temper. As we begin to talk, Desmarais's infectious enthusiasm takes over. When I tell him some high-level gossip about Conrad Black, his eyes widen, his eyebrows shoot straight up, his mouth opens in astonishment and he exclaims: "Well, what do you think of that!" He is not the richest Canadian—that honour goes to Ken Thomson—but he is the most powerful because he can make his influence and ideas felt through his unmatched personal network.

He has suffered several serious heart attacks and survived two major bypass operations. But Desmarais's sense of fun has hardly diminished. About halfway through our sessions, he launched into the previously untold story of how he saved Power Corporation from being taken over by the CPR—and just how close he came to losing his company.

———

THIS HAPPENED IN THE LATE 1970s, when Ian Sinclair was the CPR's president and CEO. "Big Julie," as Sinclair was known, was a primitive corporate marauder, his ruthlessness softened by a sense of humour and a grudging respect for his opponents. During one negotiation to buy the 25 percent of Algoma Steel held by Germany's Mannesmann for $60 million, Big Julie came face to face with Egon Overbeck, then considered Germany's toughest industrialist. Overbeck had served as a member of the German general staff during the Second World War and had been wounded in action seven times. After four hours of having his arm twisted by Big Julie, the German caved in, confessing he had met his match. (My own experience with Sinclair was typical. He at first adamantly refused to be part of the CBC's *Canadian Establishment* television series based on the first volume of my trilogy of the same name. Once he'd agreed to participate, he threw himself so enthusiastically into the project that he virtually took over its production. He invited the CBC unit into so many actual CP Ltd. board meetings that he had to swear in the camera crew as "insiders" to meet securities regulations.)

At the time Peter Thompson, one of the earliest Power partners, had a bar in his office at Power Corporation, and Montreal Establishment types would gather there on Friday afternoons to talk about what had happened during the week. Desmarais went to one of these informal gabfests and found that Ian Sinclair was there, asking heavy questions about Power. As direct as always, Desmarais demanded, "Ian, are you trying to buy my goddamn company?"

"You either sell me Northern & Central Gas or I will bloody well buy your goddamn company," Sinclair replied.

Desmarais knew that he couldn't defend himself against any onslaught by the mighty CPR, but he shot back, "It's not for sale."

And so the two men decided to spend the evening talking about it and started to drink. They went to the Château Champlain, which was the CPR hotel in Montreal at that time, and drank their way through a meal. Then they went up to the hotel's roof, where there was a private club that Sinclair belonged to, and drank there. Afterwards, the CPR CEO ordered a suite in the hotel and they drank some more. It was three o'clock in the morning by the time they finished, and both men were very drunk. They went to Desmarais's house, but he couldn't find his key—or even his pocket—and when he finally did, he couldn't find the keyhole, so the staggering pair of corporate heavies used their shoulders to break down the front door. A startled Jacqueline Desmarais threw Sinclair out on the street.

The next morning, Desmarais, feeling very hung over, reserved a room at the Queen Elizabeth Hotel and told his secretary that he was going to be at an important business conference all day. He slept for most of eight hours, but not before phoning his secretary and asking her to call Sinclair to tell him that he was at a conference all day, that Power Corporation was definitely not for sale and that he'd get back to him later in the afternoon. Finally, at five o'clock, Desmarais went over to Windsor Station to see Sinclair, who was sitting behind his desk, looking green and almost comatose, the sweat pouring off him. He had worked all day, and was so upset when his eyes focused on the smiling and vibrant-looking Desmarais that he gave up the whole scheme and Power Corporation was saved.

The anecdote tells a lot about Desmarais, but to conclude

that he built his empire by bluff would be wrong. Desmarais is extraordinarily well focused and seldom rushes decisions. When he has a significant choice to make, he'll pick up the relevant file, examine the issue from every angle, put it aside until the patience of those around him has been tested beyond endurance, then postpone the decision one more time. Desmarais allows schemes to marinate, like pickled herring.

Desmarais is always being accused of having cashed in on his good fortune, but luck had nothing to do with it. "It's the kind of luck," explains Jim Burns, Power's deputy chairman, "that strikes only when the coordinated planning, arithmetic, preparation and patience of the dozen minds that constitute Power Corporation are transformed into action by opportunity."

For the most part, Desmarais has expanded his company— and captured its original assets—through reverse takeovers. This is twentieth-century capitalism's favourite parlour trick: the target company pays for its own demise. "What you do," Desmarais explains, "is sell your assets to a company and with the proceeds buy the shares of the company that just acquired you." Simple. It's the minnow swallowing the whale, with the whale's consent. In other words, it's a leveraged buyout under a less notorious label.

"Paul has the knack of making people believe in his vision, even when it's against their self-interest," I was told by one observer of his methods. "He is probably the only businessman in Canada who can make a pitch to a board of directors for the takeover of their own company and leave them in heat."

On May 10, 1996, when Desmarais turned over the offices of chairman and CEO of Power Corporation to his sons, Paul Jr. and André, it was a genuine transfer of power. The two younger Desmarais are now running the company. But they don't own it. Their father walked out of that emotional 1996 annual meeting the same way he walked into it: with his controlling 64.7 percent of votes and 30 percent of equity shares of the company (that give him solid control) firmly tucked into his trouser pocket. Power Corporation of Canada has 12,213,693 participating preferred shares issued, with 10 to 1 voting rights. Paul Desmarais holds all of these. While his sons are in charge, it's Paul Senior's phone calls that cast deciding votes. He is chairman of the board's executive committee and holds the proxies. He plays at being retired, or as he says with an appropriate smirk, "semi-retired." But the eight bulging briefcases in his living room say otherwise.

Paul Desmarais is still *Le Patron*.

IS IT SOMETHING shrewd or needy in the man that makes him prefer the company of politicians? He collects them like rare butterflies. Most Desmarais receptions and boards of directors resemble parliamentary reunions. At one of his New Year's Eve parties at Palm Beach, his guests included Brian Mulroney, Pierre Trudeau and former Ontario premier Bill Davis, not to mention Dinah Shore, Estée Lauder, Douglas Fairbanks Jr. and former Trudeau counsellor Jim Coutts.

"To hell with people who say I do it for political favours," Desmarais says pointedly. This, obviously, is a strong incentive, but it's not the whole story. He enjoys being part of history as it is being made, especially when heads of government consult him on various policy options. He loves being in the know. Since he regards himself as a platinum patriot, he sees nothing wrong with trying to influence national policies his way. While Desmarais treats political leaders with deference, it is the kind of deference due sleepwalkers—sleeping giants who must be led, ever so gently, lest they wake up to the fact.

Conrad Black explains Desmarais's affinity for politicians differently. "I suppose we're all unlicensed psychiatrists," he once told me. "Paul has a liking and envy for the positive way politicians can get up and easily present themselves to an electorate and stand there commending themselves to the voters' good consideration. Paul really, in an odd way, is intrigued by politicians and always has been."

Whatever the reason, Desmarais has known every PM since Mackenzie King, and despite his later Liberal connections, was particularly fond of John Diefenbaker. When he was a student at the University of Ottawa, his father would come from Sudbury once or twice a year to the nation's capital on business. Young Paul had recently written to Diefenbaker, asking to see him, and had received an invitation to lunch. "I was talking to my father, boasting how well I knew Diefenbaker, while we were at the Château Laurier Hotel, when the elevator door opened and there was Diefenbaker. My father said, 'Would you present me?' So I said,

'Sure. Mr. Diefenbaker, I'm Paul Desmarais. I'm from Sudbury, and I would like you to meet my father, Jean Desmarais, who is a lawyer in Sudbury.' Dief, using his usual mangled French, said, 'John Des Mair, you've got a fine son here. I'm having lunch with him next week.' After that, I thought Diefenbaker really put the water in the ocean!"

One of Desmarais's favourite collectibles is Pierre Trudeau, who remains on Power Corporation's international advisory board. They became close only after Trudeau reached office, but plans for his candidacy had first been hatched in early 1968 at the offices of Power Corporation, at Friday-night meetings presided over by then–Power vice-president Claude Frenette. In August of that year, two months after Trudeau had swept the country, the new PM flew to visit Desmarais at Murray Bay, where he has a summer home. When Desmarais picked up the PM at the airport in one of his two Rolls-Royces, Trudeau casually inquired what it was like to drive a Rolls. Desmarais promptly stopped the car, got into the back seat and, as Trudeau took the wheel, exclaimed, "This is the first time I've ever been driven by a prime minister!" Who says he's not a power groupie?

The first time Desmarais met René Lévesque, who later became the province's first separatist premier, was comically strange. "I wanted to talk to him when he was a minister in the Lesage government because we were thinking of buying the Dosco steel mill in Cape Breton. But René didn't understand financing very well. So I called him and said, 'I'd like to come and see you.'

"He said, 'No, I can't meet you.' And I said, 'Why?' And he said, 'It's none of your goddamn business.' 'I have to see you.' 'Well,' he said, 'I can't. My evening is taken.' I said, 'I'll go wherever you are.' So finally he said, 'I'm babysitting at my house in Outremont.' So I said, 'Well, I'll come and babysit with you.' He said, 'No, no.' And I didn't even know if he had any babies or what, but he was sitting. Anyway, finally he said, 'Okay, come over and see me. I'll give you half an hour.'

"So I went over. It was a very modest home, and we're sitting in this living room and he said, 'Would you like a cup of coffee?' I said, 'Yes, thank you.' So he got up and he made the coffee. We kept on talking, and it finally got to be seven o'clock, and he said, 'Would you like a little bit of cheese?' I said, 'Yes.' 'Would you like a beer with that?' I said, 'Sure.' So we had beer and cheese and crackers. And we kept on talking, had more cheese, more beer, more crackers, and we talked about all kinds of things. I stayed there till around midnight.

"And by that time, I said to myself: 'My God, this guy is a real socialist! If he ever gets control, there will be nothing left in this place. I've got to get the hell out of this province.' I went home and called my partner, Jean Parisien, and I said, 'Jeez, I've just finished talking to René Lévesque. Boy, is that guy a goddamn socialist!'"

True to his thoughts after his initial meeting with Lévesque, Desmarais stopped making major new investments in Quebec and Canada once the separatist politician was elected as premier, and in fact did not make a major domestic investment until the spring of 1997, when he bought control of London Life.

Another unhappy experience was Desmarais's winter meeting with Conrad Black. He tried to console him—but it backfired badly. "I was in Paris and Conrad was really in the dumps. He was trying to buy this newspaper in the United Kingdom, and everything was not going right. So I called him in Toronto from Paris.

"'Well,' he said, 'I'm trying to do this and do that and the banks won't lend me the money.' 'Look,' I said, 'I'm going back to Montreal next week. I'll come and see you and we'll get more details about what the hell you're doing.' I saw all this mess and I figured I'd better talk to him and see what I could do.

"Anyway, I flew into Toronto when it was snowing. I don't remember the date. I get to the airport, couldn't get a car, had a hell of a time. Finally, I got a taxi and arrived at his place. It was seven or eight o'clock. His gate is half open, so I had to get out of the car—I'm in my shoes in the snow—and push open the gate. We get to his house and there's snow against the front door. I bang on the door; no answer. I was mad. All of a sudden, the door opens and it's his kid, Jonathan, saying, 'How do you do, sir. Come in, Mr. Desmarais. My father is waiting for you in the library.'

"Conrad is sitting there like the bloody king of England behind his desk in his pope's chair and all the flags behind him. So I said, 'Conrad, what the hell are you doing? Why are you depressed?' 'Ah,' he said, 'I'm having problems. . . . ' So anyway, he needed money from the bank and nobody would give him any. I said, 'Things have a way of working out, and you'll be okay.' It was just a friendly visit. We had a couple of Scotches. I left there about 11:30, went back to the airport in the snow, got home.

"The next day I talked to the prime minister and I said, 'Brian, jeez, Conrad's having a tough time. Why don't you call him?' And that was the end of it.

"But when I read Conrad's memoirs, he said that Mr. Desmarais came to visit me and it was quite nice of him to do that, but I resent his indiscretion in having spoken to the prime minister of Canada to tell him I was in trouble! So I called Conrad and I said, 'Are you crazy? I'm a friend of yours. You're making other people believe that I'm a shit that I would go and find out that you're not doing well. Don't you realize everybody in Canada was saying that you're going broke, and that if I talked to the prime minister of Canada, don't you think that he already knew, and did he not call you?'

"'Yes,' he says, 'the prime minister is the one who told me that you said I was having problems.'

"I said, 'You see, you're such a negative son of a bitch, such a schemer, that you always think people are after you. Why can't you believe that somebody is nice and wonderful and a great friend? One of these days, something is going to go wrong and there will be nobody there to do a damn thing for you.'

"I enjoy Conrad. I like his turns of phrase. He has the most convoluted vocabulary in the world, and he loves it. I'm like an uncle to him now and we laugh a lot, though he occasionally says some nasty things. When Conrad decides that he's going to do something, he surrounds himself with tough cookies and lets them take the rap. But he's very tough himself, of course he is."

———

WITH A SURROGATE "nephew" like Conrad Black, you learn to appreciate a mate like Jacqueline Desmarais. She is a talented singer, plays championship bridge, has a 12 handicap in golf and is the vibrant centre of Paul's life. (She has cut half a dozen privately distributed albums, including *Back to Dry Martinis* and *Songs I Love to Sing,* backed by a twelve-piece band. Her voice is a rhythmic mix of Ella Fitzgerald and Edith Piaf. She frequently sings live duets with Robert Charlebois.) "If I was to say, 'Look Jackie, I'm going to start a passenger service to the moon tomorrow,' she'd say, 'That's a great idea, babe, why don't you do that?'" her husband of forty-five years proudly boasts. "She seems to think that I can do anything." (So does *he.*)

When Paul wants to surprise Jacqueline, as he did on one of her decade-marking birthdays, in 1988, it's not a let's-order-pizza-in affair. On that occasion, he took over Montreal's Windsor Hotel. Guests gathered along its long, marble promenade, among its ornate mirrors and columns, with specially mounted gold trellises spilling freshly opened roses and fancily clad hussars opening the doors to a ballroom where a symphony orchestra was playing Viennese waltzes. Later in the evening, Ella Fitzgerald and Robert Charlebois sang for the crowd, which included the governor general, the prime minister and Quebec's premier.

When not in Palm Beach, the Desmarais family is to be found at one of three Canadian dwellings or, if in Europe, at

Claridge's in London or the Ritz in Paris. The Montreal house on Westmount's Ramezay Road was originally decorated by Lou Edwards, E.P. Taylor's daughter. The large living room, done in lemon and pale aqua, has a stunning Diego Rivera canvas as its centrepiece. Desmarais's favourite *pied-à-terre* is La Malbaie (Murray Bay), near the mouth of the Saguenay River. It was once a prestigious resort, the home of the Cabots of Boston, the Tafts of Ohio and the Hamilton Fishes of New York. Desmarais bought the house for $60,000 from Leo Timmins, of Hollinger Mines fame. It's on the Boulevard des Falaises, on a bluff overlooking the St. Lawrence. He has added a swimming pool, sauna and tennis court. The garage holds his 1906 Cadillac, a motorcycle and two Rolls-Royces, one of which is fitted with a horn that sounds like a steam locomotive. "This is the place we're happiest in," he says. Inland from La Malbaie is his château, a country estate with a hunting lodge that can accommodate forty guests, built on a wild stretch of land—a ten-thousand-acre property with fifty lakes on it—that once belonged to Canada Steamship Lines.

The Desmarais offices in Montreal are like nothing else in Canada (except perhaps Peter Munk's private study in his new Forest Hill mansion). On first impression, Power Corporation's building resembles one of the minor, outlying pavilions at Versailles; on closer inspection, it resembles Versailles itself— but with the patina of good taste. Done in a classic Louis XIV style, its creamy pillars and long, marble corridors with arching, ten-metre ceilings, and the richness of its plush velvet drapes, scattered sculptures and weathered woods, lend the place a solemn, almost churchly resonance. The walls are crowded with the most valuable corporate collection of Canadian art in the country—dozens of canvasses by A.Y. Jackson, Clarence Gagnon, Maurice Cullen, Goodridge Roberts, Frederick Varley, James Wilson Morrice (a whole wall of them), David Milne, Tom Thomson, Homer Watson, Jean-Paul Lemieux, Franz Johnston, Arthur Lismer and Jean-Paul Riopelle. The boardroom has forty-five exquisitely mounted Cornelius Krieghoffs.

All of this is a lifetime and a world away from the pool halls of Sudbury, certainly, but the popular myth that Desmarais's success was totally self-made is a bit of a stretch. He did grow up with certain privileges. The Desmarais family was well respected and relatively well heeled. Paul's grandfather had helped found the local Sacred Heart College, formed the first local Caisse Desjardins co-op and helped finance the St. Joseph Oratory in Montreal. He became a prosperous lumberman through his wooden-tie contracts for building CP and CN from North Bay to Winnipeg. His uncle was mayor of Sudbury in 1939—the only year it mattered, because that was when the king and queen came to town, so the family had their pictures taken with the royal pair. Paul's father was a prominent Sudbury lawyer who helped found Laurentian University. Out of that background, plus his own success, came the self-confidence that allowed Desmarais to grow personally and professionally without having to overcome the deference that marked his generation.

"I had no trouble going and sitting at the Mount Royal Club and telling the chairman of the Royal Bank or anybody else,

'What the hell is wrong with you that you keep complaining about "those damn French Canadians"?'" Diehard members of English Canada's Establishment regard him as a welcome ambassador from Quebec, a part of the country most of them view with only slightly more comprehension than some distant Transylvania.

With the current Liberal administration in Ottawa, Desmarais enjoys his usual gold-plated access. Apart from the fact that Jean Chrétien's daughter France is married to Desmarais's son André, he is extremely close to Finance Minister Paul Martin, who spent most of his working life at Power Corporation, running Canada Steamship Lines. (In a classic reverse takeover, Desmarais allowed Martin to buy CSL from him and even signed a bank note on his behalf to help cover the $195 million purchase price.) One of Power Corporation's senior vice-presidents is John Rae, who served as executive assistant to Jean Chrétien in Indian Affairs and managed his triumphant 1993 and 1997 election campaigns.

"Paul is a master manager of the political process," says Michael Pitfield, clerk of the Privy Council during the Trudeau years, whom Desmarais tagged to be deputy chairman of Power Corporation in 1984. The scion of a wealthy and influential Montreal family, Pitfield was a public servant most of his life, but once freed of his responsibilities (and wafted off to the Senate), he began to appreciate the private sector's role. "It never ceases to amaze me that so few people recognize that businessmen are responsible for shaping the whole country's infrastructure. The easy thing to think about Paul is that he has the politicians in his pocket, that he's a sort of master of marionettes. But he's not. He's a player. He never disengages; he never withdraws from the arena. He made an enormous fortune by age thirty-five and has ever since been engaged in the active governance of this country. Most people automatically assume that Paul's policy involvements are designed to make him richer, that he tries to control people and events to get some desired, selfish result. In fact, he's an active participant, using his power base to press for what he thinks are desirable policies. It's very important to understand that distinction."

Desmarais's most profoundly personal friendship with any politician is with Brian Mulroney, who, after he left office, was appointed to several important European boards within the Power Corporation empire and resumed his function as one of its chief legal advisers. "He may turn out to have been a great prime minister. We need more time to assess his record," says Desmarais. "If you look at the big things—Meech, free trade, our relationship with the U.S.—all that was much improved by him. The trouble is that he was too loyal to his friends, and some of his friends—people he shouldn't have been too loyal to—took advantage of him. He should have told them, 'Look, this is where you get off; I'm prime minister of Canada, so look after your interests but don't come to me.' Still, it's been a great advantage to be able to say, 'Well, I know the prime minister of Canada, and I know what he's thinking.'"

Desmarais has formed business connections between his homeland and China. He was one of the first Canadian businessmen officially to visit that country, setting up the Canada China Business Council, ably run by Jack Austin. Desmarais is in partnership with Peter Munk to develop China's gold mines and with Laurent Beaudoin to sell railway cars to the Chinese. First among Canadian businessmen, he has managed to attract major Chinese capital into Canada: $50 million to build a pulp mill in Castlegar, B.C., in partnership with one of his companies.

In Winnipeg he controls the Manitoba capital's Investors Group, the country's largest and most successful mutual fund operation (assets of $34 billion), run by Sandy Riley, which will be a major investor in London Life. Winnipeg is also the home of Great-West Life, which has assets of more than $53 billion after its London Life acquisition. A tipoff to Great-West's significance within the Power group is that Desmarais usually assigns two or three of the holding company's directors to serve on the board of each subsidiary, but the Great-West board includes nearly the whole Power house—not only Desmarais and his two sons, but also Power CEO Robert Gratton; vice- and deputy chairmen Michael Pitfield and Jim Burns; and chief financial officer Michel Plessis-Bélair, as well as Power director Don Mazankowski.

WE HAVE BEEN TALKING for most of two days. The Desmarais household is reclaiming the living room, which was our debriefing chamber. Desmarais is in his summing-up mood.

"I've been like a fisherman who goes out and puts out a net, and if he's lucky, he gets a good catch. But sometimes, even if he's a good fisherman, he gets nothing. Well, I spent a lot of time putting out nets and finally, over a long period of time, I've been lucky. But it's not just luck; it's hard work. You've got to expose yourself to the fish precisely when circumstances are favourable . . . We have a lot of capital now, much more than I ever dreamed possible, really. There are a lot of things I'd like to accomplish still. I sometimes ask myself, Why don't you stop? With everything you have, there is a corresponding responsibility—and after a while, it becomes a heavy burden. But the fascination to go on never stops . . ."

He trails off and I notice that night has fallen. There is no wedge of light remaining between the ocean and the horizon. "My enemy now is time," he says as we part.

There will never be another titan quite like this one. He was the forerunner. Long before the Canadian Establishment came along, he showed them the way. He demonstrated that you could outwit and out-harm and, if necessary, out-bully your competitors—annihilate them, have fun doing it and never feel a moment's guilt. His peers watch him, study him, try to copy him—like apprentice Sioux learning to shadow the great buffaloes—but his essence remains elusive and inviolate. In a world filled with corporate honchos who act like constipated eagles, Paul Desmarais is a refreshing exception.

I climb into my rented car and drive back to my hotel, past the darkened Palm Beach mansions. It was an interview to remember.

—1998

The Golden Couple:
Gerry Schwartz and Heather Reisman

WHEN THE LIST of Canada's highest-paid executives for 1997 was published, I noticed Gerry Schwartz's name and felt momentary sympathy for the man. True, his compensation of $18,775,640 was up 124 percent from the year before. Yes, he did manage to pay himself three times as much as, say, Conrad Black, even though the Hollinger chief had more than doubled his own pay. True, Schwartz was well ahead of Jean Monty, who runs Canada's largest corporation, BCE Inc., and Laurent Beaudoin, who masterminds the world-class aircraft and everything-else-that-moves company, Bombardier Inc.

Still, no matter how impressive, the size of Gerry's pay packet placed him behind Robert Gratton, CEO of Montreal's Power Financial Corporation, who won the year's crown with a tidy $27,395,123 stuffed into his piggy bank. There was no way to

disguise it: Gerry Schwartz had come in second. I could visual-
ize the poor guy trying to explain to his father what had gone
wrong. Hence my sympathy.

The previous year, when Onex Corporation, Schwartz's
conglomerate, made it to number 14 in the *Financial Post* list of
Canada's top 500 companies, the CEO allowed himself to feel
happy—excited even. After all, in the *FP*'s listings, Onex had come
in just behind Imperial Oil, the biggest of the energy majors, and
just ahead of Canadian Pacific, the country's defining corporation.

Now, no one has ever mistaken Gerry Schwartz for a soul
without ambition, but he does not show his feelings easily. At
moments of stress, joy, sorrow or excitement, he can appear
stiff, holding himself with what a friend describes as "the impec-
cable posture of a hand puppet." Not that morning. If he hadn't
been in his Bay Street office forty-nine floors above ground, he
might have done a little cakewalkin' in the spring sunshine, so
exhilarated did he feel. He couldn't resist calling his father in
Winnipeg to share the thrill.

When Andy Schwartz came on the line and Gerry announced
the great news, the phone went silent for a split second or three.
Then his father issued rather subdued congratulations, and they
talked of family things. The younger Schwartz knew only too well
what that hesitation meant. He had come in fourteenth, and
fourteenth wasn't first, which is what every Jewish father expects
of his son.

Now, to make things worse, he had come in second in his pay
packet, stuck at a lousy $18 mil. "There's an apocryphal story of

the kid who comes home after he gets 98 in his exams," Gerry Schwartz says. "Of course his Jewish father says, 'Why didn't you bother to think about the area where you lost those two marks? Why didn't you study that? At least for the next exam, prepare yourself.' The kid goes back, studies like crazy, comes home after the next exam and says, 'Pop, I got 100.' 'So,' the father replies, 'don't rest on your laurels.'

"The morning that *FP* list came out was a very defining moment for me," Schwartz vividly recalls. His father's "sort-of-lukewarm" voice on the phone caused all the other sort-of-lukewarm moments to well up in his memory, like the time "when I was going to law school in Manitoba. I stood first for a while, and then in the final year, I was fifth or something because I was engrossed in a couple of business deals.

"My father didn't come to my graduation or talk to me for a couple of months. He kept saying, 'You could have been first. All you had to do was work hard enough. You knew how to do it—you already proved you were smarter than the others.'"

No wonder Gerry Schwartz is so mysterious a package to contemplate from without. He's a man who honed his skills in the nastiest of shark pools, the junk-bond frenzy of the 1980s, the leveraged-buyout game that *Harper's* editor Lewis Lapham called "the capitalist system at its worst." He's a man who has been accused of outlandish greed at the expense of his own shareholders, a charge easy to level at any CEO who pays himself $75,000 every working day. He's a man ardently loved by his formidable wife, Heather Reisman, and revered for his Zen calm by his business partners. He's a man who has pulled off some of Canada's most lucrative megadeals. He's the same man who hesitated and let slip away what might have been the best deal of all.

"There is a buffed Schwartzian veneer that envelops the small tight figure within it," wrote Jennifer Wells in the *Globe and Mail*'s *Report on Business*. "It must be kept intact, and so an orchestration of the corporate and personal tableaux must be conducted." He is, in short, a Jew burdened with a Presbyterian conscience, which is a tough burden to carry for any man.

STARTING OUT IN WINNIPEG after graduating in law, Schwartz found himself articling with one firm while being attracted to the style and expertise of Izzy Asper, already a well-known tax lawyer and destined to become a broadcasting titan.

"One day Gerry just showed up on my doorstep, introduced himself, told me he was going to article with me, learn everything I knew, practise law with me and we would do beautiful things together," Asper recalls. "A bit pushy, I thought, but his determination intrigued me. I didn't have any openings, so I sent him on his way. He kept coming back until I finally caved in, and he did article and graduate with me. Then, in 1968, he decided to leave for the Harvard Business School."

While studying at Harvard, Schwartz operated a chain of small carpet stores in Winnipeg, Calgary and Edmonton and used to fly up on weekends to take care of business. Peter Herrndorf, the television guru who was at Harvard at the same time, remembers bumping into Gerry at the business school library. While everyone else was studying case histories, he was working over his companies' real cash-flow statements.

One of the advantages Schwartz enjoyed at Harvard was running the Business School's Speakers' Club. That gave him the chance to have a private dinner with each guest. One of those speakers was Bernie Cornfeld, the former New York social worker who had become the high-flying head of Investors Overseas Services, which, before its spectacular collapse, ran the world's largest group of mutual funds, with eighty-five thousand salespeople in a hundred countries on its payroll. The youthful Gerry made such a good impression that Cornfeld offered him a summer job in Geneva.

"Cornfeld looked like a little rabbi from Philadelphia," Schwartz recalls. "He knew nothing about business, knew nothing about finance, but he knew everything about what motivates individuals and what they most fear. He was Rasputin-like and could transfix you with his eyes, like he was looking into you. One day he was having a fit because one of his underlings wasn't following his marching orders. He was screaming at this guy, and the guy wasn't paying much attention until Cornfeld said, 'I'll send you back where you came from. You'll be in Kansas City the rest of your life!' The guy wilted because it was the one thing he really feared. One lesson it taught me: nobody is better than anybody else. There are no geniuses out there. It was an eye opener to see a lot of these big shots humble themselves to Cornfeld.

"I shared his office, and every trip he took, every place he went, he took me with him. It was fun, and the people I spent time with were unbelievable." Like the time Schwartz was sent to Rome aboard the Investors Overseas Services jet so he could meet with a cardinal in one of the hallowed rooms at the Vatican to dispense financial advice to the Holy See. Or another time, when the most coveted of smuggled goods appeared in Geneva. "I remember going out to the airport to meet Charles Bluhdorn, chairman of Gulf & Western. When we arrived back at the IOS mansion, Bluhdorn put his briefcase out on his knees and Cornfeld said, 'Well, Charlie, did you bring it?' Bluhdorn grinned and brought out not one, but two, giant salamis from a New York deli for Cornfeld, who hugged him and danced a little jig of joy."

Schwartz was grateful to his mentor, but not to the point of emulation, for Bernie Cornfeld was, in the words of his protégé, "a Lothario" who "could be something of a pig." Schwartz remembers the two of them leafing through a copy of *Life* magazine one evening, finding special interest in an article on bathing suits in far-away Fort Lauderdale. "There was a picture of one gorgeous, absolutely gorgeous, woman that Cornfeld kept coming back to and looking at. Three days later, she was living with us in the Geneva house. Victoria Principal, the actress who later appeared in *Dallas,* spent the summer there, and in fact, there was a picture in *Newsweek* of the three of us—Bernie, Victoria and me—sitting at the end of a long table.

"I was the young *dauphin,*" Schwartz recalls. "I had the run of the place." What became increasingly clear, however, was that Bernie Cornfeld took the same blithely reckless approach to mutual funds as he did to mutual fun. "IOS actually wasn't a scam; it was unbelievably badly managed. There were no budgets, no controls, no anything because so much money was coming in that they were always ahead of the game. We used to have dinner at his beautiful villa that Napoleon had originally built for Josephine on Lake Geneva, and Cornfeld always had four or five girls living in the house who were available to everybody. There were usually three or four businesspeople in town who we entertained in a constant round of big dinners, a party every night. The scene could get sickening. One night I was sitting there and had my feet up, just watching the goings-on, and I thought to myself, 'This is really stupid.' I just stood up and walked out the back door and headed to the office because I had left my car there. A light, misty rain was falling, and I'm walking on the gravel at the side of the road when I hear this crunch-crunch behind me. I turn around and there's Cornfeld. He puts his arm on my shoulder, walks me back to the office and says, 'I know you hate this.'"

————

AT THE END of the summer, Schwartz headed back to Harvard, got his MBA and hit Wall Street. At Bear Stearns, he was assigned a desk next to Henry Kravis, then in training to become the leading leveraged-buyout specialist in the country. Schwartz learned his lessons well and was involved in some of the first LBO take-overs. He was a good friend of the not-yet-imprisoned Mike Milken and later did three or four new junk-bond issues with the rogue trader.

Schwartz was searching for something permanently entrepre-neurial to engage his talents when Izzy Asper visited New York. While dragging Gerry to yet another jazz joint, Asper hit upon the idea of starting a western-based merchant bank. On January 17, 1977, they received a federal charter to set up Canwest Capital Corporation. Its structures reflected an intriguing marriage between institutional financiers and entrepreneurs, with the for-mer putting in most of the money but the latter making most of the decisions. Investors were pledged to stay in for ten years without taking out dividends, though results were monitored annually. By the summer of 1981, the young firm's assets had exceeded $2 billion, with revenues of $700 million. Izzy teed up the purchase of Monarch Life, through Brigadier Dick Malone, then publisher of the *Winnipeg Free Press*. But it was Schwartz who engineered the financing through the sale of preferred shares guaranteed by the Toronto-Dominion Bank.

Schwartz and Asper formed a nearly perfect working team, though their ebullience made it difficult to tell which one of them was holding the other back. When they moved in to jointly occupy the chairman's office of Crown Trust, which they bought from stuffy predecessors, they had a large Mickey Mouse telephone installed. A visitor asked Schwartz, "Why the Mickey Mouse telephone?" Schwartz replied, "Because I do Mickey

The partnership broke up over the sale of one of their best holdings, Monarch Life. Asper, ever the Winnipeg patriot, wanted to keep the company in their portfolio because it was, outside the Richardson empire, the last major Winnipeg-owned financial institution and because he saw it as a future Great-West or Manulife. But when North American Life bid for Monarch at a price that gave the partnership a cash gain of $36 million on a $6 million investment four years earlier, Izzy was voted down by his own board, nine to one.

"I've never been so wounded, despondent, almost suicidal in my life," Asper recalls nearly twenty years later. "That was my big break with Gerry. I couldn't believe it. When he threw his vote in to sell, that was the rupture of our relationship because to me it was a violation of what we had agreed to do. The only thing that makes me mad at anybody is when he or she wastes my time because it's all I've got. And here I'd spent seven years building this thing only to see it unravel."

Schwartz tells it differently. "The sale of Monarch wasn't just a loose event," he claims. "The TD Bank was pushing us very hard to repay the loans in the holding company from a U.S. investment we had made in the pay-television business—it was disastrous, way ahead of its time. TD was pressuring us to pay as a way of settling that loan. It's true that Izzy and I didn't agree, but I think it was more a matter of what we each wanted to do with our own lives than how we wanted to run the business. The board had kind of lost faith in management's ability to run the company because these losses were just mounting every week.

Once we made the decision to sell Monarch, which Izzy opposed and I supported, that was the end. But the actual sale of Monarch was simply a result of all those other things; it wasn't the triggering event."

That same unnerving dispassion is there when he is presented with the outrage of others. It's in Schwartz's voice when he tells critics how he built his current empire, Onex. The attacks have centred on the pay he has drawn out of his firm, especially during its first lean years when there was a general feeling that Onex was good for Schwartz but not so good for its shareholders. "That just burned me," he says, "because it was good for the shareholders who have gotten between 30 and 60 percent compounded returns. We took Automotive Industries public at $11, we did a secondary at $24, and we sold the company at $33. Johnstown America we took public at $9; we got out of it at $28. We took Dura Automotive public at $13, and the stock today is around $28, something like that. We took Tower Automotive public at $11, and the stock went up to $41. People have done fantastically well by investing alongside me. Secondly, we've got scads of guys who have made a lot of money either running our businesses or being in Onex itself. And in every case, they are guys who had previous careers with other people and might have accumulated a $1.5 million net worth elsewhere; with us, they've accumulated a $10 or $15 million net worth. Tony Johnson, our partner in the automotive business, for example, has probably made $50 million in the eight years that we've been together. Before that, he ran Cummings Engine for North America and probably had a net worth of $1 million. So the people that I've worked with have done well. The people who have invested with me have done well. And I've done enormously well too."

Gerry's annual income from Onex includes not only his salary, bonuses and expenses, but also the dividends he receives on the ten million subordinated voting shares he owns, plus all those multiple voting shares, which also allow him to unilaterally name two-thirds of the directors. That amounts to an additional $4.5 million or so; his annual take now seldom dips below $20 million. Up until 1994, Onex had a unique compensation package. At year-end auditors would value the portfolio asset growth, with management receiving 20 percent of the increase and Schwartz getting the lion's share of that payout.

If certain critics choose to find fault with such an enormous income, Schwartz is content to chalk it up to "Canadians' desire to bring successful people down. If I earn a $4 million bonus, that's a lifetime's income for most people, and they like to read that I'm a jerk for having done that. It makes them feel better."

As for those who would cast aspersions on his leveraged-buyout pedigree, Schwartz is equally sanguine. "There were some LBO excesses that were enormously negative," Schwartz agrees, "but the technique also had huge positives, which helped reshape American business."

Leveraged buyouts have been characterized as trading the short-term expectations of your stockholders for the short-term expectations of your bankers. Technically, they involve the purchase of an undervalued company by a small group of investors, financed largely by debt, the cost of which is borne by the acquired company, either from its treasury or by selling off its assets. (The LBO experts who do the deal usually charge a 20 percent premium or fee.) Properly done, it's as close to an infinite money machine as you can legally get, because you grow by using somebody else's money. In other words, LBOs are the corporate equivalent of that country-and-western ditty about becoming your own grandpaw.

————

SCHWARTZ HAD A TOUGH launching period with Onex in 1984 because it started as an acknowledged LBO play, making him the Canadian wizard of leveraged buyouts. This, right at the time of the aborted *Barbarians at the Gate* RJR Nabisco deal, and a whole series of Boone Pickens–Carl Icahn–Henry Kravis LBOs that left even the most adventurous investors with a bad taste. To quote more fully the view of Lewis Lapham, LBOs are like "cutting up the carcass of a sperm whale and selling off the parts. These predators repay the debts they accumulate through flash asset dispositions, sweetening the process by providing golden parachutes for displaced executives worth many millions— written off as tax-deductible opportunity costs, of course. It's neat and tidy and the capitalist system at its worst, because it destroys companies instead of creating value."

Because the LBO business in the U.S. was ultra-competitive yet super-lucrative, it attracted some questionable operators willing to accept its high risks and higher rewards. *Fortune* magazine compared running an LBO to "crossing the Atlantic on a high-speed catamaran. You're screaming along at twenty-five knots with the windward pontoon flying above the wave and the leeward hull underwater. It is the ultimate test of seamanship, recommended only for expert helmsmen."

Which some might agree describes Gerry Schwartz in action during the building of Onex. He makes no apologies. "What characterizes an LBO is two things: using the assets and cash flow of the acquired company to support a substantial portion of the purchase price in the form of debt; secondly, the original LBO firms invested other people's money and earned a fee for doing so. LBO firms were driven to sell the companies they acquired to realize a profit from their participation in the sale. At Onex, we were never really in the LBO business because we didn't fit the second characteristic, though in the early days, we bought and sold many companies to increase our capital base." Another essential difference is that Onex raises permanent capital instead of depending on temporary investment partnerships, affording it the luxury of taking a longer point of view.

Today, Onex is worth $11 billion. Gerry Schwartz makes no apologies for that whatsoever. Except maybe to his father. Schwartz and his multitalented wife, Heather, have scythed their way into Toronto society, pleased to do whatever was required to be accepted. They lead charmed lives, indulging their private and commercial fantasies, with Heather running Indigo, an exquisite book and music chain, while Gerr, as she endearingly calls him, is making Hollywood movies with artistic bounce. Once a month or so, they co-host Toronto's most prestigious literary salon in their Rosedale mansion. Its walls are crammed with medieval paintings and ancient Asian *objets d'art*. There's a Gulfstream II jet to carry them between their Nantucket and Bel Air houses. They know how to live. For Heather's fortieth birthday, Gerry flew in the Kingston Trio to serenade her. They were her favourite group when she was growing up. That year for his birthday, she gave him a red Porsche 911 Targa.

———

THE INITIAL MEETING of Gerry Schwartz and Heather Reisman, niece of free-trade negotiator Simon, is a matter of some dispute.

His version: "I was in Montreal seeing my friend Claude Frenette [the financier and Global director], when he said, 'Let's go out tonight. We'll go out with two beautiful women, and we'll have a wonderful time.' I thought that was a great idea, but I didn't know any women in Montreal. Claude said, 'Oh look, I have two fabulous women who work for me, and I'll call them both into my office so you can choose.' So he calls the first one in on some trumped-up excuse, and in my opinion, she's absolutely gorgeous. (She was Marie-Josée Drouin, later Canadian director of the Hudson Institute, a leading American think tank, and even later—after having married and divorced Montreal Symphony Orchestra conductor Charles Dutoit—the wife of Henry Kravis, the great American king of the LBOs, who had two wives to go before he would meet Marie-Josée but was at the time working with Schwartz on leveraged buyouts.) As she leaves, I say to Claude, 'Skip the second one!' He said, 'No, no, you must meet the second one.' Heather was the second woman, and that's the end of the story. I took Heather out that night, and that was it." A hundred days after they met, they knew they would be married, and a thousand days later, they were.

Her version: "Claude Frenette did introduce us at the Inter-Group office where I worked. But he introduced Gerry to me first. And Gerry said, 'That's okay. I don't have to meet the next one.' The first real date we had, he invited me to meet him in New York for the weekend. We went to see *Annie*, which had just opened on Broadway. And we weren't into the play fifteen seconds when he started crying because it's such a poignant opening, and I remember thinking to myself, Well, any guy who would cry within fifteen seconds is definitely worth getting to know better.

"There's no question that Gerry has a very, very soft centre, wrapped in lots of layers of insulation that create a legitimate interface between the essence of his emotions and what he's experiencing—the barrier between feelings and knowing. It is a really effective interface. From a business point of view, its value is that while he's always processing at an intellectual level, he never seems bogged down by an emotional reaction to something that could in any way deter his intelligent judgment in a strategic situation. His outward lack of emotion prevents outsiders from sharing his vulnerabilities, so that he comes off as much more cerebral than he really is."

If that seems an oddly analytical way for one soulmate to describe another, consider the source. At first glance Heather Reisman seems soft and shy. She is not. She is whip smart, fiercely ambitious and constantly testing herself. She profoundly loves her "Gerr" but is very much her own woman. She is an optimistic feminist who believes in the inevitable empowerment of technology and thinks that the resulting meritocracy cannot and will not be based on gender. Because of her brains, energy and forest fires of ambition, Heather will never achieve the empty glories of Jewish princesshood. Though she now enjoys a life of wealth and privilege, she knows about struggles and down times, about being a single mom without a car to take the kids to school. She dresses modestly, knowing that comfort is as important as fashion. The effect is understated elegance, throwaway cool.

The daughter of a small-time Montreal developer, she graduated in social work from McGill and worked with foster kids, helping them to cope with life and to find jobs. She married a fellow student; they had two kids, then divorced. She later dated Sonny Gordon. (Dating Harold P. Gordon, an attractive lawyer who spent twenty years as a partner at Stikeman Elliott, was a rite of passage in Montreal during the 1970s and 1980s. He now lives in New York and is a mogul of the U.S. toy industry.) Heather subsequently trained in computers and polling and eventually co-founded Paradigm, a successful consulting company with a $10 million annual turnover.

"She is really a stupendous woman," Schwartz confirms. "She is all she seems to be, but she's a huge amount more. She appears to be smart, vivacious, interested, but she's also cheerful, a great support system, a great partner, a great leader. Most people say she's the best thing that ever happened to me, and she really is. She and I are alike in so many things; our values are the same. I may not know what she's going to do, but I always know where she's coming from, and I think she always knows where I'm coming from.

"There's also a whole side to Heather that's very soft and gentle. She says I cry in movies, and I do, but try going to a movie with her. She's impossible. She talks out loud, and you really can't go to a movie with her unless there's nobody within twenty seats of you. I mean we always have somebody turning around and saying, 'Sshh!' because Heather's commenting on the film, like when somebody's about to get hurt, she's yelling, 'Don't do that! Don't hit him!'"

All tears and inner goo aside, these are the two that *Toronto Life* magazine has named the city's number one Establishment power couple. "The weirdest thing about Gerry," says his regular tennis partner, Ray Heard, "is that in the middle of winter, when it's minus thirty degrees on a Sunday morning and I'm picking him up in my Acura, he'll be waiting on his front steps, wearing shorts and a T-shirt, raring to go."

––––––––––

AT FIFTY-SIX, GERRY carries his 160 pounds on an athletic frame, plays tennis earnestly, skis recklessly and sails experimentally. His game of choice is tennis, and his partners swear that he plays exactly as he does business. "Schwartz is the most unpredictable tennis player I have ever played against. He never gives up," claims Heard, a former media executive, now senior adviser to the chairman of the Royal Bank. "He's terminally tenacious; sometimes I have him, five to three, and he'll come back from nowhere. He will return anything. I don't particularly mind if I don't win, but Gerry likes to win, I tell you."

In tennis as in business, Schwartz is a paradoxical combination of ruthless energy and inner calm. Probably his favourite literary quotation is from Pascal: "It has struck me that all men's misfortunes spring from the single cause that they're unable to stay quietly in one room." He uses that quote with the guys around the Onex offices when advising them not to jump at companies, lecturing them against the mad notion that "just because we've got money to spend, we've got to find something to buy." The maxim he coolly preaches is: You're usually sorrier for the mistakes you make than you are happy for the great deals you conclude.

His most significant recent purchase was Celestica Inc., the manufacturing and service arm of IBM Canada, which Schwartz acquired for $750 million on October 6, 1996. Of that amount, $150 million came from Onex and the balance from the Bank of Nova Scotia and the Hospitals of Ontario Pension Plan. Through multiple voting shares, Onex retains control in the company, which has revenues of more than $2 billion and unlimited prospects. "There were a dozen bidders, but we got it," says Schwartz, "because we probably have the best reputation in North America for buying divisions of large companies that are required to go on supplying their former parent company—Sky Chefs continues to supply American Airlines, ProSource continues to supply Burger King, and now Celestica continues to supply IBM. In each case, we've done well for ourselves and have very happy customers." Celestica has since expanded into Europe, and Schwartz's goal is to at least double Celestica's revenues by century's end. In the spring of 1998, he successfully sold a Celestica IPO worth $570 million, the biggest high-tech initial public offering in Canadian history.

The Celestica deal transformed Onex from being regarded as merely a fascinating conglomerate with growth potential into a certified winner that will grow exponentially from now on, with its stock soaring 62 percent in the hundred days after the Celestica purchase. Gerry's sweetest deal was his original purchase of Sky Chefs Inc., the company that dominates the oxymoronic airline food business. It is now the world's largest in-flight caterer, serving six hundred thousand passengers on 250 different airlines daily—from 139 kitchens in twenty-eight countries. Onex bought the company from American Airlines for only $19 million and seven months later sold off its airport concession division for $175 million, repaying its purchase price, as well as eliminating its entire debt load.

Other Onex holdings include ProSource, which distributes food to such chains as Wendy's, Burger King and Red Lobster and turns out revenues of $5 billion; Hidden Creek, which runs half a dozen auto-parts factories; Vencap Equities Alberta Ltd., a venture capital fund; and Scotsman Industries, which makes ice machines.

All of its activities are carried out at the operating level so that Onex itself employs only a dozen executives and their secretaries. All staff members share in Onex's generous profit sharing, expressed through stock distribution. "As a result," says Anthony Munk, one of the senior vice-presidents, "there's more pressure on people to perform. They have their own money at work, and now they're virtually running their own shows. It's amazing the impact that has on a management team. I mean, suddenly you have guys working at night, suddenly you have guys cancelling their holidays, suddenly you have guys turning the office lights off at night, suddenly you have guys driving home from work thinking about ways they can make more money for the company."

"A lot of what I do," adds Gerry, "is shape the edges of the playing field to allow the team to keep playing on it, and if the ball gets snapped to me, my job is to hand it off and put it in the hands of whoever can best run with it. The world is a very tough place; you really need to trust people."

————

HIS STAFF RESPECTS SCHWARTZ, though he can be a demanding boss. What they admire—and copy—most of all is that he does what he damn well pleases. "If you're so hung up on what people think, you end up chasing your own tail," says Munk. "The way Gerry lives exemplifies that he's different. He chooses his own time and place for vacations, his own friends. From a business perspective, he is not afraid to challenge the status quo, and in that way, there's a degree of contrariness to him.

"You can see that in some of the deals we've done. In 1990 we formed a partnership with Tony Johnson to do acquisitions in the automotive industry, though people at the time thought we were crazy because GM, Ford and Chrysler were supposed to be going bankrupt. Yet on that deal, we probably generated the greatest return we've ever made.

"There's a degree of rebelliousness to Gerry," Munk continues. "He takes pride in doing things differently from the Establishment. And I don't know whether it's from his background or because he loves the success he's attained without having to have gone through all that stuff. He's not necessarily thumbing his nose because we need the Establishment at Onex. It's more him saying, 'I'm going to do it my way, and I want to maintain a strong relationship with all of you, but you have to accept me as I am because I'm not going to conform to your ways.'"

Schwartz himself sums it up in a kind of Zen response to the global titans: "I suppose there is an Establishment, but I am so anti-establishment at heart that I find it hard to believe I would have been tricked by life into being part of it."

"I remember him as quiet, disciplined and very focused when he was in partnership with Izzy Asper back in Winnipeg," says Bill Mingo, dean of the Halifax legal corps, whose mutton-chop whiskers may be the last in captivity, outside remakes of *Mutiny on the Bounty*. Mingo knows Schwartz very well, having served on various boards with him over the past two decades. "He appeared largely uninterested in creating a business presence or empire for himself. He wanted simply to be a merchant banker who created value. I remember him mainly as possessing one of the clearest minds I've ever encountered, encompassing complex transactions effortlessly, the flow of his articulation balancing easily the nuances of his thoughts."

"His main attribute is discipline," adds Brian King, an Onex director. "If prices climb too high, deals aren't done; the adrenalin of the chase is never allowed to dominate." Schwartz has done many deals with adrenalin-pumping speed. In October 1994, Robert Lantos, the Toronto entertainment czar, called Michael Levine, the country's busiest entertainment lawyer, and asked him to arrange a meeting with Schwartz because he was intrigued by the Onex operation. "I called Gerry," Levine recalls, "and he invited us to his home for breakfast. In the middle of the meal, after Robert described his company—where he was going and what he wanted to do—quite unexpectedly, Gerry said, 'I would be pleased to advance $16.5 million for a convertible debenture. According to my calculations, that will buy me about 8 percent of your company.' Lantos said yes. And I said, 'What's for lunch?'" The stock has since skyrocketed.

———

SWEET DEAL. Yet Schwartz is the first to admit there have also been several inexplicable fumbles—and one outright choke that tears at him to this day. Among the fumbles, count his unwillingness to bid for Budget Rent A Car, which was dangled before him many years ago. The rental firm was then owned by Transamerica, whose president, Art Van Leuven, entered negotiations with Schwartz. He grew fond of the Winnipeg entrepreneur and mentored him through the process. Schwartz offered $100 million cash, plus a $25 million note. "I remember," Schwartz recalls with horror in his voice, "Van Leuven telling me in exasperation, 'Gerry, this is yours on a platter and I promise you it's a wonderful company, but the price is $150 million cash. You can't keep on trying to buy it for less. Make up your mind, and if you don't pay that, we'll hire an investment banker to do the selling.' I finally got up to $125 million cash. They opened it up and had all kinds of bidders. We revised our bid to $185 million, and the company sold for $225 million. The guys who bought it resold it for $400 million."

Another big one that got away was Schwartz's attempt, in the spring of 1995, to buy Labatt Breweries and its ancillary operations—including the Blue Jays baseball team, which Gerry badly wanted. It was a complex and puzzling heartbreaker.

"The night before we made our offer, I called and asked to see [Labatt CEO] George Taylor that evening. Taylor said no, that he and Sam Pollock [chairman of Labatt] were going to the hockey game, and he couldn't see me. "'George,' I pleaded with him, 'I have to see you tonight. It can't be tomorrow morning. It's got to be tonight!'

"'Ah, Christ, can't it wait? I'll see you in the morning . . . '

"'I've got to see you tonight.'

"'Oh, okay, come up to the hockey game.'"

The two men arranged to meet in a suite at the Four Seasons. But by now they were both in a foul mood. It was then that Schwartz told Taylor that Onex would be making a takeover bid the next morning.

The offer amounted to $940 million, of which Onex was putting in only $106 million cash, with the balance being contributed by strategic partners, including Gordon Capital, TD Securities, the Ontario Teachers' Pension Plan and Quilmes Industrial S.A., an Argentinian brewery. Schwartz intended to sell off most of the brewery's non-beer assets, then privatize it and move it inside the Onex stable. His bid amounted to $24 per share, while Taylor insisted that the business was worth a bid of $28 to $32 per share and accused the Onex crowd of trying to steal the company.

During the next few weeks, while Taylor and Labatt management were searching for a better offer, Schwartz found himself operating in a vacuum. Nobody would speak to him. "It was largely a personality thing," Schwartz maintains. "I tried to get three or four people on the Labatt's board to get me together with George Taylor to say, 'Let's work together.' And I couldn't get them to do it because George had taken the view that anybody who talked to us was a traitor, that his board should stay intact and keep up a façade of not wanting to deal with us. So the people I knew pretty well who were on the board actually wouldn't help me.

"The same thing with Peter Bronfman. I called and spoke to Peter, but George had just shut everybody down. Peter wouldn't go to bat for me. The interesting thing was that after the Labatt sale, Peter called me two or three times and asked me for favours to do with the prime minister. But he wasn't there when I needed him."

On June 6, 1995, Taylor triumphantly announced the sale of Labatt to Interbrew S.A. of Belgium, which bid $28.50 per share, though Holland's Heineken NV was also in the race. Schwartz was devastated. "It took me a long time to get over it," he admits. "In Los Angeles, Rolling Rock, the local Labatt brand, is fairly popular, and whenever I'm in a bar or a restaurant and it's on the menu or I see someone at the next table having it, it's like a little knife in my heart. I'm not kidding; it feels like that. It's the one thing I really wish I'd done. I'd love to have spent the next ten years building a beer company— building that particular one—because everything about it was right."

The smallest of consolations came during Christmas week in 1995 at a Florida dinner party at Lost Tree, hosted by Jack Lawrence, the former chairman of Nesbitt Burns, held in honour of golf pro Mike Harris, who happens also to be premier of Ontario. Schwartz found himself there with Trevor Eyton, who as the head of Labatt's former parent company, retained considerable clout on its board. Gerry had always considered him a friend, but during the takeover battle, Eyton had refused to take his calls.

Just before dessert, Eyton came up to Schwartz and asked to

have a word with him. "I know that you called during the Labatt takeover and wanted me to intercede with George," Eyton told him, "and I didn't do that because Taylor was so adamant we mustn't talk to you. Andy Sarlos called as well, asking me to help get the two of you together. I just want you to know that I consider it to be one of the great mistakes of my business career. Everybody would have been better off if you'd bought Labatt. It was the right thing to do. It was a mistake on my part, and I've regretted it ever since."

———

SCHWARTZ REMAINS HAUNTED by the possibilities. Could he have had Labatt if he'd started out with a bid of $26 or $26.50? "I don't think that was the issue," he argues, although the battle was decided by price. "We made a terrible mistake. About six or eight weeks before we made the bid, George Taylor called me and said, 'I hear all over the place you're going to make an offer for the company. That would be terrific. Let's get together; I'd like to talk to you about it.'

"Our two leading professionals, a world-renowned investment banker and our head lawyer, both said, 'Absolutely don't do it. You cannot go and talk to him. He'll take whatever you say, twist it into what he wants and you'll read about it in the newspaper the next day. You cannot go and see him until we are ready to launch the bid.' So against all my instincts, I listened to that advice. And I was stupid. Had I sat down with George when he wanted to . . . he would have wanted to be part of what we were doing. He knew his company was going to be in play. George wanted to be an ally, but the way it happened, in typical deal style, I saw him the night before the offer to notify him that we would be making a bid the next day. Of course, he was infuriated. And he then worked tirelessly, ceaselessly, to find an alternative. And I don't think it was just price. The tragedy of it is that we would have been by far a better home for Labatt than where it went. It would have remained Canadian, and the senior management team would have been owners in the company instead of continuing to be employees."

Why did the famously independent Schwartz suppress his instincts? Why did he step so far out of character by letting an emotion very much like fear paralyze his decision making? Here's an intuitive guess: what so intimidated him was the silken hand of the Canadian Establishment. Gerry Schwartz wasn't dealing with a sheik in a far-off land or some first-generation cowboy capitalist from Dallas who wore sunglasses indoors. He was dealing with the Establishment in his own country, and even though he knew it was largely a paper tiger, these were the guys who had kept him out of the Manitoba Club. These were the self-possessed WASPs who hung out at the Royal Lake of the Woods Yacht Club and thought LBO stood for Liquor Control Board of Ontario.

"Nobody is better than anybody else. There are no geniuses out there." Gerry Schwartz briefly forgot that lesson, learned so long ago in the Rasputin-like presence of Bernie Cornfeld. The price paid: he lost faith in his own judgment and allowed the Labatt guys to intimidate him, not realizing that the only thing they had over him was that they wore red blazers to the annual ball at the London Hunt Club, where most of them belonged, while he didn't have a red blazer or go to hunt clubs.

If that speculative scenario is true, how ironic a series of events for an operator many see as the walking embodiment of the muscular Canadian Establishment, 1990s version. Schwartz himself disparages the fading old-boys network. "All that Bud McDougald shit is gone," he says. "It used to be that you couldn't get a great job in a big company unless Bud said you were okay. That doesn't exist anymore. I can phone anybody in this country and get my call returned quickly. It's not that old nonsense that you have to be introduced to somebody in order to get him or her to return your phone call. I don't believe there is much disposable power floating around anymore. I can get people to call me back, but I sure as hell can't get them to do anything that's against their better interests.

"Whatever influence I have is not based on power," he rightly insists, "it's based more on notoriety. It's not because we've got forty-two thousand employees and run a $12 billion portfolio that I get a serious hearing. It's all those newspaper articles, bad as they've been sometimes. It's the notoriety that makes people take you seriously."

Right, Gerr. Of course, it can't hurt that Schwartz happened to be Canada's chief Liberal bagman for most of a decade, taking over that function during John Turner's time as leader. Prime

Minister Jean Chrétien asked him to stay on, but he demurred. Heather was co-chair of Paul Martin's first leadership bid, and both Schwartzes remain close to him. Heather almost ran for the leadership of the Ontario Liberals and remains one of the party's wisest policy resources. Whenever Chrétien hits town, the Schwartz parlour is a compulsory stop. The Schwartzes are also close to Liberal strategist Keith Davey, who even in retirement remains the political conscience of his party.

And power networking surely has nothing to do with the fact that Schwartz has earned a reputation as a take-no-prisoners fundraiser for this or that cause. "He phones me up and says, 'You bank with the Nova Scotia, don't you? Good, you've just committed to being on the tribute committee for Peter Godsoe because I'm running this thing,'" recalls Hershell Ezrin, a friend who shares synagogues as well as banks with Schwartz. "And I said, 'Well, what am I expected to do?' He said, 'We want you to buy five tables.' When I started to object, he said, 'We've got to get more than that, so I don't want to hear any of your stories.' That's Gerry."

"Schwartz is very smart," says Ira Gluskin, the investment guru, getting right down to the nub of how titans tend to keep and wield power. "He is probably smarter than anybody on Bay Street. He's got a real sense of who's important. And he knows them all."

———

"DID YOU EVER see a woman who's quite beautiful, but she's wearing a funny beehive bouffant hairdo?" Gerry Schwartz ruminates, trying to explain something about himself. "And you realize that in the 1960s, when that hairdo was stylish, she saw herself as the most beautiful she would ever be, so she maintained that style, never changing. And of course, she's quite unbeautiful now with that stupid-looking hairdo in the 1990s. People like that don't get it; they don't keep growing. You have to get a haircut at some point. You've got to put yourself into a position where you're back in kindergarten, learning." Instead of a haircut, Gerry has gone into the movie business, which amounts to the same thing. "For me, part of it is the absolute joy of being back in kindergarten," he confesses. "Here's a trade where they talk a different language, where the whole business rests on relationships, where the values are different than anything I've seen before, where it's largely a creative adventure rather than a numbers-driven process. So I knowingly put myself into kindergarten and have been trying to work my way out of it ever since. It has made me grow enormously as a person. Having to deal with creative people, creative issues, people who don't understand or care about the things that I have traditionally cared about, who don't measure success at all by the same standards that I do—that's growth.

"We made *The People vs. Larry Flynt* and lost money on it. The film had a very narrow audience, but Milos Forman, the director, and the actors who were in it and my partner, Mike Medavoy—they're all thrilled that they made it. They don't care if it lost money; they made a wonderful movie. And actually, it was a wonderful film." Schwartz put $20 million into Phoenix Pictures, a partnership with Medavoy, formerly one of the extravagant honchos who ran Sony's ill-fated Tri-Star Pictures Inc. into the ground. The new movie company, Phoenix, is due to make $60 million worth of pictures, which already includes Barbra Streisand's *The Mirror Has Two Faces*, which grossed about $45 million. "Barbra," he says as diplomatically as possible, "being the commanding force she is, many people want to accede to not only her every wish, but to what they might perceive as her every wish. Because of this, the studio outspent what it should have on promotion and our costs were enormously high, so the film didn't do well financially." That was also true for *U Turn*, the Oliver Stone movie Schwartz did, as well as several smaller films.

In his Hollywood incarnation, Schwartz has become friends with Robert Redford and bought 15 percent of his Sundance Resort in Utah. So are we witnessing Gerry's "soft, soft centre" finally oozing out, the guy who cries at movies, letting dread emotion mess up his business instincts? Not really.

"What I want to do here with Mike is build a sausage factory that makes sausages called movies," Schwartz told Jennifer Wells. "The value isn't going to be in the given movie. The value is going to be in the factory. If we can create a factory that has the infrastructure, the capability to keep on making four or five movies a year, there's a huge capitalizable value. Some other entity is going to want to own all or part of our business. There are so

many people who are desperate for the output, we'll sell 30 percent of this company for half a billion dollars."

The Schwartzes purchased a house in California to be closer
to the movie industry. They are building a replica of a 1940s
California clapboard home, with a low, shingled roof and a
couple of dormers across the top, which will appear conspicuously incongruous among Bel Air's pseudo-French châteaux
and Spanish castles-to-go, designed to show off their occupants'
importance. "It was the first property we were shown, but we
couldn't get into the house to view it. From the moment I saw
it to the day I put up the money was about six days. I don't care
about the original house; I didn't even go inside. I'm going to
tear it down, but the land is magnificent; it's four and a-half acres
right in Bel Air, and the lot is flat, as opposed to those huge hill-
sides that you can't touch."

Apart from his Hollywood ventures, Schwartz also runs
Waterloo Capital with Steve Gross, a lawyer friend from his
Winnipeg days who now does real estate equity lending, largely
in Toronto. Schwartz also controls Vincor International Inc.,
Canada's largest winery, which he acquired by coming to the aid of
Leland Verner's T.G. Bright & Co. and combining it with Cartier
Wines, which Don Triggs had spun out of Labatt. Combining
these wineries, plus the prestigious Inniskillin, Dumont and La
Salle labels, has been the industry's greatest success story.

———————

A LOT OF THE BEST VINTAGES get poured whenever Heather and Gerry alight at home in the Rosedale megahouse they have turned into a weekly salon for the hip and lit. The place is a showpiece, far removed from its days as a rundown rooming house. Gerry and Heather gutted the old pile, bought the large house next door, tore that down and extended the dream house into a tasteful château. The Schwartzes now buy mainly British sculptures and sixteenth-century Chinese pottery. Beautifully decorated, the mansion is large enough to comfortably entertain two hundred guests. (The two hundred, for example, who paid $1,000 each to be there one evening in 1995 for a Liberal fundraiser featuring Chrétien and most of his Ontario ministers. "God, it was boring," remembers Schwartz. "It was in June, and the rain just kept coming down in torrents, buckets; everybody was soaked.")

As well as his Porsche, Gerry has a Ferrari, a 1957 Thunderbird and a 1967 Austin-Healey that he restored himself. He has his certified auto mechanic's papers and is definitely eyeing a Rolls-Royce. Heather doesn't own a car; she borrows one of his.

The couple's attention to aesthetics extends to the Onex offices. For years Schwartz admired Toronto's Carswell House on the corner of Richmond and University, a Georgian building across from the law courts. He wanted to locate his offices there. Instead, he rented quarters on the forty-ninth floor of BCE's Canada Trust tower and built a Georgian office suite inside it. Nothing has been forgotten. The floor is fashioned out of rough-hewn planks of old chestnut scavenged from a 150-year-old

Alabama farmhouse. Ancient shutters surround double-hung windows, which give the appearance of being open, but aren't, because there's a plate-glass window behind each one.

"We're in the business of giving people confidence," Schwartz explains. "When a guy comes up to your office who wants to sell you his company for $600 million, it helps to be in surroundings where he can implicitly assume that we can pay for it—and he kind of understands we don't need to buy his business. So we built what is basically a theatrical set to support that thesis."

Standing in that world of Georgian fakery encased by a smooth skyscraper, listening to Gerry Schwartz theorize about the usefulness of façades, the mysteries of the man tantalize all the more. How soft, really, is the centre of any guy who's been an LBO SOB? I muse about that for a while. And then I ask him when was the last time he cried.

"I was up at IBM headquarters recently," he replies, matter-of-factly, "which is near West Point. So I drove over. It's up on a very high bluff overlooking the Hudson River and out to Tarrytown, and it's gorgeous, really magnificent. I kind of wandered around, saw the parade grounds, the superintendent's home and the barracks. Then I went up on this lookout point, and there were these brass plaques put in at the top of the stone wall. I stood there crying as I read the dedications."

For more evidence of softness, there is, as well, Heather's assurance that Gerry Schwartz really is "empathetic and sensitive to what other people go through. For example, we had a young woman who worked in our garden—I'm a very committed garden person—and one day I was talking to her, and she told me that she was so excited because she had been accepted into graduate art school in New York. I was saying how fantastic it was when she said, 'Of course, I can't go because I don't have any money. But I just wanted to see whether I could get in.'" Heather mentioned it to Gerry at dinner that night. "Without telling me first, he called her up, and said he would send her to school for two years, all expenses paid. No one," says Heather, "knows that he does such things." Another kind gesture that received no publicity was the time he gave a free office to Bob Donaldson, a leading Bay Street lawyer who got caught cheating on his expenses and was prevented from practising for two years. When Donaldson's former associates would rather cross the street than say hello to him, Schwartz helped get him back on his feet.

————

AND THEN THERE is that other mystery, the question of what professional reward will prove enough to satisfy not just Gerry Schwartz, but his father.

"I haven't actually celebrated any victories, such as selling a company for a tremendous profit," Gerry confides in a quiet moment. "One of the things that people do in this business is have these closing parties. They're unbelievably boring. It's a bunch of people who happened to work together on a single transaction and have nothing in common with each other except that they did a particular deal. So they get together, make silly toasts, drink and then go away never to see each other again. Actually, I even avoid going to our own closing parties."

One gets the impression that all the slaps on the back from colleagues will never compensate for that brief parental hesitation on the phone, that "sort-of lukewarm" tone in his old man's voice.

When good things happen, that's when Gerry's Presbyterian side kicks in. Those who have adopted that barren outlook know only too well that you must never appear happy or relaxed because that's the moment the bearded deity chooses to pounce. So if you don't celebrate too much, there's not too far to fall, should things go the other way. If you don't say you want something very much, you don't feel you've failed if you don't get it. That fear is buried deep in Schwartz's psyche. And he has no intention of tempting the fates.

"It's lousy in a way," he admits, "because you never feel the exuberant joy of revelling in your success. Like when I'm buying some company, people call and congratulate me: 'Hey, you've bought BC Sugar—isn't that great!' And I'm thinking these people don't get it. Anybody can buy a company; all you do is pay for it. What determines the success of the deal is what we do with it. We've got to fix it, make it run better, get the costs down, straighten out its market position; there's real work to do. So I never feel good when I've bought something.

"And I never feel good when we sell something, even if we make a big profit, because I don't feel that legitimate about it. Often the payoff is much bigger than I expected it would be, but

I realize that I wasn't as smart as people say I was because I didn't know I was going to make that big a profit. I didn't buy it knowing I'd make ten times the money. I wasn't a genius."

Maybe not. But take heart, Gerr. Nobody's a genius, remember?

—1998

Jimmy Pattison: Canada's Über-Entrepreneur

DURING THE EARLY 1980s, I spent a few days at Jimmy Pattison's retreat in Palm Springs, deep in the heart of California. He later purchased Frank Sinatra's sumptuous estate nearby, but this was a relatively modest villa backing onto the twelfth hole of the Canyon Golf Club. What I remember best from that long weekend (which included sharing the platform with Henry Kissinger in addressing Jimmy's "partners in pride"—the men and women who run his companies) was our departure. He lent me a car to tour the mountains above the desert, where I enjoyed throwing snowballs while still wearing lightweight cottons. After I reluctantly left both the pine forests and the palm groves, Pattison drove me to the airport, where his private Challenger jet was standing by to whisk us back to Vancouver.

We gave our luggage to a waiting porter, and as Jimmy and I were ambling toward the gates, he veered away, continuing our conversation. I found myself walking beside him as we passed a long row of pay phones. In a ritual obviously evolved from long practice, Jimmy pulled open the change slot of every telephone. He scooped out whatever coins had been forgotten and never missed a beat. I was speechless. Was this the ultimate capitalist—a man so money driven that he felt compelled to collect pay phone leftovers on the way to his multi-million-dollar private jet?

I asked why he was doing it. "Habit," he deadpanned. "My first job was as a bellhop at the old Georgia Hotel, and I made more money from forgotten telephone change than from tips. So even now, whenever I see a phone, I go for it."

That's Jimmy Pattison, sole owner of Canada's most valuable private company [now fourth largest, with assets of more than $5 billion], ahead of such well-known Canadian-based public enterprises as Power Corporation, Research in Motion and Alberta's Mannix empire. The significant difference is that Jimmy owns every share of every one of his several dozen profit centres that make up his corporate holdings. Apart from his main activities—marketing and making foods, manufacturing recreational vehicles, producing outdoor advertising and distributing magazines—he owns such eccentric assets as the Louis Tussaud's Wax Museum in Copenhagen, the global chain of Ripley's Believe It or Not! exhibition halls, a Swiss bank and a finance company in the Channel Islands.

As proprietor of a private company, Pattison keeps his earnings secret, but he has a *net* cash flow of at least $10 million a month and probably a lot more. His companies' total sales first passed $1 billion in 1984. His original target of hitting $5 billion has long been surpassed, putting him in the league that the Eatons and Bronfmans once occupied—except that he has earned every penny himself, instead of inheriting a head start—and is still in business.

Despite his vast monthly income, Pattison takes out only about $150,000 a year as a spending allowance, reinvesting the balance in his more than four dozen subsidiaries. His senior managers benefit from complicated bonus schemes based on performance, but operations are not devoted to expansion for its own sake. "Quality growth is what matters," he maintains. "Profit is only a by-product of success." What makes his companies so intriguing is that they work on the Japanese "quality circle" principle, allowing employees at every level to participate in decisions on how to keep enhancing profit margins and productivity.

His secret? "I have a basket behind my desk which lists, on a daily basis, the key indicators of each industry we're in. Every business has a soft spot, and if you want control of what's happening, you keep watching those indices. I never wait for the weekly financial statements; there's too long a lag. I just keep tabs on things like forward bookings on my radio stations, for instance. In the car business, the key is not having any ninety-day used cars on your lot. That's the kind of thing I worry about. In the food business it's volume that's critical because when you have a high fixed overhead, you've got to keep sales moving."

These and the many other indicators of how his companies are doing provide only the theoretical framework for Jimmy's management style. He acts quickly on what those indicators tell him. Every Friday, for example, he gets a list of every used car that has been on any of his lots more than ninety days. "I get rid of them," he says, "because that's where you get in trouble with bad inventory."

————

WHAT'S UNUSUAL about Jimmy is that he's not only solidly in command of his financial worth, but also acts as if he was in charge of his soul. He genuinely believes there is holy sanction involved in his success. "I represent what the free enterprise system allows people to accomplish," he once told me, "and I'm grateful to God that He allowed it to happen." Yes, he still occasionally attends the Glad Tidings Temple on Vancouver's Fraser Street, and, yes, he still prays before negotiating major business deals. But he no longer plays the trumpet at the Sunday morning services, preferring the harmonies and rhythms of one of his five Wurlitzer organs. (He has one in Palm Springs, one aboard his boat and three at his home in British Properties.)

Religious inclinations aside, it is because he is so utterly devoid of sham or pretence that his touches of self-righteousness come through as personal strength, rather than arrogance. He makes it easy for people to supply their own reasons for liking him and has surprisingly few enemies or even critics.

This unique proprietorship is made up of, among other assets, the world's largest floatplane fleet (AirBC and Trans-Provincial

Airlines) and the world's largest neon sign complex (Claude Neon and Neon Products); Canada's largest manufacturers of recreational vehicles (Vanguard, Frontier and Security), largest automobile dealerships (Toyota and General Motors), second-largest wholesale distributors of periodicals (*Mountain City News, Mainland Magazine* and *Provincial News*), largest outdoor advertisers (Seaboard and Hook); leasing companies (Courtesy, Great Pacific and Jim Pattison), supermarkets (Overwaitea and Your Mark-It), soft drinks (Crush, Hires, Sussex, Pure Spring, Wilson's); and computers (EDP Industries)—as well as real estate and energy suppliers.

He has a private room off his office, where he deals in a major way in gold and silver futures. The seven local airlines he has acquired since March 1979 have given Pattison control over a fleet of one hundred aircraft plying the B.C. coast. He insists that head office staff keep track of safety concerns and fly one of his routes at least seven days before their operations come up for budgetary discussion—and have a cancelled boarding pass to prove it. He holds leases on about sixty-eight thousand electrical signs in Canada, including most illuminated markers for McDonald's, Holiday Inn, Shell and Household Finance.

His ventures into sports and broadcasting have been less spectacular. Pattison purchased Vancouver's CJOR in 1965, but the radio station lost most of its listeners when hotliner Jack Webster moved to television. Pattison offered the slot (at $100,000 a year) to NDP leader Dave Barrett, who in the end decided to opt for the calmer world of politics. Jimmy had to settle for Social

Credit health minister Rafe Mair, who was an immediate hit—
and whose place in the B.C. cabinet was promptly taken by Jim
Nielsen, himself a former CJOR commentator. Pattison bought
the WHA Philadelphia Flyers in 1973, moved them, and renamed
them the Vancouver Blazers. Later, he relocated and rechris-
tened them once more as the Cowboys in Calgary, where they
mercifully expired. He also bid unsuccessfully for the Vancouver
Canucks as well as the B.C. Lions. (Pattison is the only member
of the Vancouver business community who uses the Texas word
"bidness" for "business," as in "Will someone please tell me why
I ever got into the hockey bidness?" He lost at least $2.5 million
on his hockey ventures.

Pattison has always maintained that the only companies he
owns that are not for sale are his radio station and the original car
dealership on Main Street. Every year there are fresh rumours
that he'll sell CJOR (which keeps losing money), but he has kept
his promise. The general manager of the station (three of them
in the past three years) is required to phone Pattison's head office
and report his daily advertising cash flow.

All these corporate activities employ six thousand people,
though only twenty-two executives report directly to Pattison.
He manages his empire with a head office staff of fourteen,
coordinated by Maureen Chant, his talented and enlightened
administrative assistant. Four times a year, Jimmy goes on fort-
night-long personal inspection tours.

———

HIS OWN WORK habits are legendary. Jimmy (nobody calls him anything else) puts in fifteen-hour days, though he sometimes quits by 4 p.m. on Saturdays. He seldom uses his condo in Waikiki because he feels too frustrated being out of touch with his office during the long flight to Hawaii. He takes few holidays. He remembers uncomfortably pacing a Barbados beach for two weeks in 1964, impatiently longing to be back at work. A leisurely fortnight he scheduled in Spain for the winter of 1971 lasted just five days, at which point he bolted for Zurich to negotiate some financing for one of his deals. His toys are two private jets and seven cars, including a 1939 Packard V-12; a Grand Ville, the last Pontiac convertible off the GM assembly line; and two limited-edition Bicentennial Cadillac Eldorados. He loves cars and bought his first model (a 1936 Austin two-seater) for $297 on his fifteenth birthday. "If I really want to relax," he says, "I jump in my car and just drive. One night I went all the way from my office to Banff."

He tries to get home on weekends for Saturday night dinners with his wife, Mary, though he doesn't always make it. In everything he does, there is reflected not so much the ambling geniality of the West Coast ethic as the supercharged tenacity of a big-game hunter who never abandons the trail. Allan Fotheringham once described Pattison as "a freckled little buzz-saw—he dresses like Nathan Detroit and thinks like J. Paul Getty."

It's not without significance that Jimmy's favourite painting is a luminous landscape of railway tracks stretching toward infinity, an appropriate reminder of his deprived Prairie childhood. When he was seven years old and Saskatchewan tumbled into the bear pit of the Great Depression, the family moved to Vancouver, where his father tuned pianos and tried to sell Packards. Young Jimmy hustled packages of garden seeds, won magazine subscription contests and eventually got a job washing cars (at twenty-five dollars a week) with the right to sell used cars for Fred Richmond Motors. That was when he also worked as a bellhop at the Georgia Hotel.

Pattison left the University of British Columbia in 1952, after having sold each of his fraternity brothers a car, three courses short of his commerce degree. He spent the next ten years or so as a used-car sales manager. In 1961 he went to see Harold Nelson, his Royal Bank branch manager, and borrowed $40,000 against the $7,000 equity he'd built up in his house and the $15,000 cash surrender value of his life insurance policy. He had to pledge all the shares of the new General Motors dealership he intended to incorporate. His first month in business, he was down $13,900; the second month he lost $12,000; the third month he made a profit of $2,000. There followed a long decade of developing his acumen, turning himself into one of the largest Pontiac-Buick dealers west of Toronto, with his automobile business eventually encompassing two blocks—just fifteen streets away from the lot where he had started out as a car washer. He introduced an unusually simple incentive for his salesmen. At the end of each month, their sales totals were tallied; the last man on the list was automatically fired.

HIS FIRST PLUNGE into the major leagues came in 1967, when he used a roundabout route (through brokers' offices in New York and Toronto) to acquire a controlling stockholding in Neon Products from a group of leading Vancouver businessmen. "It would have been impossible for me to take over the company from these men, because they were the Establishment." Neon had been formed in 1928, with the members of the original board reading like a bluebook of Vancouver society at the time: wholesaling pioneer J.P.D. Malkin; E.E. Buckerfield of the feed company; Gordon Farrell, then president of B.C. Telephone; lawyer George E. Housser; Harold E. Molson, a member of the English branch of Montreal's Molson clan who had married into the Malkin family; W.C. Woodward of the department store chain; and R.H.B. Ker, a Victoria investor. "Neon Products was made to order for a guy like me," Pattison remarked. "It was a company with the depth, history and strength for what I wanted to do—build a Canadian growth company. Besides, they turned me down for a job selling signs when I was nineteen. They told me I was too young and too small."

"He's a man with gumption, and that's why he's so successful," Jack Clyne, the province's former chief justice, said of him, while deal maker Bob Wyman defined more precisely what makes Jimmy run: "There are very few people prepared to brave the kind of risks he's taken." Peter Brown, when he was B.C.'s ace stockbroker, called Pattison his best client: "He's fantastic to deal with, very fair, very straightforward. When he's pleased with you, he tells you; when he's angry, he calls you first. Everything is always on the table. I'm a big Jimmy fan."

Perhaps the most treasured salute to the remarkable Jimmy came from, of all people, a former president of the United States. On October 14, 1980, the Pattisons were the only Canadians invited to attend Gerald and Betty Ford's thirty-second wedding anniversary at their residence in Palm Springs, California. The seventy-five guests included Frank Sinatra, Tony Orlando, Pearl Bailey, Phyllis Diller, Ed McMahon, Bob Hope and Ronald Reagan's campaign manager, William Casey. Ford had grown fond of the feisty Canadian during their occasional meetings. But even so, it came as a surprise when, halfway through the ceremonies, the ex-chief-of-state slipped the ex-used-car-salesman an exquisitely appropriate gift of his own: a money clip embossed with the presidential seal.

Being Jimmy's employee is not easy. Because work to him is the main (some say, only) reason for breathing, Jimmy tends to expect from his staff not only perfection, but also the same single-track dedication that he expends on his business affairs. His high standards can unhinge some underlings. When one of his middle-management people had a heart attack and ended up in hospital, where his pulse was closely monitored, I happened to be there when Jimmy walked in to pay a friendly visit—and, watching the wall-mounted monitor, I could see that the smitten employee's pulse rate doubled. He later told me that he felt

guilty being caught resting instead of helping the Pattison Group
meet sales quotas.

Except for manning the Wurlitzer at corporate singsongs,
Jimmy doesn't indulge in any spare time activities. He belongs
to three golf clubs but has played the game precisely three times
since leaving university. His pride and joy (to the extent of having white broadloom in the engine room) is his multi-deck
megaluxury motor cruiser that his crew takes on daytime jaunts
to the spectacular inlets around Vancouver. Yet during the first
twenty-one months he owned the boat, he slept aboard only four
nights. The only annual holiday he schedules for more than five
days is a dash to Nanaimo with his wife, Mary, to celebrate their
wedding anniversaries.

He has been and remains the West Coast's premier deal
maker. His roots are in the tough East End used-car business,
where most salesmen are born with silver tongues.

Jimmy's is platinum.

—1986

Ted Rogers: The Tycoon Who Never Rested

THE LAST TIME I felt the presence of Ted Rogers, who died of heart failure at the end of 2008, was the previous April, when I spotted his floating communications capsule, disguised as the luxurious thirty-five-metre, $10 million yacht *Loretta Anne,* anchored off Belize, a tiny Mayan republic wedged between Mexico and Guatemala. At the time the underdeveloped Creole paradise was the in-vogue destination for pre-Crash sophisticated billionaires.

Along with a few colleagues, I was in a small motor boat powered by a 150-hp outboard engine, captained by Bob Dhillon, a senior Calgary real estate operative with major investments here. We were about to venture up an alligator-infested river that snaked through a rainforest where jaguars roamed free, to visit a wilderness spa. I had thought vaguely of visiting Ted's floating vacation HQ but decided against it—not because I might be disrupting his holiday, but because I would be interrupting his latest business deal, possibly negotiating wireless rights for the planet Mars. I remembered Tony Fell, when he was head of RBC Dominion Securities, telling me that he had been invited out on Ted's vessel several times but had never seen him at rest: "Being on that boat of his was no holiday. He had a satellite telephone and was on it all the time."

Ted and I attended Upper Canada College together, and I had written up his various daredevil exploits, dubbing him the Canadian corporate world's "Riverboat Gambler," a title he amply earned by creating the country's most innovative, most quixotic and most influential media empire, based entirely on his nerve and bank loans.

This time, afloat in the Caribbean Sea, it turned out that he had a more intriguing private agenda. While I was there, Rogers secretly negotiated to purchase an island from Dhillon in the same archipelago where the Four Seasons chain was already building its first "green" hotel and near another private isle that had just been bought by Leonardo DiCaprio.

The utopia that Ted Rogers had in mind might have been his final escapist domicile, but he didn't live long enough to complete that purchase. Perhaps after half a century of galley-slave devotion to deifying his late father's inventive spirit, Ted finally realized it was time for him to take a break. That sun-washed island in far-off Belize would have been his ideal sanctuary.

On second thought, that was a dubious prediction. The Rogers mega-yacht could easily have circled the globe, but Ted never spent an uninterrupted week aboard her and even missed his own wedding anniversary after promising to spend a "second honeymoon" with his wife Loretta aboard their enchanted floating palace. *Twice.*

Summing up Ted Rogers' career is impossible because it had no discernable trajectory except the predictable arc of a yo-yo; never still, down and up, constantly veering between stunning fiscal triumphs and spine-chilling bankruptcy threats. He didn't just sell the farm—he sold it over and over again. He prided himself on being a fearless entrepreneur, the kind who thrived as much on the risk as its rewards.

In truth, he was a one-man brand being run by a one-man band.

Ted Rogers only occasionally slowed down long enough to be called an incurable workaholic, but most of the time he made that choice of category comically inadequate. To him, doing deals was life itself; everything else (except his family) was extraneous. His work habits more closely resembled the schedule of one of those donkeys that used to drive water pumps in tropical penal colonies. He never stopped. "My idea of slowing down is putting a fax in my car," he once told me. He perked up when I mentioned that I'd heard new fax machines for use on pleasure boats would soon be available—and promptly ordered one.

————

NO ONE EQUALLED his daring. He spent most of his fifty years in business guided by his viscera and the message on his personal business card, which identified his occupation as "TED ROGERS, SENIOR SALES PERSON." His profession was selling himself, and he succeeded beyond his wildest imaginings. By the end of his life, he had created a $25 billion world-class communications empire from a standing start in a whirlwind of activity that even in retrospect seemed hard to credit. His unindicted co-conspirators were Canada's bankers (mostly at the Toronto-Dominion and Scotiabank) who treated him as a black hole—in a nice way. He could extract almost any loan he demanded, and in the process somehow made these virago number crunchers feel graced that they had been asked to finance his latest flyer. Still, each transaction took its toll. Robin Korthals, then president of the Toronto-Dominion Bank, where Rogers did most of his initial banking, once confided in me that Ted had burned out fourteen of his most senior credit officers during their twenty-year association. One of his closest scrapes happened to coincide with the similarly endangered financial status of Brazil, then a Third World country that for some long-forgotten reason Canadian banks felt duty-bound to return to solvency. "No problem," Ted told a startled TD credit officer, who had questioned his suitability for yet another big, fat loan. "Just think of me as Brazil."

Rogers cited many Golden Rules to live by, but fundamentally his belief system came down to one axiom: that persuading any fiscal sorcerer with substantial amounts of *moola* available for borrowing was mainly a matter of convincing him that there was no point in maintaining things as they were. He preached that loans in his capable hands created opportunities—the chance to sponsor and exploit the profit side of newness. In Ted's lingo this implied that negotiating profitable deals was the result of an endless string of chance outcomes. If that sounded suspiciously like a lottery, he would courteously point out that you couldn't win if you didn't hold a ticket—which was why his loan applications deserved to be approved. (Do not try to reread this slowly; it still won't make any sense—but that was the kind of levitational logic that made Ted's fortune.)

The closest I came to a suitable metaphor was a passage in the journal of Simon Fraser, the North West Company fur trader, who in 1808 explored the "Mysterious Great River" on the Pacific shore (later named after him) to see whether it could be used for floating inland merchandise down to the Pacific. To reach tidewater, Fraser and his party had to negotiate the snarling cataracts that characterized the Great River's progress. They were forced to clamber across the precarious footholds in the rock faces of the canyons overhanging the raging stream, all the while portaging their canoes. "I cannot find words to describe our situation," Fraser lamented. "We had to pass where no human being should venture." During the acrobatic passage of Hell's Gate Canyon, he confided in his journal that he felt as though he was "hanging on by my eyebrows."

That phrase described Ted Rogers' financial tactics perfectly. That was why I labelled him the great Riverboat Gambler. With his corporate debts—which at one time totalled $5 billion—Rogers operated his business in a constant state of barely suppressed hysteria while—just like Simon Fraser—hanging on by his eyebrows.

Looking back, his antics contained an element of self-destruction because he always had to keep running faster in the pursuit of ever more elusive goals. But for him, that was where the excitement resided. The difference between a bird and a kite is that while both fly, only one is free, but Ted never allowed his obligations to tie him down. At one point, he ran not only out of collateral, but also out of words. He had no negotiable assets left with which to bargain. Even his usual last resort for funds—taking out third mortgages on his house and cottage—wasn't available, since he had already done that.

To cheer him on, Korthals and his TD team issued Rogers with a very special framed document that visitors to Ted's office were proudly shown, with an accompanying explanation:

We are pleased to inform you that the Toronto-Dominion Bank on the occasion of your fiftieth birthday is prepared to make available the following line of credit for your personal use, subject to the terms and conditions generally as outlined below:

Borrower: Ted Rogers.

Amount: $50 billion.

Lender: TD Bank.

Purpose: to help promote and prolong the state of good cheer and good health.

Availability: in amounts of $1 billion per year on demand subject to normal bank conditions, margin requirements and other security, interest rate to be negotiated in an amount consummate with risk.

Security: one cottage, other considerations as appropriate.

Co-signers: Loretta Rogers with John Graham [Ted's stepfather]
repayment in full at maturity, May 27, 2033, when you reach a
hundred.

We are pleased to have had this opportunity to express our
appreciation and look forward to continued utilization throughout
the terms of this loan.

"What prompted that offer," Rogers told me, "was a very critical loan in the company's early days. It was my wife, Loretta, who guaranteed it. But we didn't have much security, so we offered our cottage. Korthals told us to keep it, because it had such a good view."

That little joke was hardly typical of Canadian bankers, whose sense of humour ranks just behind that of undertakers and police sergeants. But Edward Samuel Rogers Jr. was always special. He was treated as the author—and hero—of his own soap opera instead of just another panting loans supplicant. Apart from his solid credentials as a patriotic Canadian, Rogers relied on his pedigree to get him through a wondrous life, filled equally with singular achievement, the almost sensual thrills of risking his reputation and livelihood, plus an eternally boyish sense of wonderment that he got away with it all.

————

HIS THREE BRUSHES with bankcruptcy were real. Not only did he survive to tell the tale, but each time he also persuaded the same lenders to re-open their coffers even wider so he could spend himself dry one more time. That attitude bordered on irresponsibility. But Rogers was a Texas-style entrepreneur, probably the most daring in Canadian business history. During his half-century career, that often meant launching himself on a symbolic corporate bungee jump. Only when he was floating to eternity, did he bother to look back over his shoulder to see if the rope was attached to something solid, which occasionally it was. By his own calculation, he borrowed an astonishing total of $30 billion in bank loans during his career (without a single default) and floated equity financing worth $4.5 billion.

Rogers had a disturbing habit of being sincere against his better judgment. Asked about his latest electronic vision, he would go into ecstatic detail about how he intended to electronically rewire Toronto, Ontario, Canada—or the universe. His bankers and shareholders read his remarks with a sinking feeling reminiscent of the wonderful put-down that Paul Samuelson, the MIT economist, once directed at his more popular rival, Harvard's John Kenneth Galbraith. "An unguarded comment by Galbraith," quipped Samuelson, "can send the Dow off by $2; his guarded utterances send it down $5."

In permanent overdrive, Rogers's idea of reality was whatever he claimed it to be. And he had a point. He had been right before. In 1960, while still a law student at Toronto's Osgoode Hall, he bought CHFI, the tiny, 940-watt radio station that pioneered the new frequency modulation sound at a time when only 5 percent of Toronto homes had FM receivers.

The deal set a pattern. For the next four decades, he would spot a new technology with public appeal and charge into it headlong, so that he could exploit the benefits of that first rush of interest. Most of the time it worked fine, except that the arrival of new technologies accelerated in frequency and he would still be trying to pay off the loans he required for jumping into one when another required even greater investments. By 1967 he was in the cable television business and eventually put together the world's largest cable network, with 2.3 million subscribers, including systems in the U.S. and the U.K. It was much the same story with cellular phones in the 1980s, fibre-optic technology in the 1990s and most spectacularly with iPhones, more recently. Rogers saw himself as chief sponsor and operator of the nation's electronic highway, travelling along its fibre-optics system into the future. "Only in this way can we compete against satellite transmissions and maintain a strong Canadian presence," he insisted.

That he was driven was obvious. That his ambitions might have some limits was less clear. We talked about his future many times, and the anatomy of our discourse was invariably dominated by the obsession with his father. "He died early, when I was five, and I always wanted to be in his tradition, to be as good as he was," Ted recounted. "The problem is you never feel as if you've really done it, because once you feel you have, you advance to another target."

To be ahead of your time in Canada is a bit like having leprosy: nobody wants to touch you until you're either dead or cured—so you take the plunge. Rogers took a similar devil-may-care approach to his own health. He treated his frequent illnesses not as warning signs to slow down but as annoying distractions. When he underwent serious cataract surgery in the early 1980s, Phil Lind, his best friend and chief adviser, recalled seeing company executives gathered around Rogers' bed, discussing a future cable project while their boss still had his eyes bandaged. His 1992 quadruple bypass surgery drove the medical staff at the Mayo Clinic in Rochester, Minnesota, to distraction because he was dictating letters before the anaesthetic had properly worn off.

"Ted has had everything wrong with him there is, but he just keeps beating it back—he's unsinkable," said David Peterson, the former Ontario premier who sat on his board. "Everybody has been worried about his health for the last twenty years. He can never relax. He's the only guy I know who does three things at one time. He can talk to you while he's writing something, and he'll be reading something else at the same time. Honest to God, he remembered everything in all three contexts."

IT WAS IN AN ANTEBELLUM MANSION on the lush island of New Providence in the azure seas of the Bahamas that I joined Ted and Loretta Rogers in the spring of 1994 to observe, first hand, his attempts to swallow ever tastier bites of Canada's communications sector. A five-minute golf cart ride from the legendary Lyford Cay Club, established by E.P. Taylor, one of Conrad Black's predecessors at Argus (later renamed Hollinger Inc.), it provided a safe, tax-free roost for Canadian billionaires on the wing. The Rogers compound resembled nothing so much as a stage set for a colonial governor's resplendent tropical chancellery. It was complete with elegantly rotating overhead fans, Adam tables, a sunroom done up in white wicker and pink chintz and the compulsory Sheraton dining table with ecru lace mats. The placid tableau exuded the aura of power calmly possessed and habitually exercised.

But there was nothing tranquil about Rogers himself. When I dropped in that Sunday afternoon, he was in his customary state of doing a barely suppressed St. Vitus's dance. At that point he was the harassed choreographer of corporate assets worth more than $4 billion and in the midst of his takeover of Maclean Hunter Publishing Ltd., a matter of some concern to me, since I had been a director of Maclean Hunter and editor-in-chief of its flagship magazine, *Maclean's,* and remained a substantial shareholder.

Just before hopping on his private Challenger jet, Ted assured me that there was something special about this latest takeover. "I'm a strong family man," he told me, explaining there were certain Maclean Hunter strings tugging at his mercenary heart. "Don Hunter [son of M-H's co-founder] was best man for John Graham [former chairman of Rogers and Ted's stepfather] when he married my mother," he recalled. "We used to trade ten-year budgets across our adjoining back fences. I talked him into buying CKEY. I sold his house to another friend when he bought a new one down the road. We were good pals. We would visit the Hunters' cottage a number of times every summer."

None of this stopped Ted from acquiring the company (for more than $3 billion) that had weaned me and so many others in the ways of magazine journalism. Despite his professed admiration of M-H's incumbent management, he expressed a patronizing view of professional managers taking on ownership functions, and the M-H executives soon departed.

On the subject of shares in his own company, Rogers gleefully pointed out why no freelance capitalist could ever acquire his empire. The fact was that he and his wife, an heiress to the Woolworth fortune and vivacious daughter of Lord Martonmere, the former governor of Bermuda, owned more than 90 percent of the Rogers holding company. (When Ted and Loretta decided to marry, he was so hard up for cash that he bought her engagement and wedding rings at the local Birks, not for cash but in return for running free advertising on his FM station.) Loretta provided a wonderful balance in the relationship. She was a talented amateur painter, and when Ted told her one day, after a visit to her studio, "You're such a good painter. I wish I were an artist too." She shot right back, "But you are Ted. You're one of the great bullshit artists."

What Ted accomplished was to move his stock from 70 cents to $20 since his company had gone public in 1979—despite the fact that at that point it had yet to post a profit (with the exception of one year) or pay dividends. "All the company has to do to make money is stop expanding," he told me, pointing out that his stock would be a winner when he died because surpluses would then not be constantly reinvested. (On the day of Ted's death, his family fortune was estimated to be worth $7 billion, and his stock did indeed inch up slightly.)

I was impressed, that long-ago day, with Rogers' concern about Maclean Hunter's Canadian roots and his vow not to dilute the operation's significant cultural mandate. He kept the faith. At that point I had several times described the Rogers/ Maclean Hunter standoff as an epic showdown between a Riverboat Gambler and a Village Parson. "I guess that's true," Rogers quipped just before he showed me the door. "But I don't know why they keep referring to me as a Village Parson."

————

THE DEFINING ANECDOTE about Ted Rogers dated back to the time when he was a Big Tory on campus at the University of Toronto—instead of merely looking like one, which he still did at seventy-five. Hyperactive in Conservative politics, he needed to see then–Progressive Conservative party leader John Diefenbaker on a policy issue but couldn't get an appointment. Finally, granted precisely five minutes in Dief's parliamentary office, he was squeezed in between the prime minister's more urgent chores. But when Rogers got in to see him, the Chief spent half the allocated time telling a political joke, then excused himself to use an adjoining bathroom. Realizing that his time was just about up, young Ted barged into the toilet and made his case standing next to a startled but temporarily immobilized prime minister.

Ted lived up to his income. When Rogers decided that he wanted a tennis court adjoining his stone mansion on posh Frybrook Road in Toronto's exclusive Forest Hill district, he purchased the house next door (belonging to Neil McKinnon, then chairman of the Canadian Imperial Bank of Commerce) and tore it down to make room for the courts. The story going around Forest Hill at the time was that his nervous neighbours were earnestly imploring him, "For God's sake, don't take up golf!"

Every chronicle about Ted concentrated on his father, Edward S. Rogers Sr., the inventor of batteryless radios, and with good reason. One day during a lunch we had at the King Edward Hotel's Victoria Room, I got him talking about some other ancestors, who sounded at least as fascinating. Within a month he handed me a handwritten document that, among others, identified the original clan member, John Rogers the Elder, who had arrived in England with the Norman Conquest in 1066. One of his offspring was another John Rogers, a canon of Old St. Paul's in London, who was burned at the stake in 1555, becoming England's first Protestant martyr. Eighty years later, Thomas Rogers, in a bid for religious freedom, left London for the New World and settled in Connecticut, where he became the richest man in his community. It wasn't until 1801 that Timothy Rogers, a Quaker seeking to freely practise his religion, came to Canada and settled in what is now Newmarket, north of Toronto. During his grandchildren's generation, the family divided into two distinct branches. Elias Rogers fathered a clan that became prominent primarily through St. Mary's Cement, while Samuel Rogers' family, two generations later, produced the original Edward Rogers, whose ghostly presence would dominate his son's life.

Ted's father, born in 1900, was the first amateur operator in Canada to successfully transmit a radio signal across the Atlantic and later invented the radio tube that made it possible to build AC receiving sets, doing away with bulky and expensive batteries. He founded Rogers Majestic Corporation in the mid-1920s to manufacture the sets and eventually upgraded his ham operation into a commercial station with the call letters CFRB (Canada's First Rogers Batteryless), which grew to command the country's largest radio audience. As early as 1931, the elder Rogers was granted the first licence to broadcast experimental television, but he died eight years later from overwork (and a bleeding ulcer) at age thirty-eight, when Ted was only five. (The little boy retained only three mementoes from his father: a ring bearing the call letters CFRB, which he wore daily; his dad's original tube-operated radio set; and a Valentine's card.) Young Ted was subsequently chauffeured daily to Upper Canada College, and when he was old enough, his sports car was brought around so he could drive himself home. Paradoxically—since he was a spoiled boy with a scrawny build and sickly disposition—it was at UCC that Ted learned his street smarts. "I used to box at Upper Canada," he recalled, "and I got knocked out the first year. It took me five years to win my weight. I've always been a fighter."

———

AS HE MATURED, Rogers' strength turned out to be his powers of persuasion, which in a very different context, were described by the American novelist Norman Mailer as part of an essay about Martin Luther King, who shared that talent. "He had a sweet attentive gravity which endeared him to most, for he listened carefully and was responsive when he spoke. He had the presence of a man who would deal with complexity by absorbing its mood and thus resolve its contradictions." While that was an apt description of Ted's wooing of bankers and competitors, it did not apply to most dealings with his staff. Phil Lind, Rogers Communications vice-chairman, admitted that he was a demanding, often difficult, boss: "Ted worked all the time so, yeah, you could expect calls from him at odd hours. When John Tory switched from being an executive of Maclean Hunter and joined his friend Ted Rogers in a similar role, he was surprised to find in the office allocated to him a dartboard with a picture of Ted's face on it—presumably to work off the expected frustrations with his boss. The problem with Ted was his temper. It could flare up at the drop of an extra covenant demanded during loan negotiations or for no good reason at all. His victims did not exclude his favourite banker, the TD's Robin Korthals. During one particularly desperate loan negotiation, when the latter demanded a particularly onerous covenant from the overextended company, Rogers angrily hurled his keys across the table and shouted, "Here, you run the bloody company then!"

And stormed out. Korthals later revealed that in his agitated state, Rogers had thrown him the keys to his convertible Chrysler Le Baron, instead of his business office.

————

ALTHOUGH THEY WERE his cash cow, the cable networks required injections of $1 billion a year for constant upgrading. Even their generous cash flow ($2 million a day) couldn't keep pace with Ted's ambitions for his cable network. Then, in early 1995, the integrity of the cable operation itself was threatened.

Running a large company, especially a utility like a major cable network, can be reduced to a series of occasions. And Ted's worst occasion—the nightmare that invaded his life—was the day he decided to force subscribers to buy a negative option plan. Here was this patriotic, if self-absorbed, good corporate citizen, living like a high-wire acrobat, never using—or even dreaming of using—a net. He prided himself on sublimating his ego for the public good, providing the electronic highway for much of the country, when BANG!—he became Public Enemy Numbah One.

In the past, Rogers had kept increasing the number of channels he offered and raising his monthly rates accordingly. Few subscribers objected because the only way to get a clear TV picture was to buy his service, which enjoyed a monopoly everywhere he operated. But when he decided to institute his compulsory negative option, automatically billing subscribers an additional $2.65 each month for five new Canadian specialty channels while threatening to remove some popular stations if the extra fee wasn't paid, subscribers revolted and forced him to back down.

This time Rogers had gone too far. His company's move triggered the country's first cable TV rebellion. Many subscribers cancelled his service and took him to small claims court. His offices were picketed; politicians were cheered for proposing legal challenges that would turn his marketing gimmick into a crime; newspaper editorialists lashed out at "government-sponsored, elitist arrogance." The country went berserk. Vancouver novelist and playwright John Gray was moved to comment that Canadians, normally docile even when "faced with declining medical services, separatists in Quebec, high unemployment, a seventy-cent dollar and the loss of the cod fishery, stood up, dug in their heels and drew a line in the sand over their right to receive CNN and The Sports Network on their basic cable." "What I found interesting about the protest," he went on, "was that these expressions of collective rage are usually reserved for governments. In a way, the tone of the protests revealed that to many people, the cable television monopolies have become a kind of government. The demonstrations were an admission on the part of consumers that somebody up there could meddle with their feed. If they didn't like what was offered, all they could do was squawk."

"The fury of the cable protest," wrote *Maclean's* editor Robert Lewis (who later became a Rogers executive), "serves as a warning for establishments everywhere, whether corporate or political.

The people of Canada have been in a grumpy mood, starting with the rejection of the Charlottetown Accord in the 1992. The same volatility was evident in the rout of the Conservative Government in 1993 and the reaction to the cable companies. It is an era when people do not trust their leaders or, generally, the country's elite."

"I was stunned," Rogers confessed when it was all over. "Now I know how those turbot must have felt swimming toward the Spanish fish boats. From now on, our customers will determine what level of service each one of them will get." It was a small skirmish in a long war, but there was little doubt who had won, and it wasn't Ted.

———

THERE WAS SOMETHING of the mountaineer in Rogers' countenance, something about his eyes that had the permanent poached look of living on the edge of an abyss, and looking down too often. He was in so many ways a false extrovert—as transparent as the dye jobs of his hair, which turned an embarrassing apricot as he grew older. More characteristically, he was remote and private, an unquiet spirit who never made peace with himself. He was terminally baffled by his inability to find some form of exemption from the laws of cause and effect that taunted him, taking the edge off his triumphs.

If I could choose a final epitaph for that irreplaceable man, it would run something like this: When George Leigh Mallory, the first man to climb Mount Everest, was asked why he wanted to conquer the great mountain in 1924, he shrugged and famously replied, "Because it is there." Nearly seventy years later, on September 29, 1988, when Stacey Allison became the first American woman to scale the great peak and was asked the same question, she smiled and shot back, *"Because I'm here."*

That reply served Ted Rogers well. So much of what he accomplished was an offshoot of his physical presence. Being there, nurturing his vital signs, taking a lead in any action that was in play, gambling on the future, being the token Texas entrepreneur in a Canadian sea of porridge-weaned WASPS who had been toilet-trained to believe that being careful was the ultimate virtue—those are his essential legacies.

————

IT WAS NO ACCIDENT that in later years, much of Ted's planning had to do with settling his enormous estate. As his heirs, his son Edward and daughters Lisa, Melinda and Martha, would become the company's owners, with Ted Samuel Rogers III being appointed CEO of the holding company that controls an overwhelming majority of the voting stock. Nadir Mohamed, a Tasmanian whose family originally came from India, became head of Rogers Communications Group.

Ted ended his autobiography by offering this valid advice: "Throughout my life, my business drive has been to get my father's name back as a leader in communications. Most of my financial efforts have been to survive. Risky levels of debt were a consequence, not a choice. I am truly amazed how well it has turned out! If my life has a lesson for others, I think it is that everyone has a shot. Don't follow a dream; live it. No matter what it is you want, take your best shot. Be passionate and work hard, maybe harder than you ever dreamt, but the opportunity is there. You've got to be lucky at times, and having a supportive spouse and solid family sure helps."

Too many Ted Rogerses would have made this country ungovernable because, ultimately, they might have bankrupted or even maimed one another in the hunt for ever more daunting challenges. But we were immensely fortunate in having had one.

May Edward Samuel Rogers II rest in peace. He sure as hell deserves it.

—2008

Arthur Child: Calgary's Renaissance Man

IT IS 4:15 P.M., Christmas Eve, at Maple Bay, a small harbour on the east side of Vancouver Island, forty miles north of Victoria. Light rain is falling. Nothing stirs in the mist over the water. Fishing boats and pleasure craft have tied up for the holiday season. The mountain at the entrance to the bay is hidden in a low cloud, obscuring the mouth of the harbour. Suddenly a watcher on shore hears the beat of diesel engines, and a vessel appears out of the fog, its radar scanner revolving atop the mast, heading for the docks at the head of the bay. It is a small ship such as the shore-watcher has not seen before. The silhouette is that of a wartime corvette assigned to hunt submarines. But instead of grey paint this ship has a pale green gleaming fibreglass hull. The superstructure is light gold, set off with stainless steel railings and wide glass shatterproof windows. Two diagonal stripes, one dark green and one dark red, lend a rakish dash to the hull. Radio aerials stand against the sky above the high wheelhouse. The vessel slows down and then comes alongside one of the piers. A slight figure in yellow oilskins, rubber boots, and blue toque stands on the stern step until the dock is within a few feet, then jumps ashore, secures a line with a couple of turns, and races to do the same with the bow line. The captain, in an orange rainsuit, steps out of the wheelhouse, looks over the side at the lines, and shuts down the engine.

That description came from the log of a forty-six-foot motor vessel out of Canoe Cove named *Cybele III*. It was written during the boat's shakedown cruise in the winter of 1980–81 by owner and skipper Arthur James Edward Child. In his shorebound manifestation, he was president and chief executive officer of Burns Foods, Alberta's largest private employer. Here at sea, about an hour's flight from Calgary by private jet, he was very different from the stalwart, square-looking, Dickensian gent who, besides riding hard herd on annual food sales of $1.5 billion, presided over the Canada West Foundation, the country's most effective and most conservative think tank.

Closer inspection of *Cybele III* yielded telling clues to Child's character. For one thing, instead of flying the Canadian maple leaf designated for small craft, this boat was proudly displaying the Blue Ensign (Union Jack in a field of blue), especially made for Child by the Annin flag company in Toronto. It was his gesture of protest against the Liberal party's imposition of a new flag in 1965. During the same voyage, while docked at the Nanaimo Yacht Club, Child noted with satisfaction: "Club members who saw our ensign made very disparaging remarks about the Canadian flag."

The boat also revealed a great deal about Child's personality and work habits. First of all, he was very much in command, standing there in his wheelhouse, hugging himself against the chill of the day. He was never a noisy man, but his body language spoke for him. This vessel was built to his exact specifications right down to the walls of hand-rubbed teak in every cabin. His love of detail was exemplified by its engine room, which on most boats this size is a greasy pit into which the owner sends befuddled mechanics on annual inspection forays. Not on *Cybele III*. This engine room was fifteen feet wide, with ample space to walk around and poke at the two outsize 310-hp 6–71N Detroit diesel engines and the Onan generator, which produces 7,500 watts, making the ship independent of shore facilities. The carpeted engine room was as neat and innocent of bric-a-brac as Child's desk back in his Calgary office.

There was another parallel between Child's business life and his boat. He believed in the privilege of the proprietor, he privatized Burns and, typically, he not only owned his boat, but also bought a major interest in the Canoe Cove Manufacturing yard near Sidney, B.C., that had built her. *Cybele III* was an expression of Child's personality, containing as it did the best of materials and equipment without a touch of hedonism or ostentation. The pleasure cruiser had style, but for the professional sailor only.

What the vessel's utilitarian lines did not reveal was the romantic side of Child's nature. This was not exactly what he's

known for in Alberta. One of his former associates summed up
the more commonly held view of the man with the unoriginal
comment: "When Art Child says, 'Jump,' you ask, 'How high?'
on the way up."

But here, cruising through Spieden Channel down to the
San Juans, a very different Child was noting in his log:

> *Spieden Channel has vicious tidal currents, of no concern to a boat*
> *of our size but spectacular to behold, especially if the wind is going*
> *in the opposite direction. On a dark and stormy day, the tidal turbu-*
> *lence of Spieden Channel conjures up the adventures of Ulysses and*
> *his Greek sailors when they dared the Strait of Messina and faced the*
> *terrors of Scylla and Charybdis. On this sunny day, however, there*
> *were no monsters waiting for us on either side of the Strait.*

As *Cybele III* nosed her thirty tons around Limestone Point
into San Juan Channel off Orcas Island, Child took a moment
to reminisce about his love of seafaring and why he chose this
journey as a maiden voyage. He set down his private impressions
in the ship's log:

> *I grew up in the Thousand Islands, those southern outcroppings of*
> *the Precambrian Shield which choke the ten-mile source of the mighty*
> *St. Lawrence River as it emerges from Lake Ontario. In winter there*
> *was easy access to any island over the ice, but the real delight was the*
> *sparkle of the summer sun on the channels between the islands. The*
> *channels gave each island its separate privacy yet enabled small boys*

in small boats to explore any beach or cove. The Thousand Islands of the St. Lawrence have a sheltered and mature beauty, in contrast to the wind-swept rocks of the Thirty Thousand Islands of Georgian Bay, whose bare shoulders make one want to stand tall against the elements, as do their lone pines defying the cold north winds. By contrast, as a victim of long frigid winters, I have enjoyed the warmth of cruising among the mangroves of the Ten Thousand Islands that protect the west coast of Florida southward from Marco Island. There the complete absence of human presence and the stillness of the clear water between the myriads of islets, mere footholds for mangrove trees and oysters, compel one to turn off the noise of the outboard motor and paddle silently between corridors of bright shiny green foliage.

The San Juan Islands have nothing in common with the island groups of the inland rivers and lakes, or the green hummocks along tropical coastlines. Broken off from the northwest corner of the state of Washington, and sheltered from the open Pacific Ocean by the massive barrier of Vancouver Island, the San Juans are like a husky group of individuals who just happen to have been thrown together. Some of the larger members of the group are big and mountainous; others are fairly flat and extensively farmed. The shores of most are rocky and forbidding, and large islands like Blakely have little habitation because only fir trees can cling to the mountainsides. The general impression of the San Juans is dark green, the colour of the dense growth of spruce and cedar and Douglas fir. The impression of dark forest and grey granite is heightened when there is rain and fog, which is most of the time, but on a sunny summer day the sailor's spirits are lifted by the bright iridescent leaves and white flowers of arbutus trees and the glimpse of wildflowers where the forest opens at the water's edge.

There are no wave-created beaches in the San Juans because the violent ocean is fifty miles away. But in any case the water would be too cold for swimming. The visitor is entranced by the deep and steep inlets of Orcas Island or the bays that hide behind many of the headlands. A school of porpoises may put on a show as you thread a channel, and every stretch of water is host to thousands of seabirds: ducks, herons, cormorants, coots, seagulls, and many others. The San Juans convey a vivid impression of lush forest growth and teeming wildlife above and below the water. Harbour seals and fishermen compete for the schools of salmon, and shellfish are everywhere for the gathering.

———

ARTHUR CHILD WAS the most interesting and certainly the most important non-oil businessman in Alberta. He turned seventy in 1980, but instead of entertaining thoughts of permanent retirement on his boat, he launched a five-year expansion designed to take Burns well past $2 billion in sales. He put in a daily average of ten hours behind his desk, including Saturdays and Sundays, and his company's official biography insisted: "Arthur Child has no social or sports interests whatsoever. For the most part, his time is spent at his office, his home, or travelling on business."

That was a gross distortion of Child's eclectic mind and unusual background. After graduating from Queen's University, he read early French literature at Laval; lived in Europe; taught himself German, Russian and Spanish; wrote a PhD thesis in economic history; studied at the Harvard Business School and wrote two books. He served as treasurer of the Canadian Authors Association (Hugh MacLennan was secretary), and in 1951 he helped save the group from financial collapse.

He has been a pilot, performing aerobatics in his own Tiger Moth, and he undertook several lengthy voyages as captain of his two previous *Cybeles*. His house had the largest private military library in the country. He took regular trips to Washington for private Pentagon briefings on the world situation, was a member of London's prestigious Institute for Strategic Studies and believed strongly in applying military analogies to business. He admired Julius Caesar ("whose qualities of leadership applied equally well to business as to military matters") but had little patience with modern management-by-consensus techniques. Child blamed the U.S. defeat in Vietnam on the fact that its officer corps relied on such fancy nonsense as systems analysis, decision models and management by objective. Officers, he contended, must be gentlemen, and their most essential skill is knowing how to die well. Child believed in leadership by example. That, and discipline. "If you read the history of India, you would see how discipline and organization and the demand for perfection enabled the Indian Army . . . to defeat native armies twenty, thirty times their size. Discipline, the desire for perfection, high standards, sound training . . . are all worthwhile principles in the military and in business."

He made use of that military knowledge in reorganizing the Burns company when he arrived in 1966. The company had been founded by Patrick Burns of Kirkfield, Ontario, and Odanah, Manitoba, when Calgary was little more than a North-West Mounted Police outpost, and he got the contract for supplying meat to the railway gangs building a spur up to Edmonton. The Burns firm was sold in 1928 to Dominion Securities and eventually found its way into the portfolio of Howard Webster, the Montreal investor. It was losing $375,000 a month when Webster persuaded Child (who became chief auditor of Canada Packers at twenty-eight and in 1960 had moved over to rescue Intercontinental Packers in Saskatoon) to take over. Child fired fifty-seven of the ninety executives at head office, wrote off packing plants in Regina, Prince Albert and Medicine Hat, and diversified into restaurants (Murray's), catering (Crawley & McCracken), groceries (Stafford Foods), vegetable oils (Canbra Foods), tanning (A.R. Clarke) and trading with Japan. By 1974 sales had tripled and profits stood at $4,571,000.

When he joined the company, Child sank all his savings into Burns shares so that by 1978 he owned 4 percent of its stock. That was the year he and Webster decided to go private by forming a new company (WCB Holdings) to buy up the public's shares for $50 million. Writing in the *Financial Post,* Richard Osler speculated at the time that Child's stake, which had moved up to 25 percent, was worth $10 million. The value of his investment multiplied many times since, and Child was delighted with his privatized status: "My friends who head up large public corporations invariably say to me, 'Gee, I wish we could do that.' Being private has a lot of advantages for any chief executive officer. Your business is your own. You don't have to disclose anything to anybody; you don't have analysts calling you every week, which is a bit of a bother."

Unlike many of his Calgary colleagues, Child had spread his influence across the country, as senior vice-president (and substantial investor) in the Quebec-based La Vérendrye Management, which owned the Télé-Capital radio and television network and Brazeau Transport, the province's largest trucking operation.

He was equally contemptuous of Pierre Trudeau and Joe Clark, believing that Brian Mulroney would bring sanity back into the political process. "People are quite happy to go their own ways," he told me, defining the Calgary ethic. "We won't let anybody take liberties, but we're not looking for distinction as such. Business is fun to people out here. But we're very realistic, very hard-nosed when it comes not only to our companies' investments, but also to our own portfolios. No real estate operator, broker or anybody like that could even get the time of day from me. I make my own decisions."

———

ART CHILD WAS a contented man. He was rich, had virtually no public profile, pushed his political ideas through the Canada West Foundation and his private impulses through half a dozen personal investment trusts. His name seldom surfaced in lists of

Alberta power brokers, yet he was as influential as any of them and more interesting than most.

It was aboard his boat that Child came closest to the essence of himself. As he wrote in the final entry of his log describing the maiden voyage to the San Juans: "While most ex-sailors or would-be sailors can only sit at home and dream of islands and blue water, *Cybele III* makes it possible for us to cruise a thousand miles of coastline—a far journey for the small boy who once ventured in his tiny skiff across the channels of the St. Lawrence."

———

IT WAS TRUE that Child invested most of himself in his work and that he turned the once insolvent Burns Foods into a $2 billion corporation that became Alberta's largest private employer. And it was true that while Child deliberately maintained no public profile outside his company, he also led a fascinating private life, worth describing now that he has passed away, at eighty-six.

An unpretentious gent with a wry sense of humour and a romantic's soul, he was kind to strangers and ruthless with competitors. His chief vanity was to wear a red toupée that fitted his head so awkwardly he must have known it was a bad joke. He came daily to his office until six months before he died and was already well into his eighties when he experienced one of his greatest thrills.

He had been a skilful flyer, performing impressive aerobatics in his own vintage Tiger Moth, and when a visiting American fighter-jet pilot heard about his flying skills, he allowed Child to pilot his supersonic jet fighter. He started to lecture the octogenarian on how the ejection seat worked, but Child interrupted: "I won't need that," he gently cautioned. "At my age, if I get into trouble, I'll just ride her down."

—1996

Sir Christopher Ondaatje:
The Knight Who Explored Africa

The parallels are striking. When Conrad Black went to war with Prime Minister Jean Chrétien over the right of Canadians to accept British titles, Conrad decided that it was worth becoming Lord Black of Crossharbour, though he was forced to give up his Canadian citizenship as the price for the foreign honour. He left the country of his birth and original fortune with a soliloquy that amounted to "good riddance." Two years later, another Canadian financier who writes books and ran a Toronto publishing house (just like Black) was granted a British knighthood, but instead of a public shootout, nobody said a word and there was no problem about his retaining his Canadian citizenship.

His name is Ondaatje, now Sir Philip Christopher Ondaatje, and since retiring from his Bay Street brokerage (for the second time) in 1995, he has become one of England's most generous philanthropists. Over the years, Sir Christopher has given away more than $60 million to British and Canadian museums, universities and cultural foundations.

When I dropped in recently to see him at his luxurious Sloane Square flat, he told me the full story, which makes it very clear that the former prime minister had it in for Black long before he was publicly disgraced over his alleged corporate shenanigans. "In April of last year, my wife Valda and I were invited, with some ambassadorial couples, to stay at Windsor Castle," Ondaatje told me. "We were treated royally, given a suite and waited on hand and foot. The queen was unbelievably friendly and spent a lot of time with Valda and me. After dinner, for nearly two hours, she personally gave us a tour.

"A few weeks later, I got this letter from Downing Street saying that they were going to recommend me for a knighthood and would I accept? I wrote back and said I'd love to, but I wanted to make it very clear that I will not give up my Canadian citizenship and left it at that. Nothing happened. So I was living in this question mark world because I knew about the Conrad situation and Chrétien was still prime minister of Canada."

On June 14, 2003, Ondaatje's name appeared on the list of new knighthoods. From that moment on, he was officially a knight but still a Canadian. That same evening, the Westons invited the Ondaatjes to Fort Belvedere, the estate they lease near Windsor Castle, where Galen was throwing a gala to celebrate his wife, Hilary's, sixtieth birthday. It was attended by three hundred international celebrities, including the queen and Prince Philip. "After dinner Valda and I got up, and the queen made her way to where we were standing," Ondaatje recalled. "Before I could greet Her Majesty, she grabbed both of my hands and asked if I had heard from the prime minister of Canada. I said that I hadn't. 'Well,' she replied, 'let me tell you, he's certainly been in touch with me and let me tell you my advice to you is to let me handle this my way.'"

"They let it happen for me, and I feel more Canadian than ever," Sir Christopher concluded. "Canada made me. It's an incredibly bloody great country."

That story hasn't been told before, but it says as much about Ondaatje's rising reputation as it does about Black's downfall. Born in Ceylon (now Sri Lanka) seventy-one years ago, Christopher Ondaatje has become known as "The English Patron," a play on his more famous younger brother Michael's award-winning novel, *The English Patient*. "Most people in the financial business seek power, and sometimes it brings them down," he told me. "I always wanted money and I was good at finance, but I didn't want power because it's an ego trip."

————

AS I LEFT his flat, I noticed a prose fragment in one of the half-dozen books he has written that seemed to sum up the man and his dreams: "The world of tomorrow will change and as if tomorrow were a foreign land, we must set out in search of it. No man is totally confined by his own time, and no man can move into the future without understanding the past. The future—as always—can only be grasped by those who are ready for it."

Ondaatje spends most of his time between expeditions giving money away. His Canadian causes include Massey College at the University of Toronto, Pearson College on Vancouver Island, Ontario's Lakefield College School, Toronto's Royal Ontario Museum and Nova Scotia's Chester Playhouse, among many others. In London he has helped finance a wing named after him at the National Portrait Gallery and a theatre at the Royal Geographical Society, while providing $35 million to establish a foundation for the development of learning and international understanding.

Since he is a Conservative, his most unusual gift was $4.5 million he gave to the British Labour party in 2000. "Tony Blair is a middle-of-the-road conservative in my opinion," he maintained. "I thought he was worth backing because he was the right person at the right time. He is leading the Labour party but has kept the unions out. How much more right wing do you want me to be? The last person I liked was Margaret Thatcher."

A tall, rangy man with a mercurial personality, Ondaatje is one of those rare birds who follows his own flight plan and knows exactly where he is heading. No wonder the empire city's chattering classes have adopted Sir Christopher as their model Canuck.

—2004

Seymour Schulich: Champion Philanthropist

"I'VE BECOME SOMETHING of a psychiatrist to half a dozen rich guys who have come to me for advice," confides Seymour Schulich, the Montreal-born mining magnate who has donated more than $15 million and is in the process of giving away another $10 million. "The people who consult me have made good money in the investment industry and are having thoughts about doing something with it. I mean, any fool can give his money away, but the trick is to get some leverage for it. That means forming partnerships with governments, other donors and the leaders of the receiving institutions."

The easygoing Schulich outlined his donation philosophy at his unpretentious downtown Toronto office. "Everybody wants their life to have some meaning," he says. "The big mistake people make is trying to fund something by themselves. If it's significant, you won't have enough money to do that, no matter who you are. Even John D. Rockefeller couldn't. What you must do is become a catalyst by providing the large lead gift for a capital campaign which has matching elements. That's how you get that all-important multiplier effect."

Schulich, who grew up poor and Jewish in Montreal, struck it rich in Nevada. A McGill University science graduate, he personally has never discovered an ounce of any mineral but has instead cut himself into the action through royalty arrangements and now shares ownership in some of the region's richest mines, including royalties from Peter Munk's Goldstrike property. His company, Franco-Nevada Mining, has been one of the biggest price gainers on the Toronto Stock Exchange in the past decade. Schulich, who keeps a six-shooter in his desk as a gag, has lived in the same suburban Toronto bungalow for twenty-two years with his one and only wife. Yes, he has driven a Cadillac, but it was ten years old when he traded it in for a Ford. "I've never learned how to spend money on myself," he confesses. "It makes me very uncomfortable."

Schulich made news in 1995 when he donated $15 million to establish a business school named after him at Toronto's York University. It has since grown to be the largest and most prestigious graduate business school in the country, led by Dean Dezso Horvath, a high-octane Hungarian with two PhDs who never lets up and has won Schulich's admiration because they share the same motto: both men would rather ask for forgiveness than for permission.

"We train five thousand managers every year and graduate one in three of Ontario's MBAs," he says. "And yet we have the oldest and most outdated facility of all the major business schools in the country. It's great to have scholarship, but if your students are studying in tents, it's not too good, especially during those Canadian winters. So I'm putting up a lead donation of $5 million to put up a new school building. But it's not a naming gift. I'm hoping to attract someone who will put up a matching amount to have his name on the building."

Schulich's next move is his donation of another $5 million to upgrade the coronary unit at Toronto's Sunnybrook Hospital. It's an ideal example of his "multiplier" theory at work. The Ontario government has already promised $7 million, and a public campaign is expected to raise another $14 million. "What I saw in Sunnybrook," says he, "is the same thing I recognized at York. Both institutions have lots of room to expand. Sunnybrook isn't like the downtown hospitals, all hemmed in. Like York, it also has a great leader, chief cardiologist Dr. Brian Gilbert, who can take the project forward and make it significant beyond its geographical boundaries. We'll end up with 152,000 square feet of a world-class facility devoted to cardiac care. It's going to be called the Schulich Heart Centre, the last damn thing I'm putting my name on."

Most of the money now flowing into Toronto's health and educational facilities originated in the Nevada gold fields. Peter Munk, who has sponsored a major heart institute at the Toronto Hospital and the Centre for International Studies at the University of Toronto, made most of his fortune digging up Nevada's rich Carlin Trend, as did Joe Rotman, the generous patron of the University of Toronto's newly revived School of Management. "After Munk built a heart centre, I felt every guy in the gold business should have one," Schulich deadpans. "There's a lot of Nevada money running around Toronto.

"A hundred years from now, it won't matter how much money you had in the bank, what kind of car you drove or what kind of house you lived in. But the world may be a better place because you helped some people achieve a better education and improved health care."

When he is giving money away, an activity that currently occupies much of his energy and most of his thoughts, Schulich always recalls a marvellous French saying, which, translated, means: "You can't tow a safe behind your hearse."

— 1999

Peter Bronfman: The Bronfman Who Hated Money

THE MOST SECRETIVE member of the Bronfman family, the
Canadian distilling moguls who once earned the title of being
"the Rothschilds of the New World," walked alone. His persona
was charged with corrosive sensibilities and retroactive grievances that marked him as an outcast, even in the Baroque gallery
of this neurotic clan. There was about him none of the loose
amiability of his cousin Edgar, who walked into a room with a
gracefully endearing lope, or of his cousin Charles, whose nour-
ishing quest for certitude charmed one and all.

More than a little miscast as a Bronfman, Peter was so sensitive that after his father's house burned down in the summer
of 1977, he spent the next six months trying to recover from
what his doctor diagnosed as a "sympathy low-grade fever"—
even though he'd spent some of the unhappiest times of his
life growing up in that cold Victorian pile next to patriarch Sam

Bronfman's Belvedere Palace. To be a Bronfman was never easy. "I grew up in a castle on a hill on Belvedere Avenue in Montreal's posh Westmount district, and I wasn't really aware of what was going on. I had no friends and no real relationship with my parents," he would recall over an espresso we shared. "I had a nurse for five years when I was very young, and when we happened to meet in Ireland much later when I was twenty-eight, we just fell into one another's arms and hugged and hugged."

Peter's fatalistic view of himself and life in general was summed up in this fragment of an essay written about the nihilistic turmoil of the mid-sixties by the New York journalist Gay Talese, which was Peter's favourite literary selection: "One must be *seen* to exist, for now there is no other proof. There is no longer an identity in craft, only in self-promotion. There are no acts, only scenes. Peace marches are masquerades. News is staged for camera crews. Critics dance with their eyes closed. Nothing is happening. It is a meaningless moment in history."

Peter's personal theology held that the ability to marvel at life was a gift of heaven and that such enchantment was difficult to achieve and even more difficult to share. A loner with a million complexes, his greatest joy was walking by himself through the fluorescent desolation of city streets in late-night rain, investigating the radiant miscellanies along the way. "Peter is rather antisocial," noted Jacques Courtois, his Montreal lawyer. "He enjoys the company of a few personal friends but shuns large receptions or gatherings; he has a strong dislike of ties and jackets, let alone dressing in black tie."

Except for being close to his children, Peter was an urban hermit. Despite numerous invitations, he managed to visit cousin Charles, who lived less than five minutes up the Westmount hillside, no more than twice a year. He saw cousin Phyllis, whose house was twenty minutes away in the other direction, three times during the last fifteen years. "It might be better if I were more outgoing, a little more gregarious," he admitted. Peter's solitary ways sometimes got him into trouble. Among the many other assets in the $2 billion business empire over which he and his brother, Edward, presided was sole ownership of the Canadiens hockey team and the Montreal Forum. During a home game against the Bruins on May 7, 1977, Bob Wilson, a Boston radio commentator, was sitting high up in the press gondola with his technician when a person he later described as "a tall lanky fellow, very leisurely dressed, with open shirt and sports slacks" plunked himself down between them. "The guy didn't say anything, just sat down and calmly watched the game, gesturing to show his approbation or disappointment. I was looking for a way of telling him to get the hell out of there, that he had no business in the press box, but the many commercials kept me constantly 'on mike.' He left near the end of the first period before I could say a word, so I asked the usher on duty if he knew who this impudent guy was, acting as if he owned the place."

"He does," the guard informed the embarrassed commentator. When he returned to watch the second period, Peter explained to Wilson that he could relax during games only by sitting next to somebody with an open microphone, so he couldn't yell even when he felt like it. Occasionally, he was so overcome by emotion that he had to leave his seat to watch the game on the colour TV in the directors' lounge.

———————

NOW AND THEN Peter's determination not to display emotions in public turned in on itself. He could be sardonic in his observations of the privacies of others. This streak in his makeup was probably best documented in a description he wrote in his diary about a flight home from Israel in September of 1976:

Sitting in El Al's first-class section, the plane about to take off from Tel Aviv to New York on a recent morning, I was beside a middle-aged Israeli woman who informed me that she and her husband were flying free, since he was an El Al employee. No sooner had I recovered from this mild hurt than she followed up with, "My husband is over there, sitting beside Mr. Eban." Congratulating her on his good fortune, I learned that she was thankful she wasn't sitting there, since she couldn't possibly imagine what she might say to the great man, who had been Israel's foreign minister.

Just then, an El Al steward came by and informed her that, unfortunately, she and her husband would have to move into economy to make room for two paying first-class customers who had just come aboard. Turning to me, he asked if I wouldn't mind sitting beside Mr. Eban, as he didn't want to separate the newly arrived couple. I asked if he would consider having Mr. Eban move back to the now-vacant seat beside me, since he was sitting up front near the clatter of the bar and the traffic that soon would be flowing to and from the washroom. Understandably, the steward was reluctant to ask Mr. Eban to move, so I picked up my briefcase and seated myself beside him.

Extending my hand, I introduced myself, thinking the name might possibly remind Mr. Eban of the time in 1967 when, shortly after the Six-Day War, he spent a few hours in my parents' home in Montreal prior to addressing a large audience on the Israeli-Arab conflict then being hotly debated at the UN. On that occasion, he had mumbled some phrase in reply to my attempt to exchange a few words, his gaze remaining fixed midway between the top of a small Sisley painting and the ceiling. I remember thinking at the time that I perhaps shouldn't have intruded on the thoughts of a man at stage centre of world attention. All of this flashed through my mind as I extended my hand, which he shook, mumbling a phrase very similar in tone and content to that which I had heard some nine years before. The smile, too, was pretty much of the same vintage.

Realizing that Mr. Eban was undoubtedly preoccupied with matters of significance—though not necessarily as critical as during the 1967 situation—I determined to let him go back to leafing through the dozen or so Hebrew and English newspapers on his lap. When breakfast was served and, some hours later, luncheon as well, I commented briefly about the meals being offered and was met inevitably with the same diplomatic smile that seemed to be his trademark. I assumed that this packaged response to queries and approaches from the unwashed masses was for the purpose of discouraging discussion so that he could be alone with his thoughts. His system was certainly effective. I only bothered him one more time to ask for a few sheets of paper from the scratch pad that he kept nearby for intermittent jottings, so that I could write down these words about how we had lunched together.

Peter Bronfman published none of his writings, but there existed a slim, mimeographed volume simply entitled *Poems 1969–1970. The Cocktail Party* graphically screamed out his hatred of empty social occasions:

> *Hello! The bar's over there!*
> *Good-bye! Going so soon?*
> *Gotta go home and throw up!*
> *Terrific! Keep well!*

———

ALTHOUGH PETER WAS an active chairman of the Jewish General Hospital, he frequently found himself battling the group think of Montreal's Jewish community. When Arthur Pascal, the unofficial dean of Quebec Jewry, accused him of ignoring the collective views of the community, Peter exploded. "Listen, I've heard that bullshit all my life. It means nothing. People who are exposed to it at the age of twenty instead of five, they may take it seriously. But I don't care and won't let you get away with pulling that stuff on me!"

Peter was separated from his first wife, Diane Feldman, in 1973, and three years later married Theodora Reitsma, a vivacious Dutch blonde with faintly sucked-in cheeks who seemed constantly to be sheltering a smile, turned like a sunflower toward the sun. His children were educated in outstanding private schools, but Peter lived in astonishing modesty. Until he moved into a downtown Montreal apartment, his main residence was a $90,000 townhouse on Trafalgar Place, seventy-five feet *outside* Westmount's eastern boundaries. He drove an ancient brown Mercury, and his only real luxury was a valuable art collection that included canvases by Chagall, Lawren Harris and Alfred Pellan, as well as a carload of exquisite pieces of Eskimo sculpture. (The carvings so dominated the house that Jack Pierce, the president of Ranger Oil and a good friend of Peter, once commented that the Bronfman living room reminded him of "the duty-free shop at Gander airport.")

Peter hated to spend money. Edper's chief Toronto link was Trevor Eyton, a canny lawyer with Tory Tory DesLauriers & Binnington, who tended to whisper his legal advice and in the summertime kept a telescope in his office permanently trained on Olympic Island in Toronto Harbour so he could watch his daughters taking sailing lessons at the Royal Canadian Yacht Club. He vividly remembered relaxing with Peter in a Vancouver hotel room when Peter took his shoes off. Eyton noticed not only that he had a hole in one sock, but also that the socks had previously been darned in several places. During a train trip Peter and I took (by coach) on the CNR's Rapido from Montreal to

Toronto, when I bought a cheese sandwich, Peter suggested we should share it. When his wife, Dora, ordered half a lobster as an appetizer for dinner at Toronto's Hyatt Regency Hotel (of which he owned 37 percent), Peter became so nervous that he started fidgeting with his wedding ring and finally dropped it with a loud, symbolic clang on the pewter serving plate.

"I don't think I'm secure enough to spend the kind of money my cousins do or live in houses like theirs," Peter confessed. "I've always sort of felt, 'Gee, look at all the money that person's spending. I guess he knows he can always make it.' A strong part of me keeps saying to myself, 'My God, the money just came to me; maybe it could all disappear some day.'"

———

HIS FATHER, ALLAN, was a stubborn character but no match for Sam, the autocratic chief of the clan who gradually shunted Allan off into looking after the family philanthropies, although he remained a senior vice-president of Seagram's until 1975. A former colleague recalled being in Sam's office just after the outbreak of the Second World War, when Allan came in decked out in the uniform of a private in the Canadian army. On his way to a ten-day reserve training course at St. Bruno, near Montreal, he shook Sam's hand, executed a smart about-turn, marched to the door, saluted and was gone. Sam could hardly contain himself. "Ah, look at the fucking hero," he exclaimed. "You'd think he'd just won the war. Christ, they get a few more like him and Hitler's got a chance!"

It was one of Sam's eternal grudges against his brother that during the immediate postwar reconstruction period, when Allan donated a boatload of flour to a French city, he was decorated with the Legion of Honour. "How come he didn't send the flour from both of us?" Sam asked anyone who'd listen. "He does everything else jointly, for Christ's sake. Hell, he doesn't know enough to get out of his own way, and now they give him the goddamn Legion of Honour." Allan didn't say a word, but he always wore the scarlet pip that denotes the French decoration proudly in his buttonhole.

Sam had his revenge. His excommunicating Allan's sons from Seagram's hallowed halls triggered a primal feud that split the family into warring camps. Allan himself was quite content to play a complementary role in the distilling giant's corporate affairs, but he never stopped hoping that Edward and Peter would be counted among its operating heirs. Instead, Sam chose specifically to exclude them, even before their abilities could fairly be appraised. Cousin Minda remembered being puzzled by the tension that began to build up between the neighbours on Belvedere Road. "When we were smaller, we thought our cousins would go into the company. Later, we knew how things stood." Cousin Charles's summary was more succinct: "Pop didn't want them in the business."

The actual *coup de grâce* that drove Allan's branch of the family out to pasture took place in the summer of 1952, shortly after Peter graduated from Yale. "The boys came to me," Allan recalled, "Peter first. He started to cry and asked me, 'How is it that I can't get into the company?' So I told him." Sam and Allan had placed their Seagram stockholdings into Seco Investments, a private company controlled jointly by their family trusts, Cemp and Edper. But the ownership was not evenly split; Sam had 2.2 million shares and Allan 1.1 million. This two-thirds majority allowed Sam to issue instructions barring Allan's children. The decision was taken during a memorable shouting match between the two men. "Sam was really mad at me," Allan recalled, "and when Sam gets mad, he can go back four generations."

Even though he'd won, the fact that there had been some minor challenge to his supreme authority made Sam so angry that during the next twelve months, he refused to exchange a single word with his younger brother. "For a whole year," Allan recalled, "he used to walk by my office, which was next door to his, and never stopped to talk." No member of either family crossed the tailored lawns between the Belvedere mansions. Eight years later, Sam struck another blow. Having ejected Allan's sons from any proprietary function in the company, he decided to strip them of half their holdings. Seagram's was at the time selling on the open market for $28 per share. Sam set out to purchase 600,000 shares of Edper's holding of 1.1 million at $26 per share, claiming that he was entitled to a "quantity discount" for such a large block. Peter and Edward accepted because the offer had been accompanied by what they read as a clear warning that their refusal would strip their father of his only remaining power base—the Seagram vice-presidency. This bold move raised Sam's holdings to 2.8 million shares, which, with two subsequent two-for-one stock splits, brought him to more than 11 million shares of his family holdings. At the same time, Edper's stake in Seagram was reduced to 500,000 shares, which, following similar splits, eventually left Allan's family with only 2 million shares. Peter and Edward immediately sold them off, claiming with ill-concealed pride that "there are lots of better investments around."

———————

SAM CALLED PETER into his office in the winter of 1969 to confront him with a large pile of press clippings, praising the rise of "the other" Bronfmans.

"What the hell are all these?" Sam demanded.

"I don't know," Peter replied. "I don't ever answer reporters' calls. What they write isn't my fault."

"Your private office still connected to the Seagram switchboard?"

"Yes. But we pay all the long-distance bills separately."

"Well, you better get off. Right now."

The last shreds of the umbilical cord between the two families had been cut.

Peter was then forty. He and Edward had accomplished little. They'd put up an office building in Montreal at 2055 Peel Street, bought a few bowling alleys, purchased an interest in a minor printing house and sat around too frightened to take any risks lest they make a mistake. But now there could be no more excuses. Their uncle Sam's brutal finality brought with it a flood of fresh perceptions. Suddenly, they weren't nearly so afraid anymore, realizing that there was no easy way out, not in the middle of a life, that the power to change and grow resided within each individual, not in his external circumstances.

Peter and Edward Bronfman conducted Edper's operation with what they called "informed intuition," perusing monthly budget sheets of their associated companies, interviewing prospective promoters trying to earn their finders' fees. Harold Milavsky, president of Trizec, a major Edper holding, says, "Peter gets good people, trusts them and gives them their head. His secret is that once they've proven themselves, he allows them full authority as well as full responsibility. At Trizec, for example, we report to him only at quarterly directors' meetings."

Peter came to maturity very late, and it wasn't until years later that he finally managed to catch up with himself. "When I was twenty-four, I was acting like sixteen. I didn't start working until I was well over twenty, so I didn't have a very realistic view of what life was all about. At forty, I was still eight to ten years behind, doing and thinking things that people I know and respect were doing at thirty. But now I'm past my hang-ups and enjoying life."

The incident that finally began to liberate Peter Bronfman in his quest for identity was a conversation with his son, Bruce. Six years old at the time, Bruce wanted to know exactly what being a millionaire was all about. "I tried to explain it," Peter recalls vividly. "I told Bruce about our family history, our business and asked him how he felt about being a millionaire."

Young Bruce considered the matter carefully and replied, "I'm very proud."

The answer deeply impressed Peter because it seemed such a healthy reaction. "Up in the castle where I grew up, the three things we never were allowed to talk about were money, other people and sex. What else is there?"

————

THE EDPER GROUP of companies that Peter and his brother, Edward, founded was turned into an astonishingly diverse and successful $18 billion empire, employing sixty-four thousand people. When Peter died in 1997, the firm's top executives trumpeted their late chairman's "corporate statesmanship" and "selfless leadership." Peter would not have had much patience with such sentiments. "I happen," he once told me, "to have a very low threshold for bullshit." What he meant was not so much to denigrate his corporate successes as to affirm his personal priorities. He spent most of his life becoming his own man, allowing the roaring boy deep inside to take command and cut himself loose from the constraints of his upbringing.

Sam Bronfman, the dynasty's father and Peter's uncle, could make boys out of men, and with Peter he almost succeeded. Just after Peter graduated from Yale, Sam made it very clear that there was to be no place for him or his brother. Command of the giant distillery was ceded directly and exclusively to Sam's two sons, Charles and Edgar. Allan's reduced nest egg of Seagram stock was enough to provide his sons with seed money to start their own, initially tiny conglomerate. But Peter never forgot the slight.

His conglomerate, which at different times has included such well-known firms as John Labatt Ltd., London Life Insurance Co., Brascan Ltd., Noranda Inc. and Royal LePage Ltd., took up most of Peter's working time, but his heart and spirit were never in it. He attended only the occasional, compulsory corporate cocktail party. He would stand at the back of the room, hunched over in a penitent position, sipping his flat ginger ale, silently praying for relief.

The business venture he enjoyed most was ownership of the Canadiens hockey team and the Montreal Forum from 1971 to 1978. His respect for the players knew no bounds. Only a few months before he died, he flew to Montreal for a private visit with a former star forward (Floyd Curry, suffering from Alzheimer's). The Habs won four Stanley Cups during the seven years he owned the team. After he sold it to Molson's and bought, through Labatt's, the Toronto Blue Jays instead, the baseball squad won two World Series.

Peter came to maturity only in 1985 after marrying his third wife, Lynda Carroline Hamilton, a Vancouver management consultant, who fulfilled his quest for security and love. He spent the best decade of his life in their country place, a converted one-room schoolhouse in Palgrave, Ontario, where his gentle nature was allowed to flourish.

Peter died just one day short of being presented with the Order of Canada in a special bedside ceremony by Governor General Roméo LeBlanc. Jack Rabinovitch, one of his best friends, reminded Government House that Bronfman had contributed to "aspiring young artists" and pronounced a moving eulogy of his pal. June Callwood, the Toronto social activist, praised "his inspiring decency, compassion and commitment." But the most significant letter came from cousin Charles Bronfman, Mr. Sam's son, the man whose inheritance Peter had so envied. "Peter," Charles wrote, "is a man who has carved a place for himself in Canadian history. He well deserves the recognition of being included in the Order of Canada."

Peter Bronfman had come home at last.

—1996

The New Wave: Navjeet Dhillon Goes Gold

AN IMMIGRANT AND a new breed of Canadian entrepreneur, Navjeet (Bob) Dhillon, was born a Sikh forty-three years ago. Unlike his peers, he is a master scuba diver, expert spear fisherman and professional-level salsa dancer. Dhillon meets none of the preconceptions of his race or religion and prefers yoga and meditation to religious observance. He refuses to wear the traditional Sikh turban, owns a cigarette racing boat in which he sweeps across the Gulf Stream into Cuban harbours and is about as far removed from the usual taciturn, non-communicative Indian business leader as it is possible to be.

As a businessman, he boasts that he will become North America's first Sikh billionaire—and is three-quarters of the way there. His publicly traded real estate conglomerate snaps up apartment buildings in Saskatchewan, Alberta and Ontario, and on the side, he markets luxury beach lots in the Central American playground of Belize.

A barrel-chested, perpetually tanned extrovert who lives in a palatial $2 million house on a mountainside overlooking Calgary, Dhillon justifiably describes himself as having "a triple A–type personality." He has never been interviewed before, except for two-minute segments on business channels, and is inordinately reserved about his personal life, which he insists must remain private for religious reasons. Apart from his official shyness, his frantic schedule allows few quiet moments to discover balance in his life. "When I'm travelling alone on plane rides, that's the only time I have for myself," he told me. "On those four-hour trips from Toronto to Calgary, I can reflect on my future. I'm always writing notes to myself and sketching out business plans. But I do meditate, which gives me calmness."

————

HE ALMOST DIDN'T have a future. "I was diagnosed at one time with cancer, but I beat it," he reveals. "I got my clean bill of health three years ago. I also beat racism in Alberta and the odds of a falling capital market. What drives me is the second wind in my life when I went through chemo. Now the stars are realigning. My personality is a fabric of my family, being an immigrant and conquering cancer.

"If you ask me what religion I am, I would say I am a Sikh," he says. "But if you ask me whether I am a real, practising Sikh,

I would say that would be a false statement. I am more spiritual than religious. Sikhs were persecuted like the Jews. They've always been at war. For hundreds of years, we guarded the foot-hills of the Khyber Pass, beating off the invaders who came from the north. When you're fighting for your life, generation after generation, you develop a survival instinct, as I have. The image of being Sikh is that it's orthodox-oriented, but it actually is very liberal. You go to a Sikh temple, and they sing songs like the Southern Baptists and invite you in for a meal. When the Canadian Legion wouldn't allow turbaned Sikhs into their halls, they didn't realize that we've won more Victoria Crosses than any other group. Sir John A. Macdonald even suggested bringing in a Sikh battalion to protect Canada from the Americans."

Although he considers India to be his homeland, Dhillon was born in Japan. His grandfather Saproon Singh Dhillon had migrated from Punjab to Hong Kong at age sixteen. There he eventually became a trader and established the North China Shipping Co., which exported goods to Japan. That was where Dhillon was born in 1965. Six years later, the family moved to Liberia to tap the trading markets of West Africa. During the 1970s, when a bitter civil war erupted in that unstable repub-lic, the family lost everything and sought refuge in Vancouver. It was not a happy time. Racial slurs were regularly directed at the youthful Bob as he walked to school.

The family relocated to Calgary, which they found to be no more welcoming, and his mother was fired from her job at the post office strictly because of its racist attitude. "Now, this is a fact," Dhillon insists. "We fought the case with the post office, a Crown corporation, and won. I don't want to give you a story about someone hitting me in a bar or somebody calling me a Paki and pulling my hair—these are things that happen because some guy behaves like an idiot. I'm telling you about an institutional fact. My mom fought the case in court and was reinstated a year later."

The family soldiered on in Calgary. "It was tough getting a job," Dhillon remembers. "There were only stereotyped positions available for the Sikhs, and it was really hard to break through the glass ceilings. For example, we were banned from any front-line positions in offices, and no oil companies would hire me." With no obvious prospects, he decided to go into business for himself. In 1984, at age nineteen, he bought two houses, fixed them up and sold them for an $18,000 profit. That was his modest grubstake. For the next fifteen years, he bought and sold Calgary real estate worth about $150 million, a hectic pastime better known as flipping. "I worked out of the trunk of my car with a cell phone," he remembers. "What drove me to work seventy hours a week or more was that my family had lost everything in Liberia after the coup, and I vowed it would never happen again."

His first success was to establish the grand-sounding Pan-Pacific Mercantile Group, which he hoped to spin into a major distributor of three dozen North American brands throughout South Asia. It never happened, but until recently if you ordered a Bloody Mary anywhere east of Hawaii, you'd have flavoured it with Tabasco sauce that was distributed by Bob Dhillon.

He underwent a significant sea change in 1996 when he decided, at age thirty-two, to spend two years getting his executive MBA at the University of Western Ontario's Richard Ivey School of Business. Larry Tapp, then the school's dean and now a director of Dhillon's companies, described him as "a very direct, driven guy." In May of his first year, he incorporated a numbered Alberta company that would become his main investment vehicle. "I used every available course at Ivey to formulate the strategy for Mainstreet," he recalls. "Whether it was building a brand, running an efficient operation, financing growth or making a speech, I thought about the lessons in terms of what they meant for Mainstreet." When he graduated, his company went public, and he began buying properties to hold instead of flip. Once back in Calgary, he moved his office out of the car trunk to the main floor of one his buildings, which was also used to store construction supplies.

———

IN THE PROCESS of moving in new directions, Dhillon came up with every entrepreneur's wet dream: a neglected yet accessible real estate niche that could profitably be filled without having to raise new capital. The building industry was polarized into local mom-and-pop-size operations running a few buildings and, at the other end, the giants—the Bronfmans, the Reichmanns, Brookfield, Trizec and others. In between was where Dhillon wanted to be. He became a consolidator of multi-family, mid-tiered residential rental properties, starting in Alberta, then moving west to Vancouver and east to Toronto. During the past seven years, Mainstreet Equity (of which he owns 41 percent) has mushroomed from 276 units to nearly 4,000, with a portfolio worth more than $300 million. The year 2000 was particularly stellar, with the *Globe and Mail's Report on Business* magazine ranking his company at the top of its list of Biggest Profit Gainers, recording a stunning 15,791 percent increase.

His technique is to buy buildings that require drastic repositioning, such as one in Calgary's Forest Lawn area, which had sixty deserted cars and trucks in its derelict parking lot, holes in living-room walls and all the telltale signs of having been a druggie hangout. Dhillon invested $2.3 million, doubled the rents and turned a slum into a middle-class complex. His fix-ups do not break any luxury barriers. Expenditures are calculated to the nearest penny. (Replacing toilets with modern, low-volume fixtures, for example, reduces water consumption from 6 gallons per flush to 1.6; substituting 60-watt light bulbs with $20 fluorescent lights reduces annual electricity consumption from $30 to $8.) He doubles rents, and three-quarters of his pre-renovation tenants usually move out, but the increased cash flow covers the cost of the upgrades.

Fifteen years ago, when he was looking around for something interesting to fill his non-existent spare time, Dhillon discovered Belize, a tiny former British colony bordered by Mexico's Yucatan Peninsula and Guatemala to the west. It was an English-speaking democracy with little poverty, and still virgin tourist territory. With only 280,000 people, it boasted all the trimmings fit for ex-pats: offshore banks protected by privacy laws, a diving paradise second only to Australia's Great Barrier Reef, dozens of Mayan ruin sites and 540 species of wild birds. "We were in Calgary before it was the centre of the universe, and oil was less than $20/barrel," he says. "We went to Edmonton before the tar sands were a buzz and to Saskatoon before it became Saskaboom. We were also one of the first professional developers into Belize."

Dhillon purchased a 2,300-acre island and marketed beach lots, only a few with price tags of under $1 million. Leonardo DiCaprio is a neighbour, and Madonna is said to own a nearby estate. When Dhillon is not skippering his fifty-five-foot yacht into the surf (occasionally crossing over to Cuba), he is negotiating to purchase an 88,000-acre patch of jungle for more development. His original island is now worth well over $100 million. "Belize will be the next St. Bart's without the Eurotrash," Dhillon says. "It has the best fishing, the best diving, the best sailing, white sand beaches and the kind of lifestyle we all dream about."

The one constant in Dhillon's cheerful litany is his unstinted praise for the country of his choice. "I owe my success to Canada. No matter how bright I may be," he confesses, "if I wasn't in Canada, I wouldn't have had one-tenth of the success anywhere else in the world. I owe my start to Alberta because it was not a closed shop like some of the other places. If you create a business model there that has a success pattern, you can branch out to other parts of Canada. The rest of the country can learn some-thing from Alberta, which is that the number one economic engine is lower taxes. Let the people be free. Governments cannot create jobs. Governments cannot create anything."

———

IN THIS TIME of cholera, few CEOs have the nerve to express confidence in the future, even about their own companies. A dramatic exception is Dhillon, who spent $25 million buying what he decided was the best bargain on the stock exchanges: shares in his own company. His offering wasn't altogether successful because a quarter of his shareholders decided to hold on to their investment, even though he was offering a substantial premium of over the listing price.

About a year before the Great Recession, Dhillon decided to gear up for the next cycle and was one of the few Canadian CEOs who planned for a downturn, though he could not know how serious it would turn out to be. His apartments, often occupied by former house owners whose properties had been repossessed, provided a healthy cash flow ($47 million in 2008), and his assets ranged in worth down from their peak at $625 million, depending on the state of the stock market.

"Why did the pendulum swing the other way so fast—was there a flaw in the whole system or is it just truly free enterprise and that's the way it is?" he asked when I interviewed him in a downtown Calgary hotel during the Great Crash. "There's another aspect that nobody talks about. Is there too much concentration of capital in too few hands—I'm referring to the institutional money in a G8 country like Canada—and that's why these cracks appeared in our capital markets so suddenly. This is something that somebody should definitely look into. Is the wealth concentrated among, perhaps, fifty portfolio managers in Canada? Maybe there should be ten thousand."

Still, Dhillon remains positive about the American financial system compared to Canada's: "The way the Americans do things is they take direct action, and they'll flush their bonds, their distressed real estate, their foreclosures, out of the system so quickly, and if this happened in Canada to that extent—which it hasn't—we would debate it, prolong it, dance, into a prolonged recession. Flushing out the bad assets will create a new generation of billionaires." Himself included, one assumes.

Within the Canadian real estate world, his firm remains a mid-size company with a future. Dhillon admits, "I've got to be at about $5 or $10 billion before anybody will recognize me," but he intends to double his holdings in the next five years and he has another advantage. "I'm now learning *kundalini,* which is a higher level of yoga," he confides as we part company. "I'm a very spiritual individual. Meditation combined with yoga means I can live forever. Literally."

—2005

PART 4

Okay, They're Not Canadian, but They're Still My Heroes

Stan Kenton: Artistry in Rhythm

WHEN I FIRST emigrated to Canada from Czechoslovakia
in the early 1940s, I used to put myself to sleep listening to the
Eaton's catalogue radio I got for one of my teen birthdays, and it
turned out to be the most significant formative influence of my
young life. I couldn't speak much English then, but I soaked up
the historical CBC radio documentaries, turning myself into a
hip nationalist in the process.

Late at night, long after my parents thought I was asleep, lying
there with the radio turned right down (its dial light removed
so there would be no telltale glow), I tuned into other, more
exciting worlds that followed the earnest history lessons. The
midnight airwaves were filled with remote pickups from ball-
rooms across North America where the big bands were swinging
high, and it was their music that first opened the way for me into

the culture of the new world to which I had so lately and so fortunately ventured. When I finally fell asleep after three or four hours of CBC documentaries and the big bands, I would dream about John A. Macdonald, Woody Herman, Mackenzie King, Tommy Dorsey, Wilfrid Laurier and Charlie Barnet—somehow sure that this would always be my country and my music.

Then one night in the late summer of 1942, I picked up a Mutual Broadcasting Company remote from the Rendezvous Ballroom in Balboa Beach, California, and heard Stan Kenton for the first time. The music came pouring out of my little radio like a hailstorm. The sound engulfed me with its azure beauty, the soloists cutting into the static of the airwaves in dissonant outbursts, like voices shouting into the wind. Right then and there, my obsession with Stan Kenton's music began.

I have performed it, studied it and listened to it ever since. I had tapes of it along with me during those out-of-body train rides during the Diefenbaker election campaigns; heard it when I was reporting the Israeli wars, crouched in foxholes along the Suez Canal; and I've written every word of all my books with the Kenton band coming in loud and clear over my earphones, splitting my head open and making me deaf, but also charging me with energy and providing the musical cadence to my prose.

Kenton played piano, but the band was his real instrument, and he used it like a playwright with his own versatile stock company. It was Kenton who first moved American music beyond its "polka dots and moonbeams" phase into more meaningful rapport with the changing, fluorescent North American environment. He believed that rock music would eventually evolve into jazz because that was the only direction it could grow.

When Stanley Newcomb Kenton died in 1979, he was a lion in winter—defiant in his going but well beyond his prime.

During the late forties and early fifties, Kenton's orchestra was the biggest jazz attraction in the world. Though he kept his sound evolving and his band travelling, Kenton spent the last decade of his life careering around the continent, still making converts but reduced to playing one-night stands at shopping-centre openings, musty nightclubs and other neon snake pits on the North American road.

He lived for thirty-eight years on a band bus, suffering the vagabond's indignities of little sleep and bad food, drinking a million cups of tepid coffee and eating all those stale Danishes— dealing with the greedy souls of scruffy promoters while having to prop up musicians trying to dredge new sounds out of exhausted psyches.

What made his gruelling schedule bearable were the nightly concerts when the old man would bound up on the bandstand, shout "Let's go!," strike an imperious triad on the piano and bring in the trumpet section with a chop of his right elbow. The sound of that music would melt away the years and energize him into a groove that took no enemies.

What Kenton demanded from his musicians was that they broaden the harmonic, rhythmic and structural boundaries of the band's arrangements so that each composition would trigger their ruminations. The best of the improvisors would grope for a melodic line, pursue it, then explore and soar with it, like astronauts dangling in the moonlight.

The Kenton band, which opened the 1941 season at the Rendezvous Ballroom in Balboa Beach, California, was a hybrid offshoot from the Jimmie Lunceford rhythm machine. But Kenton's own jazz charts moved quickly to the harmonic values and polyphonic inventions of Bartok, Stravinsky and Darius Milhaud. London's Sadler's Wells Ballet choreographed his avant-garde arrangements for Grace Kelly's wedding, and several French and Italian art films were built around his music. Much of the thematic pseudo-jazz that now serves as background music for avant-garde films and television series can be traced to Kenton's influence.

The best of his scores sounded as if they might have been torn out of a late Dostoevsky novel, the bravura fanfares from his ten men of brass counterpointed by the deep-mouthed empathy of the smoothest saxophone section in the business. His piano solos, all slides and whispers, had a smoky, three-o'clock-in-the-morning quality about them. He could transform Sondheim's "Send in the Clowns" into a lyrical comment about contemporary social values; his dirge-like version of "Here's That Rainy Day" became a tone poem, its chord structure as poignant as the touch of lovers' champagne glasses.

Kenton's many critics claimed his concerts were about as spontaneous as a cathedral mass. The satirist Mort Sahl captured the band's tendency toward the pretentious with the line "When Stan Kenton spills a cup of coffee, he doesn't say,

'Somebody help me clean this up.' He says, 'Look, I have created a mess!'"

It certainly wasn't music to make love by, and it didn't always swing. "There are many more emotions that can be portrayed and felt in jazz than just swinging," Kenton once explained to me. "For some reason, the critics haven't been able to communicate with my band. But I don't worry about it. Most of that crap I just let go in one eye and out the other."

The fundamental intent of jazz is to entertain and recharge the spirit with sensory awareness. No music depends so much on the individual players and their ability to improvise. Ideally, jazz performers are spontaneous, non-repetitive poets expressing themselves through their instruments. But what Kenton demanded of his musicians was that they carry the spirit of his composers' ideas into their own musical ruminations. That was the essence of his art, and that is why his music will survive.

But for those of us who followed his career and admired his music, the Kenton sound will never replace the Kenton presence. His passing marked not just the close of a musical era but a kind of death in the family. "We play life," Louis Armstrong once said of jazz, and that was exactly the affinity we felt with Stan Kenton's music—its lustre and eloquence, its rage and its unfulfilled promise.

—1973

Diana: The Luminous Life That Defined an Era

WATCHING THE FUNERAL of Diana, Princess of Wales, I was reminded of a passage by John Masefield, one of England's great poet laureates, in which he described the attack fleet of the Royal Navy leaving Moudros, on the Greek island of Lemnos, during the First World War. The mighty flotilla of warships was bound for the dramatic invasion of the Turkish seaport of Gallipoli, a defining moment of the conflict. "They left the harbour very, very slowly; this tumult of cheering lasted a long time," Masefield wrote. "No one who heard it will ever forget it . . . and those who were left behind in Mudros trimmed their lamps, knowing that they had been for a little time brought near to the heart of things."

Princess Diana's funeral had that kind of momentous mood about it. We watched, knowing that what we were seeing was the end of a storybook saga that went terribly wrong, right down to the crashed Mercedes where it ended. Personal grief was what we felt, not the cloying diffidence that most Canadians display for the royals during their stilted Canadian tours.

This was the burial of a spirited woman who had survived heavy psychological abuse by her unfaithful husband and met life more than halfway. She had fought for such worthy causes as the destruction of land mines, thus turning the publicity she generated to good use. She was the role model that the lesser members of the House of Windsor might have envied—if they possessed the brains or the guts to pursue it. The most photographed individual since the invention of the camera, the Princess of Wales was mourned not as some cold, distant apparition on official platforms, but as a sprightly presence with looks and charm to burn, who refused to become the sacrificial virgin that the Royal Family insisted on recruiting for the ungainly heir to the throne.

Apart from his unwillingness to maintain his marriage vows, the goofy Prince Charles's greatest failing was that he understood almost nothing about maintaining the monarchy's essential mystique. For one thing, he never stopped talking, whether it was about his sexual adventures when he was in the Royal Navy or his erotic fantasies about inhabiting the nether regions of his long-time mistress, Camilla Parker Bowles. "Many a thing we'd like to tell him," the British royal watcher Julie Burchill pointedly wrote about Charles in her *Guardian* column. "Many a thing he ought to understand. But how do you get him to shut the fuck up and listen to any voice save that of himself and his groupies? How can a man with such huge ears hear so very little?"

A good example of Charles's maladroitness was his pro-
nouncement that modern architecture had done more damage
to London's skyline than the Luftwaffe during the Second World
War. "Really?" asked Burchill. "How many children have London
architects burned alive?"

Charles earned most of the credit for his often awkward and
almost always inappropriate behaviour, but he shouldn't bear
the brunt of the blame for being an emotional cripple. I clearly
recall seeing a documentary on the Royal Family that showed a
youthful Elizabeth II arriving home after a lengthy tour abroad.
There was the six-year-old Prince of Wales so excited to see her
that he was literally jumping up and down with glee. Yet the
Queen welcomed her joyful little boy by solemnly shaking his
hand. It takes several lifetimes to survive such an upbringing.

Diana had obviously read the situation correctly and decided
that divorce was essential to her survival. She understood that
her power flowed not from regal titles or her marriage to the
future king, but from her personal popularity, and that this was
transferable to real life outside the palace. It was this connection
with reality—Diana's decision to opt out of the essentially phoney
business of being a royal—that mesmerized so many fans when
she was alive, and it was the reason why her funeral attracted
such astounding throngs of mourners. She had reached into
our psyches and allowed us to vicariously enjoy her boundless
humanity, her sense of mischief and her magic presence.

Diana, Princess of Wales' posthumous glory will not save
the British monarchy. The passing of Diana leaves the Queen

presiding over a house of horrors that makes the Addams family seem refreshing by comparison. One imagines Her Majesty rolling out of her canopied bed each morning, afraid to turn on the telly in case the BBC might be detailing the unspeakable act a family member has committed with yet another fugitive from the gene pool. Only the Queen Mother, at ninety-seven, still seems emotionally alive and kicking.

Canadians' connection with British royalty has always been more spiritual than constitutional. For generations, the British monarchy was an essential touchstone for Canadians: the ultimate expression of how to behave and a symbol of what to believe in. That invisible bond relied on a delicate balance of reciprocal illusions that has now been shattered.

With the Princess of Wales dead and buried, we are no longer enthralled by the royals. Canadians have demanded nothing of the British monarchy except to keep the faith. Diana's funeral ended all that. It's time for Canada to ditch that inbred family of promiscuous mediocrities, still pretending to reign over us.

—1997

Václav Havel: Politics of the Improbable

I MET HIM only once, but I've never forgotten my private moments with Václav Havel, the secular political saint whose personal courage and effective guidance freed Czechoslovakia of its Communist yoke. Our meeting took place in Ottawa in 1990, when he was on his way to Washington to address a joint session of Congress and didn't have much time. But he was glad to meet someone who could speak Czech, so he wouldn't have to rely on his interpreter. (She was a tiny Asian woman he kept tucked under his left shoulder, who was so good at her job that as local well wishers talked to him, she would repeat what they said to Havel in Czech, lip-read his answer and reply almost instantaneously in perfect Oxford English.)

From our brief exchange, I recall only two fragments. "I've learned never to be surprised by anything," he replied when I asked how it felt for a beleaguered playwright to suddenly find himself a famous president. To my question about the secret of politics, he shot back: "Write your own speeches and express hard truths in a polite way." Then he paused and added: "Of course, everyone is replaceable."

I'm not so sure.

Havel was one of those rare conscience-driven politicians we couldn't afford to lose. He kept himself removed from the darker tricks of his craft and was never impressed by the fumes of fame. Havel believed that character is destiny and that it was therefore essential to live a principled life, even at the risk of being imprisoned for his beliefs—which he was.

A scruffy-looking man with once ginger-coloured hair and an orange moustache (one friend joked, "Václav looks as if carrot juice is flowing through his veins"), he enjoyed a highly developed sense of the absurd. His plays were absurdist creations in mundane settings with universal characters. Havel started writing when he was thirteen, but Czech theatre was closed to him until the Velvet Revolution of 1989, of which he was the chief animator.

He led the peaceful overthrow of the occupying Russians and that winter assumed Czechoslovakia's presidency. This meant moving into Hradcany Castle, a huge pile of palaces and cathedrals overlooking the Vltava River, which bisects Prague. Just eight months earlier, he had been serving a four-year sentence in a Communist prison a few kilometres away.

He had been the spiritual catalyst of the bloodless revolt that swept the Communists out of power, and now he was the country's first democratic president since 1938. Being a playwright, one of the first things Havel did was to make sure everyone wore appropriate costumes. He asked his friend Theodor Pistek (who won an Academy Award for his couture in the movie *Amadeus*) to design properly pretentious royal blue parade uniforms—complete with toy sabres—for the castle guards. When they were delivered, Havel tried one on and yelling, "Let's go scare the cooks!" ran into the castle kitchens, waving his pretend weapon. He later got fed up with soldiers stomping around the castle to regal marching music and had another of his friends compose a jarring melody in seven-eight time that no one could possibly march to, then insisted it be played for the changing-of-the-guard ceremonies. Hradcany Castle is so huge that Havel sometimes resorted to getting around the place on a scooter, but after the first few weeks in office, he reluctantly agreed not to come to work in jeans but received visitors wearing a polka-dot tie. (His first press secretary was Michael Zantovsky, whose claim to fame was as the author of the only study in Czech of the films of Woody Allen.)

As president, Havel granted amnesty to thirty thousand prisoners, presided over the peaceful withdrawal of Soviet troops, defied public opinion by supporting the reunification of Germany, masterminded the Czech Republic's NATO application and generally brought some badly needed enlightenment to a country that had not known democracy for five decades.

But his main contributions were his evocative speeches, written by himself on a manual typewriter. Probably the best was his 1990 New Year's message: "For forty years, on this day, you heard the same thing in different variations from my predecessors: how our country was flourishing, how many tons of steel we produced, how happy we all were, how we trusted our government and what bright perspectives were unfolding in front of us. I assume you did not nominate me to this office so that I, too, would lie to you. Our country is not flourishing . . . Entire branches of industry are producing goods that are of no interest to anyone . . . A country that once could be proud of the educational level of its citizens spends so little on education that it ranks today as seventy-second in the world."

He went on like that for about ten minutes. Then came his seminal point: "Let us teach both ourselves and others that politics does not have to be the art of the possible, especially if this means the art of intrigues, secret agreements and pragmatic manoeuvrings. But that it can also be the art of the impossible, that it is the art of making both ourselves and the world better."

"Man," Havel wrote from jail, "is nailed down—like Christ on the cross—to a grid of paradoxes. He balances between the torment of not knowing his mission and the joy of carrying it out."

Václav Havel did both. We are all the better for his historical presence, and we miss his impish presence in world affairs.

—1998

Margaret Atwood: The Corrugated Madonna
From *Sometimes a Great Nation: Will Canada Belong to the 21st Century?*
Toronto: McClelland & Stewart, 1988

The Tempestuous Vision of Irving Layton
From *Defining Moments: Dispatches from an Unfinished Revolution*
Toronto: Viking (Penguin), 1997

A Fond Farewell to Robertson Davies
From *Defining Moments: Dispatches from an Unfinished Revolution*
Toronto: Viking (Penguin), 1997

The "Fillum" Moguls Who Made Me
From *Here Be Dragons: Telling Tales of People, Passion and Power*
Toronto: McClelland & Stewart, 2004

Terry Fox on the Run
From *Sometimes a Great Nation: Will Canada Belong to the 21st Century?*
Toronto: McClelland & Stewart, 1988

Jack McClelland: The Authors' Publisher
From *Sometimes a Great Nation: Will Canada Belong to the 21st Century?*
Toronto: McClelland & Stewart, 1988

Hugh MacLennan: Charting Canada's Psyche
From *Sometimes a Great Nation: Will Canada Belong to the 21st Century?*
Toronto: McClelland & Stewart, 1988

Remembering Pierre Berton, the Big Foot of CanLit
From "Big Foot of CanLit," *Maclean's*, October 22, 2001

June Callwood: A Passion for Compassion
From "A Passion for the Fight," *Maclean's*, April 30, 2007

Jack Poole: The Shy Birth Father of the Vancouver Olympics
From "Driven by His Dreams for Others," the *Globe and Mail*, October 23, 2009

Marshall McLuhan: Calling Planet Earth
From "The Table Talk of Marshall McLuhan," *Maclean's*, June 1971

Ralph Allen: The Man from Oxbow
From *Home Country: People, Places, and Power Politics*
Toronto: McClelland & Stewart, 1973

Homage to Christina McCall
From "Remembering Christina," *National Post*, May 4, 2005

Michael Ignatieff: The Count Comes Home
New

Pierre Trudeau: Phantom of the Canadian Opera
From *The Canadian Revolution, 1985–1995: From Deference to Defiance*
Toronto: Viking (Penguin), 1995

Lester Pearson: A Good Man in a Wicked Time
From *The Distemper of Our Times: Canadian Politics in Transition, 1963–1968*
Toronto: McClelland & Stewart, 1968

Walter Gordon: The Troubled Canadian
From *The Distemper of Our Times: Canadian Politics in Transition, 1963–1968*
Toronto: McClelland & Stewart, 1968

Frank Underhill: A Liberal for All Seasons
From *Home Country: People, Places, and Power Politics*
Toronto: McClelland & Stewart, 1973

Judy LaMarsh: The Gutsy Charmer with Class
From *Sometimes a Great Nation: Will Canada Belong to the 21st Century?*
Toronto: McClelland & Stewart, 1988

Peter Munk: The Man for All Seasons
From *Titans: How the New Canadian Establishment Seized Power*
Toronto: Viking (Penguin), 1998

For the Love of Andy (Sarlos): Of Casinos and Markets
From *Defining Moments: Dispatches from an Unfinished Revolution*
Toronto: Viking (Penguin), 1997

"Young Ken" Thomson: The World's Shyest Multi-Billionaire
From *Defining Moments: Dispatches from an Unfinished Revolution*
Toronto: Viking (Penguin), 1997

David Thomson: Fortune's Child
From "Fortune's Child," *Maclean's*, May 6, 2002

The Immaculate Passions of Nelson Davis
From *Sometimes a Great Nation: Will Canada Belong to the 21st Century?*
Toronto: McClelland & Stewart, 1988

Paul Desmarais: King of the Establishment
From *Titans: How the New Canadian Establishment Seized Power*
Toronto: Viking (Penguin), 1998

The Golden Couple: Gerry Schwartz and Heather Reisman
From *Titans: How the New Canadian Establishment Seized Power*
Toronto: Viking (Penguin), 1998

Jimmy Pattison: Canada's Über-Entrepreneur
From *Sometimes a Great Nation: Will Canada Belong to the 21st Century?*
Toronto: McClelland & Stewart, 1988

Ted Rogers: TheTycoon Who Never Rested
From "Ted Rogers: A Visionary Leader," *Maclean's*, December 8, 2008

Arthur Child: Calgary's Renaissance Man
From *Defining Moments: Dispatches from an Unfinished Revolution*
Toronto: Viking (Penguin), 1997

Sir Christopher Ondaatje: The Man Who Explored Africa
From "Our English Knight," *Maclean's*, June 14, 2004

Seymour Schulich: Champion Philanthropist
From "How to Give Away Money," *Maclean's*, May 17, 1999

Peter Bronfman: The Bronfman Who Hated Money
From "Peter Bronfman: The Gentle, Lonely Tycoon," *Maclean's*,
December 6, 1996

The New Wave: Navjeet Dhillon Goes Gold
From "A Second Wind: Real Estate Honcho Navjeet Dhillon is Flying
High after Beating Cancer," *Maclean's*, December 16, 2005

Stan Kenton: Artistry in Rhythym
From *Home Country: People, Places, and Power Politics*
Toronto: McClelland & Stewart, 1973

Diana: The Luminous Life That Defined an Era
From "A Short Life That Defined a New Era," *Maclean's*, September
15, 1997

Václav Havel: Politics of the Improbable
From "Saluting the Playwright Who Became President," *Maclean's*,
August 17, 1998

Index